THE DRAMA OF OUR PAST: MAJOR PLAYS FROM NINETEENTH-CENTURY QUEBEC

Although the general evolution of French-Canadian theatre in the nineteenth-century has been described previously in some detail, the plays themselves have remained largely inaccessible both in French and, especially, in English. *The Drama of Our Past* fills this void by presenting, in English for the first time, ten plays which together cover the major genres and themes treated by local dramatists throughout the century.

These plays include *Anglomania* (1803), the first play with an explicitly Canadian theme and setting to appear since the seventeenth-century; the politically inspired *Status Quo Comedies* (1834); *The Donation* (1842), the first play by a Quebec-born writer to be produced and published in Canada, and *A Country Outing*, by the same author, which deals with French-English relations; *Felix Poutré* (1862), the most popular of the plays in public performance; and *Archibald Cameron of Locheill* (1868/1894), the best known and most frequently staged of the college plays.

The Drama of Our Past provides an introductory essay for each play, situating it in the social, historical, and political context in which it was composed and performed. Together the essays and plays offer a connected history of Canadian drama in French for this period. The plays are presented in their full and most authoritative versions, in translations which convey both the sense of the original French and its flavour and spirit. The texts themselves take many forms, ranging from stilted literary convention to parody of local dialect, from solemn political harangue to earthy comedy. What emerges is an indigenous drama more original, impassioned, sophisticated, and entertaining than has hitherto been credited.

L.E. DOUCETTE is Professor of French at the University of Toronto, and author of *Theatre in French Canada: Laying the Foundations, 1606–1867*.

THE DRAMA
of
OUR PAST

Major Plays from
Nineteenth-Century Quebec

Translated and edited by
L.E. Doucette

UNIVERSITY OF TORONTO PRESS
Toronto Buffalo London

© University of Toronto Press Incorporated 1997
Toronto Buffalo London
Printed in Canada

ISBN 0-8020-4140-X (cloth)
ISBN 0-8020-7985-7 (paper)

Printed on acid-free paper

Canadian Cataloguing in Publication Data

Main entry under title:

The drama of our past

Includes bibliographical references and index.
ISBN 0-8020-4140-X (bound)
ISBN 0-8020-7985-7 (pbk.)

1. Canadian drama (French) – Quebec (Province) –
Translations into English.*   2. Canadian drama
(French) – 19th century – Translations into
English.*   I. Doucette, Leonard E. (Leonard
Eugene), 1936–   .

PS8315.5.Q8D72 1997   C842'.408   C96-932166-X
PQ3915.5.E5D72 1997

University of Toronto Press acknowledges the assistance to its publishing program of the
Canada Council and the Ontario Arts Council.

This book has been published with the help of a grant from the Humanities and Social
Science Federation of Canada, using funds provided by the Social Sciences and Humanities
Research Council of Canada.

Contents

Prologue

This volume contains five full-length plays and five short playlets that have been chosen to represent the broad range of dramatic writing in nineteenth-century Quebec.

Some 175 plays written in French survive from that period, in one form or another. Only half a dozen have ever been translated into English, and even these are becoming increasingly inaccessible.[1] Thus, while it has been possible to read *about* the drama of nineteenth-century Quebec in English,[2] access to the texts themselves has not been possible without a sound reading knowledge of French and without the services of a major library. The principal aim of this book is to remedy the situation.

By any criteria, the plays retrieved here are the most important of the century. At the same time, this work is intended as more than a mere anthology: the essays that introduce each play seek to go well beyond the individual texts and to provide a connected history of Canadian drama in French during the nineteenth century. Read in chronological order, which is how they are presented here, the plays demonstrate the evolution of dramatic forms between 1803 (most probable date for the completion of Joseph Quesnel's *Anglomania*) and 1894 (date of first publication of *Archibald Cameron of Locheill*), and at the same time enable an assessment to be made of the contribution of each text and of each author to the development of a native theatrical tradition.

Before the nineteenth century, theatrical performances had taken place – at times frequently – in French Canada, but drama (in the restricted sense of the texts on which performance is based) was, with the rarest of exceptions, imported from the mother country. Four texts that are more or less Canadian survive from the period preceding 1800: Marc Lescarbot's quaint *Théâtre de Neptune en la Nouvelle-France* (*Theatre of Neptune in New France*), performed in Acadia in 1605, published in France in 1609, and translated into English several times in the twentieth century;[3] the anonymous *Réception de Mgr le vicomte d'Argenson*, composed by the Jesuits at Quebec and performed in 1658 by their pupils to welcome the newly arrived governor, and interesting for its use of native Amerindian languages and its political content;[4] the thin poetic text performed by female students for Bishop Saint-Vallier in 1727;[5] and Joseph Quesnel's innocuous operetta, *Colas et Colinette, ou le bailli dupé* (*Colas and Colinette, or the Bailiff Confounded*) staged in 1790, published in 1812, and translated into English in 1974.

Theatre did not return to Acadia until the 1860s, but it was a fairly common cultural phenomenon in the colony along the St Lawrence from the early 1640s to the end of the seventeenth century. Public performances leaned towards plays currently or recently popular in Paris, notably the works of Corneille, Molière, and Racine, while the semi-private theatrical sessions in the Jesuits' and Ursulines' schools preferred edifying works composed specifically for pedagogical institutions in France. But as the Catholic Church consolidated its authority in France and its hegemony in New France, the growing hostility it displayed towards public theatrical performance caused problems in the colony, culminating in Governor Frontenac's memorable confrontation with Bishop Saint-Vallier in 1693–4, occasioned by Frontenac's announced intention of staging Molière's controversial *Tartuffe*. On the face of it, Frontenac won the battle, since he was paid handsomely by the bishop in exchange for his promise not to stage the play. But theatre lost the war, for Saint-Vallier proceeded subsequently to ban performances everywhere in the colony, and his interdiction continued to impede the development of a native dramatic tradition until the last decade of the nineteenth century.

There were other factors inhibiting that development, most notably the absence of printing presses in New France during its entire history, the small population sparsely scattered over a huge territory, and the weak attachment of its transient cultural élite to the new country. The Conquest brought presses, encouraged urban growth, made access to France difficult, and considerably diluted the Catholic Church's influence, at least for a few decades. It is not surprising, therefore, that theatre reappeared almost immediately. Performances by garrisoned troops had long been part of the British military tradition, and their offerings in Quebec City and Montreal were generally in French (Molière's plays in particular), attracting spectators and, soon, local amateurs eager to appear on-stage with British officers. Within a few years independent local troupes were organized (Joseph Quesnel, for example, was able to join a francophone company in Montreal shortly after his arrival in Canada in 1779, and he helped establish, ten years later, the more ambitious troupe which staged his *Colas et Colinette* in January 1790 along with five other plays from European French repertoire). But by the latter date the Church, having demonstrated its hierarchy's loyalty during the War of American Independence, felt sufficiently secure of its renewed authority to intervene, at first publicly from the pulpit, then privately – and very effectively – through the confessional. It would continue to exert a braking effect on the development of a native theatrical tradition for another hundred years.

In the interval the French Revolution and the ensuing Napoleonic Wars had made the cultural and political situation even more difficult for francophones in Canada. It is in this context that Quesnel's *Anglomania* was composed and circulated discreetly in the first decade of the nineteenth century. A hybrid work – ultra-conservative in form, but highly topical in content – it melds the cultural inheritance of pre-Revolutionary France with the hard realities of contemporary Lower Canada, while maintaining a bemused and fairly objective tone. Surprisingly, the play remained not only unpublished but also virtually unknown until the twentieth century.

Between the date of Quesnel's text and 1834, that of the *Status Quo Comedies*, the only drama written by local authors was political in inspiration, adversarial in intent, and not destined for performance. In no other occidental society is armchair political drama of this sort the first and most vigorous indigenous genre to develop; it was spawned by the election campaigns of the 1790s, and was nourished by the partisan newspapers that shaped the public opinion of francophones, starting with the foundation of Quebec City's durable *Le Canadien* in 1806. For the rest of the nineteenth century this tradition continued to mature, highlighted by the *Tuque Bleue* comedies of 1848 that attacked George-Étienne Cartier and his politics of compromise and bicultural cooperation, by the clever and amusing *Dégringolade* series lampooning Sir Allan MacNab and his cabinet and the bibulous John A. Macdonald during the ministerial crisis of 1856, and culminating in Elzéar Labelle's delightful *Conversion d'un pêcheur de la Nouvelle-Écosse*, satirizing both sides in the recent Confederation debates.[6] The five *Status Quo Comedies* included here are the best known and most typical examples of political theatre, a genre that survived well into the 1970s in Quebec.

The texts of the *Status Quo Comedies* are from 1834, three years before the Patriote rebellions that were to change radically the way French Canadians perceived themselves and their country. The 1830s had also seen an increase in direct literary and political influence from France as a result of political turmoil in that country. Expatriate European francophones, such as Firmin Prud'homme, Leblanc de Marconnay, and Napoléon Aubin, all helped to inject new life into local theatre, the first two by composing, performing, and publishing plays in Montreal, the latter by founding Quebec City's seminal troupe, Les Amateurs Typographes, in 1839, the company that would stage Pierre Petitclair's *The Donation* in 1842 and remain active for at least two more decades.

The two plays by Petitclair included here reflect recent changes to the situation of French Canadians, with the Durham Report and enforced union with Upper

Canada having brought new political structures and new frictions. In *The Dona-tion* the author's misgivings are muted, to the extent that their expression had gone unperceived until my own research revealed their existence. In *A Country Outing* conflict is transposed from the covertly political to the public cultural level, as the insidious threat of inundation by English values, customs, and speech is identified and castigated, much as it had been in *Anglomania*. On another level, the most obvious influence on the form of *The Donation* is that of contemporary European melodrama, whereas *A Country Outing*, first performed fifteen years later, is less derivative and much more sure-handed than its predecessor. It was a significant building-block in the construction of an indigenous dramatic tradition.

The next important step was the rehabilitation of Canada's own history, memo-rably achieved by Louis Fréchette with his *Félix Poutré* in 1862, by far the most popular play in public performance for the rest of the century. Dealing with the Patriote rebellion of 1838, still a vivid memory for many of the play's spectators and readers, Fréchette's drama was the first to tap what would almost immediately become the most fertile vein for French Canadian dramatists until the 1930s: the history of their own country, often idealized as a result of such later historians as Lionel Groulx. This obsession with the patriotic, nationalistic retelling of the past would eventually prove counter-productive, resulting in the publication of scores of ephemeral titles and a widening hiatus between composition and performance. But *Félix Poutré*, despite its many deficiencies, succeeded in galvanizing public attention as no other play before it had done, to the benefit of stage arts in general.

In the 1860s, with the completion of a North American railway system linking Montreal and Quebec City with New York, Boston, and Philadelphia, Quebec's two main cities became part of a continental theatrical network, as touring troupes from France began to add them to their itineraries. Despite frequent condemna-tions from the pulpit, these tours soon had a profound effect on local audiences, actors, and dramatists, notably in the work of playwright-politician Félix-Gabriel Marchand, whose five plays capture the lighter spirit of Parisian fare without offending local moral sensitivities as the repertoire of visiting troupes so frequently did. Other local authors, less gifted or at least less confident, merely 'adapted' French plays for local tastes, their adaptations frequently consisting in excisions of anything remotely likely to offend, Ernest Doin, J.G.W. McGown, and Régis Roy being the best known practitioners of this re-packaging. Until the First World War these two disparate veins – solemn historical theatre and light, unsubstantial adap-tations – prevailed, to be displaced eventually by cinema, burlesque, and radio drama.

But 'private' theatre, in this case the plays performed in Quebec's system of *col-lèges classiques*, which was extensively developed by the mid nineteenth century, continued to thrive. The tradition of school performances goes back to the seven-

teenth century in Quebec, but had virtually disappeared after Saint-Vallier's condemnation of all forms of theatre in 1699. It re-emerged in the 1780s, and
continued its modest existence until the death in 1825 of theatre's most resolute
opponent, Bishop Octave Plessis. Reports of more and more ambitious college theatricals are frequent thereafter, and these reports were often given prominence in
local newspapers. For the most part the texts continued to be imported, but there
are notable exceptions, beginning with a verse tragedy written by a student and
performed by fellow-students for a select audience in 1844; the text of *Le Jeune
Latour* (*The Young Latour*), by twenty-year-old Antoine Gérin-Lajoie, was published the same year.[7] Appealing to nationalist sentiment and high moral principles, the play obviously touched its élite audience deeply. More typical of college
fare is Father H.-A. Verreau's *Stanislas de Kostka*, an edifying if boring depiction of
the life of the Polish martyr, performed at another college for a restricted public in
1855. Later, more talented authors specialized in the genre, attaining some degree
of recognition for their efforts: Father J.-B. Proulx, whose five plays range in topics
from the life of an English king and saint (*Édouard le Confesseur*, 1880) to an effective attack upon the evils of alcohol (*L'Hôte à Valiquet*, 1881) and a humorous
depiction of student life (*Le Mal du Jour de l'an*, 1882); Father E. Hamon, who
contributed to the official campaign for colonization of Quebec's entire territory
with his propagandizing *Exil et patrie* in 1882; and Father S. Brault, whose prosely-
tizing *Le Triomphe de deux vocations* (1897) returns to a more traditional concern
of college theatre, recruitment for the priesthood. The play chosen here to represent this important aspect of nineteenth-century drama in Quebec is an adaptation
of the best-known novel of the century, Philippe Aubert de Gaspé's *Les Anciens
Canadiens*. The dramatic text drawn from it, entitled *Archibald Cameron of
Locheill, or an Episode in the Seven Years' War in Canada (1759)*, became easily the
most popular play for the college stage, generating various imitations and continuing to be performed well into the 1930s.

In light of their importance it may seem surprising that none of these texts has
previously been translated into English (and, indeed, most of them are rarely read
in French). The way would-be dramatists perceived dramatic forms tells us a good
deal about the vision French Canadians had of themselves and of their role in a
rapidly changing North American context. Authors obviously sought to write what
they thought would or should interest the public. Publishers printed what they
thought would serve the public's – or their own – interests. And the public
decided, in different and less scrutable ways, what it wanted to read or see performed. Predictably, at the thematic heart of all of the plays – except one, *The
Donation* – that are retained here is the original and enduring conflict between
French and English, between the established authority of a conquering nation and
the resolute will of a conquered cultural-linguistic group to survive. There is, then,

a significant element of modernity visible here. The perception of specific threats and the perspective on specific events may change, but the essential dilemma for French-Canadian cultural survival remains constant, from the healthy satire of *Anglomania* through the shrill adversarialism of the *Status Quo Comedies* to the elegiac nostalgia of *Archibald Cameron of Locheill.*

Three of the translations included here (the *Status Quo Comedies*, *The Donation*, and *A Country Outing*) were first published elsewhere, in the now defunct periodical *Canadian Drama/L'Art dramatique canadien.* I wish to express my gratitude to the long-serving editor of that journal, Professor Eugene Benson of the University of Guelph, for permission to reproduce them here. I offer my sincere thanks as well to Henri Pilon for the careful attention with which he has edited my text. His extraordinary knowledge of historical sources and his sure sense of style have helped me avoid a number of errors of fact and infelicities of expression.

THE DRAMA OF OUR PAST

I

Anglomania, or Dinner, English-Style

INTRODUCTION

1. The Play and Its Author

Although it seems certain that Joseph Quesnel's short verse comedy *L'Anglomanie ou le dîner à l'angloise* (*Anglomania, or Dinner English-Style*)[1] circulated discreetly among his friends and neighbours in the village of Boucherville – and perhaps more widely – in the first decade of the nineteenth century, it was not published until the twentieth.[2] For once, the long delay had nothing to do with the notoriously Canadian difficulty of finding a publisher for something as ephemeral as a play text. In this case it was because the foolish Anglophiles whose excesses are here so humorously depicted were modelled too closely upon prominent citizens of the little community in which Quesnel himself had been living since 1793. In the strained atmosphere of Lower Canada during the Napoleonic Wars it would have been unwise, impolitic, and perhaps even dangerous for him to seek publication of the text as it stood. For unlike the other three plays by Quesnel that have survived in whole or in part, this is a text whose theme and whose characters are rooted firmly in the precarious realities of his time – in this case, life in Lower Canada at the beginning of the nineteenth century.

The play's author was the best known writer in the colony in his day. Born in the Breton town of Saint-Malo in 1746 to a prosperous merchant family, he had received a solid classical education there at the Collège Saint-Louis. From the age of nineteen Quesnel had devoted himself to the family's business. This involved travel to four continents, broken by a lengthy stay in Bordeaux (1772–9), where an uncle was a well-established trader and ship chandler. After France intervened directly on the American side in the War of Independence in 1778 trade with the rebellious colonies seemed attractive to French merchants. But Quesnel's plans for quick profit were rudely interrupted the following year when the British Navy intercepted his ship, laden with supplies for the Americans, off Newfoundland.

Brought to Halifax, he managed, through his family's connections with Swiss-born Governor Frederick Haldimand, a transfer to Montreal where within a year he had married into a family with roots in Saint-Malo and important commercial connections in Canada. With only brief interruptions, Quesnel would remain here until his death in 1809, his mobility restrained first by the American war and then by the effects of the French Revolution, the Consulate, and the Empire.

There is no doubt that for most or all of the thirty years he spent in Canada Joseph Quesnel's heart lay elsewhere. The new British colony had offered him amnesty, opportunity, then refuge from the excesses of Revolutionary France, from which his own family and friends suffered (a cousin, for example, went to the guillotine and the family's properties in Bordeaux were confiscated). But the cultural attractions he had learned to love in France were rare indeed in French Canada in the last quarter of the eighteenth century. He had developed an early passion for music and theatre in particular, and was active on the amateur stage in Montreal soon after his arrival. So, when an intermission in international hostilities allowed him an extended visit to France in the winter of 1788–9, he sought every opportunity to satisfy his passion, especially in the theatres of Bordeaux, an important provincial cultural centre. On his return to Canada he brought with him not only a contract for importing wines and other French products but a firm resolution as well to introduce some of the cultural amenities of his former homeland that he most missed: music, theatre and poetry. After his semi-retirement in 1793 he was able to devote much of his time and energy to them.

2. The Social and Political Context

For the first three decades following the signature of the Treaty of Paris in 1763 relations between English and French-speakers in Canada remained generally workable, despite strains induced by the regular influx of British merchants, traders, and placemen, and especially by the waves of Loyalist immigration from the south after the advent of American independence. Even the initial stages of the French Revolution aroused for a time more tolerant interest than alarm in Canada as in Britain. English attitudes began to change radically, however, as the political situation in France deteriorated, exacerbated by the execution of Louis XVI in January of 1793. Three weeks later France and Britain were officially at war, and they would remain so for most of the next twenty years.

With Britain legitimately concerned for its own survival, it is not surprising that fear and mistrust of everything French soon rose to fever pitch among anglophones in Canada. Their sentiments were not entirely unfounded: the colony's innately precarious situation, with British forces constantly preoccupied elsewhere, was aggravated by the existence of a robust anti-British faction in the United States and by memories of the solid alliance between France and the American rebels during the recent War of Independence. In the early 1790s clandestine clubs sympathetic to the French Revolutionaries were active in Montreal and fear of their intentions was fomented by passionate appeals to Canadians by the French ambassador to the United States, Citizen Genet. Rumours circulated of a planned invasion along the Richelieu River, to coincide with the arrival of a large French fleet that would regain mastery of the St Lawrence.

On the other hand, the Catholic clergy in Canada repeatedly expressed its gratitude to God and the British Crown for saving Canada from the terrors of revolution, regicide, and religious persecution, most notably in public prayers and thanksgiving ordered by Bishop Denaut to commemorate the defeat of the French fleet at Aboukir in 1798. His coadjutor, the future Bishop Plessis, expressed the Church's attitude in a public sermon on that occasion, asking rhetorically, 'Alas, where would we be, brethren, if this country, by an unfortunate reverse, should return to its ancient masters?'[3]

Informed francophones consequently found themselves torn between ancient and new loyalties, between their cultural and their political homelands. This heightened tension within and outside the numerically dominant but politically marginalized French in Canada was particularly felt by the seigneurial class and the landed gentry, to which Quesnel now effectively belonged and which now found itself excluded more and more from the councils of government. This tendency was exacerbated by the arrival in 1799 as official administrator of the colony of former career soldier Sir Robert Shore Milnes, who would remain in the position until 1807 (although he had returned to England two years earlier). To the extent that *Anglomania* is based on real people and real attitudes – and that extent was considerable, as we shall see – the governor referred to so frequently in this play has to be Milnes.

All of Milnes's advisers were convinced, and they soon convinced him, that the only viable solution to the colony's problems lay in the rapid assimilation of the *Canadiens*. To this end various strategies were proposed, the most notable being a project devised by Anglican Bishop Jacob Mountain in 1799 for financing a free, 'public,' English-language school system, in which the language would be taught to French-Canadian children. The plan was implemented in 1801 by a statute that established the Royal Institution for the Advancement of Learning. As the historian J.-P. Wallot has observed, 'In practice the statute conferred absolute control of public education in Lower Canada upon the civil administrator and his minions.'[4] Milnes also sought, with much less success, to abolish or radically modify the seigneurial system, thereby allowing English-speaking settlers to establish themselves in the hitherto exclusively francophone areas the seigneuries represented, with the same aim of diluting French influence and eventually assimilating the *Canadien* element.

Yet Governor Milnes was far from being the Francophobic ogre some historians have sought to make of him. As Wallot points out in his article in the authoritative *Dictionary of Canadian Biography*:

Milnes was a sociable man, interested in arts and letters, and he enjoyed receptions which Lady Milnes, reputed to be beautiful and charming, graced by her presence ... Skilled at maintaining ambiguity, he forged links with some of the Canadians, even though he was secretly advocating their assimilation.

It is this social aspect of Governor and Lady Milnes that is emphasized in Quesnel's play, along with the influence their British manners and customs had upon some impressionable French Canadians in the early nineteenth century.

3. Quesnel's Theatre in the Context of His Time

In the fall of 1789 Quesnel had been a moving force in the foundation of the first theatrical company in French Canada since Governor Frontenac's ill-fated household troupe a century earlier. Following a tradition then still in vogue in France Quesnel's group styled itself a 'Théâtre de Société' or 'Upper Society' Theatre, the French term implying a connection with the cultural élite of the colony.[5] But Quesnel and his friends had misjudged or forgotten the firm opposition by the Catholic Church to public theatre, in effect for all of French Canada since 1699. This had been the result of the confrontation between Governor Frontenac and Bishop Saint-Vallier in 1694 that had led to the prohibition of all public theatricals anywhere in the colony five years later. After the Conquest, as long as the Church's role was still insecure, it could do nothing about the French plays performed publicly by British garrisons in Quebec City and Montreal, and it had to tolerate the occasional performances by local amateurs whose interest had been aroused by the garrisons' performances (some local francophones participated in their performances as well). But by the later 1780s the Church had reason to feel more secure, and began to exert its moral authority more openly.

Thus, when Quesnel and his friends announced their ambitious repertoire (eight plays in five double programs) for the country's first true theatrical 'season' of 1789–90 in Montreal, they immediately met with outright condemnation from the pulpit and with threats of the withdrawal of the sacraments from any parishioner who attended the performances. Although Quesnel and his troupe managed, by strenuous protest, to have the public condemnation withdrawn, it was replaced by a far more effective medium: the confessional, where penitents could be firmly but privately dissuaded from frequenting theatrical performances. Certainly the Church was not exclusively responsible for the virtual invisibility of indigenous theatre over the next few decades (factors such as population dispersal, the weak educational and economic situation of francophones, and the lack of a previous theatrical tradition were, taken together, probably just as important); nevertheless, its resolute opposition to public theatre was no doubt significant for those who, like Quesnel, continued to adhere to the Catholic faith throughout troubled times.

For this and other reasons, Quesnel's original Théâtre de Société did not survive beyond its first season, a highlight of which was the performance of a play he had recently completed, *Colas et Colinette, ou le bailli dupé*. A light, semi-pastoral comedy with frequent musical interventions (Quesnel termed it an 'operetta'), it represented a type of musical entertainment very popular in France since mid-century.[6] The first sample of the genre produced in French Canada, it would become in 1812 as well the first play by a Canadian resident published in this country.[7]

Apart from the venue of its performance there is little that is specifically Canadian and even less that is contentious about *Colas et Colinette*.[8] The lack of Canadian reference is visible as well in his second play, *Les Républicains français* (*The French Republicans*) (1801), but this time the political content is inescapable: it is a savage parody of the excesses of the French Revolution, penned by a man whose life had been seriously disrupted by it. *Les Républicains français* represents a hybrid genre whose closest connection is with the permissive *parades* that were so much a part of eighteenth-century theatrical tradition in France, a phenomenon closely connected with private *théâtres de société*. In every respect, it is as French as the wines Quesnel imported in the hope of enhancing his fortune. Apparently never performed, the text remained unpublished until 1970 (it appeared in an English translation in 1982).[9]

Anglomania was the last of Quesnel's plays to be completed (the partial text and score of another operetta, to be entitled 'Lucas et Cécile,' have also survived). It is the only one with an explicitly Canadian setting and a theme that remains as topical for francophones in Canada today as it was when Pierre Petitclair dealt with it again in 1857 in his *A Country Outing*, a translation of which is also included here.

4. Characters and Setting

Critic and historian John Hare first carried out the detective work that has resulted in the identification of the real characters involved in Quesnel's fictive setting.[10] Unknown now except to historical specialists, they were figures of some importance in their day. And they included the most prominent poet of the age, Joseph Quesnel himself, disguised here as the comic 'Monsieur François.' 'Colonel Beauchamp' is a certain Louis-Joseph Fleury d'Eschambault ('Monsieur de Chambeau,' as an English diarist called him, 'Chambeau' or 'D'Eschambault' easily becoming, by inversion, 'Beauchamp'), aide-de-camp to Lieutenant-Governor Milnes.

D'Eschambault, whose family had been impoverished by the Conquest, was also lieutenant-colonel in a British regiment and apparently a shameless proponent of the innate superiority of all things British. 'Monsieur Primenbourg' ('First in Town'), similarly, is Joseph-Louis Boucher de Montarville, seigneur of Saint-Denis-sur-Richelieu and the most prominent resident of Boucherville, just across the St Lawrence from Montreal. His mother, the 'Dowager Primenbourg' in our play, is Louise-Renée de Pécaudy (1712–1800); his daughter Lucette is Marie-Françoise, still unmarried in 1803. The commonsensical officer 'Vielmont,' identified as 'a relative of M. Primenbourg,' is in reality François Vassal de Montviel (Montviel reversed into 'Vielmont'), whose father had been killed during the battle for Quebec and who in 1803 was a semi-retired captain in a French-Canadian regiment (he would later be made adjutant-general of the Lower Canadian militia and achieve some prominence in the War of 1812). The real Montviel had helped found the Théâtre de Société in 1789, and was step-brother to Boucher de Montarville (Monsieur Primenbourg), since Montviel's mother had married Montarville's father after her first husband's death following the battle of Sainte-Foy in 1760.[11] Dr Pennkrève or Pancrève (Pan: 'all'; 'crève': die) is Georg Stubinger, a surgeon and apothecary who had served with the Hessian troops stationed in Canada and had taken up residence in Boucherville. Finally, the hapless poet, Monsieur François, is a figure who appears elsewhere in Quesnel's work and is generally identifiable with the author himself.[12]

But, as in any good satire, the characters presented by Quesnel are all, to some extent, caricatures of these real-life counterparts. Surely Boucher de Montarville was not as uncritically accepting of his son-in-law's ridiculous Anglophilia as our Monsieur Primenbourg proves to be, or as fatuous as the incident involving Monsieur François and his horse paints him, or, for that matter, as prompt to see the error of his ways and to readjust them radically. This is legitimate exaggeration for comic effect, as old as satire itself. Similarly, the colonel, the doctor, and the poet François are as exuberantly overdrawn as the character-types created by Molière, or by Aristophanes and Plautus before him. And in much the same way, the neat structure of the piece, with its artificial resolution reminiscent of many classical comedies, is an improvement on 'real life' that is imposed by the author. This is a play in which the fictive-comedic dimension prevails, as indeed it must in order to justify the text's resuscitation.

As to setting, it is ironic, given the characters and situation, that the play has so little else reflective of Canada (or, for that matter, of European French literary tastes at the turn of the century). Its verse form – rhymed alexandrine couplets – is the most traditional characteristic of French classicism, of the age of Molière, Racine, and Corneille. Predictably, the apparent intent that informs the play is also identical with that of Molière, as with that of the poet Horace seventeen centuries before him: *castigare ridendo mores*, to curb social excesses by exposing them to ridicule. Its structure responds also to classic dictates: the unities of time and place are rigidly observed (the duration of the action is identical to playing time; that action – all verbal – takes place in one office or ante-room, with every entrance or departure constituting a new scene). The unity of action is observed as well, although less rigorously (the amusing digressions that introduce Doctor Pennkrève and the poet François illustrate Primenbourg's foibles and those of the colonel, thus linking them, loosely at least, to the central theme). In short, this is a play whose form and aesthetic values would have been fully familiar to French audiences a century and a half before its composition.

5. Language

Anglomania represents an exception among the plays included here in that the language of Quesnel's characters does not include a single typically Canadian word or turn of phrase. There is no reference either to New World geography (indeed, the word 'Canada' is used only once and is made to rhyme derisively with Kamchatka in Far Eastern Russia, consonant in late eighteenth-century parlance with remoteness and lack of civilization). Apart from the hilariously deformed speech of Doctor Pennkrève there is little to distinguish the French spoken by any of the other characters.

Finally, since there is nothing poetic except the form in Quesnel's original text, I have here translated it into prose. As a result the constant, distracting inversions of syntax necessary for placement of rhyme in the French text disappear and the rhythms of normal speech are more easily approximated. Otherwise, here and in the other play texts that follow, the intent is to remain as close as possible to the spirit and diction of the original text without being slavishly dependent upon it.

JOSEPH QUESNEL

Anglomania, or Dinner, English-Style

CHARACTERS

Mr Primenbourg, a French-Canadian Seigneur
Mrs Primenbourg
The Dowager Primenbourg[13] [Mr Primenbourg's mother]
Lucette, daughter of Mr Primenbourg
Colonel Beauchamp, son-in-law of Mr Primenbourg
Doctor Pennkrève
Vielmont, a military officer, relative of Mr Primenbourg
Mr François, a poet

Setting: *Mr Primenbourg's country home. The stage represents a room decorated English-style, alongside which is an office where Mr Primenbourg and the Colonel are conversing.*

SCENE I
Mr Primenbourg, The Colonel

Colonel: I repeated your fervent request so often that he's decided to accept the invitation, for tomorrow.

Mr Primenbourg: Colonel!! So tomorrow – at last! – I shall have the honour of hosting our Governor at dinner!

Colonel: Yes, dear father-in-law, tomorrow.

Mr Primenbourg: What an honour! And you say Her Ladyship will accompany him?

Colonel: Yes, for certain.

Mr Primenbourg: I'm ecstatic – no matter how much trouble we'll have to go to – I'm so delighted that my heart is fairly bursting with joy! Oh, even though I'm a rich man, if anyone had ever told me I would play host to someone they call 'Your Excellency,' I would never have believed it!

Colonel: Well, I certainly believe you on that score! And that's what comes from having a son-in-law like me. In fact, ever since that lucky day for you when I married your daughter, thereby embellishing your family name by linking it to mine, with typical selflessness I've thought only of your own good. Which, just between the two of us, is something you really needed. You just didn't have the style, the elegant manners, required of a landed gentleman with an income of twenty thousand francs. You were completely unknown to the power brokers, the social élite! In fact, the only people you were known to associate with were your own relatives. And good heavens, what relatives! Oh – nice, kind, polite folk – second to none as far as that's concerned – but not the least bit *fashionable*! As far as your social standing was concerned, they were nothing but an obstacle. That's why, first things first, I put the run to all of them. Everything started to improve the moment they disappeared, too, and I'm quite pleased with the progress you've made. I'm even hopeful of making you a real presence in the Governor's court!

Mr Primenbourg: And every day I thank my lucky stars for all you've done for me, Colonel! How ridiculous I must have seemed, really! My wife, my house and furnishings, my clock, even my table-settings – nothing was English! Everything about me reeked of the Middle Ages! But I took your advice: following your directions, I changed my dishes, had cutlery and serving-ware melted down, substituted copper for my gold plate and pewter for my silverware – in short, I managed to introduce some taste into this household!

Colonel: Yes, and you're all the better for it. But I see Madame is coming this way.

Mr Primenbourg: And here's my mother with her.

SCENE II
Mr Primenbourg, Mrs Primenbourg, The Dowager, The Colonel

Mrs Primenbourg: Well well! my son-in-law! Good day to you – I didn't know you had returned.

Colonel: I've just come for a brief visit, to see the family.

Mrs Primenbourg: You're always welcome here.

Dowager: How is our daughter?

Colonel: Oh, the same as usual. Yesterday, tea at the old General's house; tomorrow I've been invited, along with her, to tea at the young Baroness's ...

Dowager: May the good Lord forgive me for saying so, but I'm afraid you're going to kill her with all that tea! In the good old days when the French ruled here we were all so healthy – and I ask you, did we ever drink tea? Never! Except maybe as medicine, when someone had a migraine. But these Englishmen of yours drink tea morning, noon, and night, whether they like it or need it! They'd rather be caught dead than be caught without tea! And that's why you see them all with pale faces, weak stomachs, and a skinny, starving appearance, instead of the rosy complexions everyone had in our time! That's what this stupid habit of theirs has led to!

Mr Primenbourg: Mother! For my son-in-law's sake you really shouldn't make such a scene for no good reason! You should realize that tea served by a *General* would never harm even the most sensitive stomach!

Dowager: That I don't believe.

Colonel: Being invited to tea by the upper class is a special favour, Madame, to which only people of a certain station can aspire.

Mrs Primenbourg: Just the same, ask her to take care of herself.

Mr Primenbourg: All right, but I think she should continue to accept these invitations. Let's change the subject. Do you know who we're going to have to dinner tomorrow?

Mrs Primenbourg: I believe we're going to have my sister and my first cousin – they've agreed to come to dinner tomorrow.

Colonel: (*aside, to* Mr Primenbourg) Those two wouldn't fit in too well. As you're well aware, sir, with a governor you must ...

Mr Primenbourg: (*aside, to the* Colonel) Quite right. (*Aloud, to his wife.*) My dear, I'm sure your sister knows how happy we always are to see her. She knows both she and our cousin are always welcome at our table. But we can't have them to dinner tomorrow!

Mrs Primenbourg: What a shame! And why not?

Mr Primenbourg: Because of this bit of news, Madame: Our Governor and his retinue are going to do us the honour of dining in this house tomorrow!

Dowager: Well! Is that any reason to exclude one's own sister? What a *dis*graceful way to show one's social graces!

Mr Primenbourg: Mother, this is not just a family dinner, to which everyone is welcome, as is!

Colonel: Since only people of certain refinement are to be invited, surely one is entitled to invite only whomever one wishes ...

Dowager: Really now, Colonel! What a nice way of putting it! And whom then, in your opinion, should we invite to this dinner, if our own sisters, cousins, and other relatives aren't to be included?

Mr Primenbourg: Mother, I beg of you, don't get yourself all overwrought! Our son-in-law has no intention of offending you, but we can surely discuss whom we're going to invite. And – no offence to you – we should try, as he says, insofar as possible, to make this a dinner English-style.

Dowager: English-style or not, the main thing is to treat people properly, with due consideration. Style has nothing to do with it!

Mr Primenbourg: You're too set on the old-fashioned ways of doing things, Mother.

Dowager: The old ways weren't any less sensible, believe me!

Mr Primenbourg: That may well be. But since we are fortunate enough, at present, to be English, let's take pride in that fact and follow English customs to the extent possible.

Dowager: Well, as far as I'm concerned, son, I shall continue to follow French customs. It's a waste of time arguing with you. Go ahead and arrange your banquet any way you wish. As for me, I want no part of it. Good day to you.

Mr Primenbourg: (*watching her leave*) I do despair of ever bringing mother around to accepting fashionable manners!

Mrs Primenbourg: I'm sorry to see her leave so abruptly.

Mr Primenbourg: At her age, she's entitled to be a bit stubborn.

Mrs Primenbourg: Yes, but there's no need to make her angry! I'm going to go with her.

SCENE III
Mr Primenbourg, The Colonel

Colonel: How distasteful it is to have to struggle constantly against their preju- dices! But I know you always follow my advice; in fact I won't hesitate to say – no flattery intended – you're the only one around here intelligent enough to let your- self be governed by me.

Mr Primenbourg: Well, it wouldn't be very intelligent of me *not* to follow your advice, since even the Governor and Her Ladyship value it so highly!

Colonel: My dear father-in-law, I told you that in confidence, and it's something that it would be unwise to repeat elsewhere since it might make people think I'm vain. Let's change the subject, and talk about tomorrow instead. Between the two of us, let's choose respectable people, who will bring rank and prestige to the dinner table.

Mr Primenbourg: Which is not such a challenge for us, after all; it's something we can manage rather easily ...

Colonel: As for you, you certainly are as elegant as any of the fine bourgeois folk I got to know in France ... But it's quite another matter, as far as the English are concerned. Especially when it comes to court manners and customs!

Mr Primenbourg: I'm not familiar with court manners, it's true. But I could invite my sister and my brother-in-law. When they were young they travelled a lot, visiting France, London, and Paris ...

Colonel: How can you still mention 'France,' when we're talking about taste and refinement? As I've already pointed out, your relatives are really not fit to appear at a dinner like this one.

Mr Primenbourg: We *have* to invite my sisters, my brother, and my nieces. To my mind, they're the only ones – apart from myself – who can consort with the upper class. Moreover, since the Governor is bringing ladies along, surely you'll agree that a few women will have to be ... Oh, I hear someone coming! It's that Doctor of yours.

SCENE IV
Mr Primenbourg, The Colonel, Dr Pennkrève[14]

Doctor: Vell vell, Gurnel! Your humple serfant ...

Colonel: Good day to you, Doctor!

Doctor: Vile I am doink my rounts I learn mit bleasure zat you are here. I gongratulate Meinsieur Brimenpurk: for zat I am barticularly bleased!

Mr Primenbourg: Please sit down, Doctor. There's a chair.

Colonel: How have you been?

Doctor: Fairy goot!

Colonel: I'm happy to hear that.

Mr Primenbourg: And your patients?

Doctor: Not too bat. I cure zem all, egzept zose who inzist on dyink, in spite of mein efforts! But I can't cure efferypody ...

Colonel: That's for sure.

Doctor: I haff had four gaces of bleurisy to dreat – unt only zree of zem diet on me!

Colonel: (*to* Mr Primenbourg) Three out of four! That's a good record, I guess.

Mr Primenbourg: Yes. But let's leave medicine aside for now. Doctor, I would like your advice on something.

Doctor: On vat?

Mr Primenbourg: On cooking. We've invited the Governor for dinner here tomorrow. Tell me, what do we need to make a good pâté?

Colonel: They say the ones you make are excellent.

Doctor: Gurnel, since you haff gonfitence in me, I can come domorrow unt I vould be honourt to perform a bâté, if I can, to ze Goffernor's daste.

Colonel: Talent such as yours will take you a long way, my friend. It's always a good idea to show off one's skills for others.

Mr Primenbourg: Can we count on you, then?

Doctor: On mine honour, chentlemen. Zee you domorrow!

Mr Primenbourg: We'll see you tomorrow.

SCENE V
The Colonel, Mr Primenbourg

Colonel: Well, there's one good thing arranged for the dinner!

Mr Primenbourg: I've see him display his skills more than once. He's so obliging!

Colonel: I think so, too. Well! here's someone else coming ...

Mr Primenbourg: (*aside*) Oh! It's Monsieur François. I'd like to tease him a bit, just to have some fun.

SCENE VI
Mr Primenbourg, The Colonel, Mr François

Mr François: Don't stir yourselves on my account, gentlemen, I pray you. I was just coming to say hello to Monsieur de Primenbourg.[15] (*To the* Colonel.) Then I heard you were back in these parts ...

Colonel: Good day, my dear friend.

Mr François: And I'm your friend, too. We are each as fond of the other as the other is, I believe.

Colonel: Well, I'm certainly grateful to you for saying so! My dear father-in-law, here you have one of my protégés: I've been looking after his interests for twenty years now. A fine citizen he is, well deserving of my consideration.

Mr Primenbourg: (*aside*) And the biggest liar in the whole world!

Colonel: How are you? How goes the poetry? Are you still writing any?

Mr François: Frankly, poetry is an art that no one appreciates in this country. I'm so disgusted with all of Canada that I'd gladly go write my rhymes in Kamchatka, for next to nothing!

Colonel: Now what's the cause of this bleak mood of yours, my friend?

Mr François: You ask? In the twenty years that, inspired by Minerva, I've been following the dictates of the god of poetry, what have I ever received as compensation for my efforts? How many times have I graced the pages of newspapers here with my poems on the military defeats of France? How many times have my poems, like good lawful subjects, glorified Britannia's victories?

Colonel: Indeed, my good friend, I believe your poetry deserves to be rewarded by the state, in our national interest. As sworn protector of every good citizen, I intend to intercede for you with the Governor. But in order to secure his goodwill right off, I would like to be able to show him some of your work. So tell me: what fine things have you written lately?

Mr François: 'Great God, for George III'[16] ... do you know that one?

Colonel: Do I know that one! A charming song, one you hear in all the clubs and taverns as soon as people have had a few drinks! It's based on the English 'God Save the King.' There's no doubt loyalty drips from your rhymed couplets. I'm certainly a fervent defender of your talents, but I didn't realize you were such a stout royalist as well. Actually, I'd like to obtain some consideration for you from the king himself.

Mr Primenbourg: Just a moment, Colonel – I'm against that idea! Perhaps my opposition will come as a surprise to Monsieur François, but I feel I must express it.

Mr François: But what have I done to make you angry with me?

Mr Primenbourg: You've taken liberties with the truth in your poems, and, I must say, that's made me quite displeased!

Mr François: Well, you know there *is* a thing they call 'poetic licence' – and that's something I'm more familiar with than you are ...

Colonel: Would you mind telling me what this is all about?

Mr François: ... all you have to do is read Horace's statements on that ...

Mr Primenbourg: As far as horses go, I'm an expert on them!

Mr François: And the critic Boileau[17] – just read what he has to say on the subject!

Mr Primenbourg: When it comes to horses, there's not much you can tell me!

Mr François: But when it comes to poetry, you should bow to me!

Mr Primenbourg: Instead of writing lies, you'd be better off not writing at all!

Colonel: Gentlemen! Let's at least agree on the topic! One of you is talking about poetry, and the other about horses. And I really can't fathom what it is you're both referring to!

Mr François: Well, as far as I'm concerned, if I've been wrong I'm ready to admit it.

Mr Primenbourg: Perhaps you remember, Monsieur, that in an insolent tale you invented you gravely insulted me, whom you disguised under the name of d'Imberville.[18] You wrote that one day I was about to leave for town when I saw you coming with some poetry you wanted to read me; and that I whipped my horse to get away as fast as I could!

Mr François: Oh, now I see what you're getting at! ...

Mr Primenbourg: There's obviously no need to tell you anything more. You know who the author of this malicious poem is. But luckily my horse is well known also, and I can prove, despite your attempt at humour, that what you report is nothing but a lie. The fact is, for a good six months I thought I had *lost* my whip – it had been hanging up in the stable! So tell me, Colonel, haven't I a right to complain?

Colonel: You don't have to worry about tales like that as far as our governor is concerned – he's not easily taken in. He's aware of your reputation as a connoisseur of horseflesh. On the other hand, I must admit the tale *was* rather funny ...

Mr Primenbourg: To invent a story as nasty as that, you have to have an unhealthy penchant for satire!

Mr François: So here I am, already tried and condemned! Oh, please, Monsieur, before they hang me, would you allow me to speak? Is that really the reason why you're unhappy with me? Why didn't you tell me so, sooner? I have a gift for embellishing things that has no equal anywhere. I can take a horse like Don Quixote's Rocinante, and make of it Alexander the Great's Bucephalus! And certainly I had no intention whatever of insulting you. How was I to know you were so sensitive on that point? For me, it would have been so easy to make amends for my crime: all I had to do was change a word, perhaps a rhyme, and put, for example, that

Prancing, and neighing, and all hot to trot
Your horse, *without whipping*, took off like a shot.

Mr Primenbourg: That's the truth, and that's what you should have said, instead of making my horse an object of ridicule!

Mr François: All right, then, let's be reconciled on that point. I'll see that it's changed.

Colonel: Come, dear father-in-law, let's have it end there. Our friend recognizes his mistake. The distress he caused you, he caused unintentionally. I know his character – he's not nasty, deep down! But how long can one resist one's natural inclination?

Mr Primenbourg: Hum! – a fine 'inclination' – towards libel!

Mr François: Forgive me, Monsieur. I write only in jest, and to get a laugh from my readers. The Colonel will vouch for me: he's fond of adding a poetic touch to his speeches, and is as expert in poetry as he is in politics. And he knows that a poet, when he's carried away by his inspiration, often stretches the truth a bit in his depictions. Indeed, the well-spring of wit that stings, but pleases and amuses, often arises directly from that aspect of his muse! I'll leave it up to him: let him act as arbiter between us.

Colonel: My word of honour, I don't think the case could be better put! I know the author of an excellent work (it's a poem – in verse – entitled *L'Aréopage*).[19] Nobody writes poetry like that man![20] But you really should hear him speak on that subject. Really, his views are identical to yours; and, in fact, each of you rhymes almost as well as the other! That's the way the muse rations out talent to a poet, so that boldly he'll sting, he'll mock, he'll move you, or he'll simply write nonsense. In a word, writing in prose or in verse is not the same thing at all. The poet always exaggerates. And frankly, dear father-in-law, in that little tale of his, I think you did well to come off with nothing worse than one crack of the whip!

Mr Primenbourg: Do English poets enjoy this same sort of poetic licence?

Colonel: In England, they're just as malicious as they are in France, but nobody pays much attention to their banter.

Mr Primenbourg: All right, in that case I won't say anything more. I forgive you for everything, and no hard feelings.

Mr François: But please excuse me, gentlemen, for dropping in unexpectedly like this. You were discussing important business, and I shall leave you to it. But I'd like to come back and talk with you tomorrow.

Mr Primenbourg: (*aside, to the* Colonel) He intends to come back again tomorrow. Is he looking to be invited to the dinner?

Colonel: Let's make sure he doesn't come. (*Running to the door.*) François, my friend, we won't be here tomorrow! Come back some other time!

Mr François: All right.

SCENE VII
Mr Primenbourg, The Colonel

Colonel: If we invited him, he'd have to eat in the kitchen.

Mr Primenbourg: If only he were an officer in the militia, we might be able to honour him with an invitation.

Colonel: Invite a poet to dine with a governor? That would be fine company for him, indeed!

Mr Primenbourg: Frankly, seeing your fondness for him and your friendship, I was afraid for a while that he *would* be coming to the dinner!

Colonel: Confidentially, I don't think very much of the man. He's not a bad sort, and I've known him for a long time. But he's the type of chap you only want to see occasionally, and only receive socially when there's no one else about; the type it's better to flatter, than to be bitten by!

Mr Primenbourg: That's the best way to treat him. You certainly do know how to deal with people ... Oh, here comes Lucette!

SCENE VIII
Mr Primenbourg, The Colonel, Lucette

Lucette: Welcome to you, dear Colonel Beauchamp! How naughty of you to surprise us like this – and how sweet of you, as well! How's your family? How about your youngest little daughter, is she being good? Does my sister dine with Her Ladyship very often? My, how happy we all are with this government! May I return with you, dear little brother-in-law of mine?

Colonel: Any more questions to ask me, my dear sister-in-law? Come, give me a hug. My wife is not as spry as you are. The doctor has ordered her do a bit of walking, and not to attend so many balls because they make her ill.

Lucette: That's a shame. But a bit of exercise will certainly do her good. I love to walk, myself, and in fact I don't think there's anything better for one's health. But how can ballroom dancing be bad for her? I've certainly never tired from it!

Mr Primenbourg: At your age, daughter, one never gets tired. But just you wait – one day ...

Lucette: Papa! Are you serious?

Mr Primenbourg: Let's change the subject – we've other things to talk about. You have to get ready to offer our hospitality – here, in this house, tomorrow – to ... the Governor and Her Ladyship!

Lucette: *Her Ladyship* is coming here?!

Colonel: Just as he says, Lucette. Don't forget to primp for the occasion!

Lucette: Will you give me advice on how I should look?

Colonel: Yes indeed. I'll have your hair done the way the Governor's circle does it.

Lucette: Fabulous! That's always the prettiest style. But tell me, dear brother-in-law, is your sister coming?

Mr Primenbourg: We're certainly not going to forget her, since she'll be hostess at the dinner!

Lucette: You couldn't have made a better choice. Oh, I'm really happy about that: she's the one who really knows English customs!

SCENE IX
Mr Primenbourg, The Colonel, Lucette, Mr de Vielmont

Colonel: (*interrupting* Lucette) Hush! I see Vielmont coming. – Well! Good day to you, my friend!

Vielmont: Have you been here long?

Colonel: A couple of hours.

Vielmont: My aunt told me you were here. I ran into her a little while ago, in a terribly irritable and unhappy mood. She complained to me about young people today, who are now so different from when she was young. And about the fact that everybody's copying English customs and tastes. That frivolity is in vogue, and that thriftiness is forgotten, and I don't know what else. She's complaining about the fact that everything in general is topsy-turvy nowadays. As you can guess, she sticks to her old prejudices! But I suppose at her age she's entitled to speak her mind as freely as she wants ...

Colonel: Do you know the reason for all these complaints of hers?

Vielmont: No – and frankly, I'm not interested in them. But she did mention some sort of English-style dinner that's to be given tomorrow. Anyone else but her would just have laughed at such a silly idea, but the old lady is getting on, and tends to get worked up over everything instead of laughing off the idiotic things that go on these days.

Mr Primenbourg: Mother often likes to contradict, just for the pleasure of it ...

Lucette: That's true – grandmother likes to take an opposite stand on things.

Vielmont: As though it made any difference whether a dinner was served Turkish-style, or English style, as long as it's a good meal ...!

Colonel: Pardon me, no, you're quite wrong there, my friend – Turkish and English styles can't be compared. They're quite different!

Lucette: Golly, I can believe it! I heard it said at the [Governor's] Château that the Turks are not even Christian!

Vielmont: I don't know what to respond to that. I speak my mind, and that's all there is to it.

Colonel: That's not very politic on your part. You should at least show a bit more circumspection and some respect for English customs. I know your preference for French tastes in everything: deep down, you think the same way your aunt does. And that's why I've told you, as a true friend, the only place where you'll ever achieve any prominence is among Frenchmen – that's the right place for Monsieur Vielmont!

Vielmont: Now there's a dire prognosis indeed from Monsieur Beauchamp! How can I ever lead a happy life after a sentence like that! Please be charitable enough not to mention that to others. I'm quite aware you are a talented courtier – you like that life, and you're welcome to it. But let's change topics, and talk instead about the Château. Any news from there, Colonel? They say there's nothing interesting in the mail?

Colonel: Who says that? There's been a battle fought, and the French lost two of their generals, two thousand infantrymen, and four thousand horses with their riders. It's a decisive blow. The French can only go on the defensive now. Our troops are pushing back the enemy everywhere, and within two months you'll see them at the very gates of Paris!

Mr Primenbourg: Excellent! The Lord be praised!

Lucette: I'm delighted to hear that! Her Ladyship will probably have a reception to celebrate, and you'll be invited, and me too!

Vielmont: I'm afraid, my dear Colonel, that your source may not be all that reliable. I've read all the newspaper reports on the French troops and – unfortunately! – all I read about is their brilliant victories. In fact, after what happened in the latest engagement, it's believed that a truce will soon be sought, and an end put to the war![21]

Lucette: That's too bad! Then what will happen to the reception?

Colonel: How can you contradict me like that? I tell you, we've won a victory! And in a case like this, who's to be believed, you or me?

Vielmont: Whichever one is telling the truth.

Mr Primenbourg: Really, Vielmont, sometimes you're as stubborn as the devil! Can you really claim to be as well informed on the latest news as my son-in-law is? You know what sort of position he has in government!

Vielmont: I've heard about that. They tell me it's really lucrative.

Mr Primenbourg: And, moreover, honourable!

Vielmont: Is it true that you have rights to all the leftover food from banquets?

Colonel: Yes indeed! In fact, that's my best source of income, since it allows us to live opulently, without expense!

Vielmont: Then you really do have a wonderful position! Since you get to taste all the Governor's food, no doubt you also get to share all his secrets. Well, consider me a fool if ever again I dare to disagree when you announce political news to us!

Mr Primenbourg: Well said, Vielmont, and that's a good resolution to make. You should never contradict anyone without realizing the source of that person's information. You were in the wrong!

Vielmont: Oh yes, as wrong as a person can be! I'm quite embarrassed at my own audacity! So goodbye, Colonel. The French troops –

Colonel: – Have been defeated, thank heavens!

Lucette: Fabulous! So no doubt Her Ladyship will give a concert, or a ball, or a dinner, or a country outing!

Colonel: I'll take it up with the Governor.

Vielmont: As for me, I can't expect to be honoured by an invitation. But I must hurry and tell the newspaper that what it's published is a lie. So, gentlemen, without further ado – goodbye, Lucette.

SCENE X
Mr Primenbourg, The Colonel, Lucette

Mr Primenbourg: We certainly silenced him on that topic!

Colonel: I'm pretty sure I was the one he wanted to get at, and unless I'm greatly mistaken his quarrelsome mood isn't without connection to his aunt's remarks.

Mr Primenbourg: He's always had a bantering wit, and he's not going to change.

SCENE XI
Mr Primenbourg, Mrs Primenbourg, The Dowager, The Colonel, Lucette

Mrs Primenbourg: (*holding a letter*) Oh! my dear Primenbourg! Oh! you poor man! I've come bringing sad news. In this letter ...

Lucette: What is it, Maman?

Mr Primenbourg: Who's it from?

Dowager: Her Ladyship is not coming.

Colonel: Her Ladyship!

Mr Primenbourg: But – why?

Mrs Primenbourg: This letter will explain.

Dowager: All I can tell you is that the special courier told me so.

Lucette: What a pity!

Colonel: What a setback!

Mr Primenbourg: What a terrible disappointment! I'm crushed!

Lucette: Her Ladyship is not coming!

Mrs Primenbourg: And all the expenses we've incurred will be for naught!

Mr Primenbourg: (*impatiently*) Here now, let's see the letter. It would have been a far sight better not to have promised to come! (*Looking at the seal.*) It's from the Governor ... Let's see what it says

Monsieur,

We had planned on coming to your home tomorrow, and having the honour to dine[22] and spend the day with you and your whole family. But, following information received from your dear son-in-law Colonel Beauchamp, my aide-de-camp, we have decided to put off this charming occasion since your family will not be present. Her Ladyship wishes, as do I, that your family members be present.

What does this mean?

Mrs Primenbourg: What did you do, son-in-law?

Colonel: I am just as surprised as you are by this letter. His Excellency has certainly changed his mind!

Dowager: No, he hasn't changed his mind, I assure you. The Governor wanted the family's company, and didn't want all this fuss and bother. I told you so.

Mr Primenbourg: What an unfortunate turn of events! Now we won't have the great honour we were looking forward to!

Colonel: It's only been postponed, dear father-in-law. Cheer up – I'll take care of everything. But not a word about this ...

Mrs Primenbourg: Everyone will be offended!

Colonel: Then we'll do our best to make amends. If we have to invite certain people, we'll invite them.

Dowager: Now just think for a minute! What a fine scheme that was – announcing that certain people were absent, when they're right here! Doesn't that strike you as a bit odd?

Colonel: Frankly, I thought it was all right. The people you're talking about certainly aren't familiar with English manners, and since it was to be a dinner ...

Dowager: What a fine excuse that is! Is my family any less cultivated than others', then? Even if your English manners aren't to their taste, aren't they well-bred enough to be invited anywhere you might wish?

Mrs Primenbourg: Mother is quite right.

Mr Primenbourg: (*after a moment's reflection*) I think so, too.

Colonel: So I'm left all alone, like some village idiot? Now that you've changed your mind, I can see that soon I'll be the one blamed for this whole mess. Well, I may have been the cause, but quite innocently! And the whole thing can be made good without too much trouble. Let's get rid of this letter, and I'll take upon myself the honour of inviting everybody, in the Governor's name. I'll have the credit for this favour, and you could even intimate to them, on the sly, that the invitation has come about through my intervention.

Dowager: (*aside*) What vanity!

Mr Primenbourg: I hate beating round the bush like that! Besides, they wouldn't believe me. Better to say nothing, than try to pull the wool over their eyes. What do you think, Mother?

Dowager: Very well said, son! Enough of these roundabout tactics. If you take my advice, you'll swear off these foreign fashions and ridiculous snobbery. As I've always said, you're far too gullible! Everybody is to be judged on his or her own worth: let the English stay English and let us remain forever French!

Colonel: Monsieur doesn't need any advice on that account. He knows what's appropriate and what's not ...

Dowager: He may have changed his tastes on your advice, Colonel, but he now sees his error!

Mr Primenbourg: You're quite right. I've come around to your view. (*To the* Colonel.) I'm sorry to disappoint you, but I've made up my mind.

Dowager: Well done!

Colonel: Can this be true?

Lucette: (*aside*) What! Papa wants to de-English us! (*To the* Colonel.) Try to defend yourself, at least! There are thousands of good arguments you could raise!

Colonel: No, I've said enough and more than enough, for anyone who knows how to appreciate good taste and elegance.

Lucette: You must admit, on that point my brother-in-law is right, Papa! When it comes to elegance, there's nothing like an Englishman – especially when he's dancing!

Mr Primenbourg: Silence, daughter!

Lucette: Really! I've got rights, too!

Colonel: How to explain such a sudden change? What! – You're actually returning to your old ways? Well, you'd better be prepared for negative criticism from the English. Thanks to me, you've acquired a certain reputation among them. Are you prepared to say goodbye to the advantages resulting from that?

Mr Primenbourg: No, I understand the advantages of being known to them. I know how to appreciate them, and their customs. But I also see that we can retain their esteem without abandoning our forefathers' traditions. I admit that I was completely wrong with regard to all that. But if I was wrong, you're the one responsible! First you're convinced my family is unworthy of attending a dinner like this one, and then here we have His Excellency honestly wanting to meet them and insisting that they be present! So style has nothing to do with it, although it's English 'style' that's been draining my purse and turning my household upside down! Well, I'm going back to my old ways, whatever gossips and critics may say! I'll invite the Governor, along with my family, and a lot of other people I want to invite to brighten up the dinner table, though you may grumble about it. After dealing with serious matters, comic relief is welcome. You can't go on talking about politics all the time, so my first aim will be to amuse Her Ladyship. And all the decent folk hereabouts will help me achieve it – I'll invite all the Germans and French in the village.

Colonel: All right, I fully support this worthy project, dear father-in-law, and I hereby applaud it wholeheartedly. Did you really think you'd be punishing me by doing that? No, no – I see nothing in your plan that I don't approve! There's no such thing as festivity without fun, and our Governor certainly likes lighthearted entertainment. You want to invite the French and the Germans? Bravo! A great idea: their different languages, tastes, and personalities, not to mention their different appearances, should all combine to encourage merrymaking! To start with, Mont Frédérick[23] will probably take us all around Germany in some long speech during which he won't neglect a morsel of food as he gulps down his champagne! He'll tell us about Altendorf, Frankfurt, Bamberg – and especially about 'ze gourt uff ze Tuke von Würtemperk,' where he got to know 'an olt tuchess' – and he'll even reveal to you privately what the duchess has on her rump.[24] He's an amusing chap – has seen everything, read everything. There's not a single ruler anywhere who doesn't know him. He'll even swear that his dreams are reality! And right next to him will be dear Doctor Pennkrève, solemn, sterile, polite, well-versed in more than one trade (he recently qualified for a certificate as armed bodyguard). So he'll talk to you about cooking 'shtews,' and, in the same breath, about galloping consumption, 'frigassées,' 'ultsers unt pharmasoiticals,' and charm everyone with his delightful French. Beside him will be my good friend François. His gloomy look, behind which he conceals his lunacy, runs the risk of throwing a wet blanket on the party, but since he's both poet and musician, people will forgive him for his grotesque appearance. He really loves to criticize poetry (between the two of us, he's even made fun of *L'Aréopage*!)[25] But in fact his whole knowledge of poetry doesn't amount to a hill of beans. The verdict is in on that poem – it's a thing of beauty, and always will be! Apart from that, he's rather a good sort of chap, though sometimes a bit of a clown. He'll fit in quite well with the guests you've mentioned, along with any others you want to invite. And to end things on the right note, how happy I would be if Lucette were to sing her English arietta! Nothing could possibly be better than that to round off the dinner. As a finishing touch, *coronabit opus*![26]

Mr Primenbourg: I would agree to that. And she's got dozens of songs – in French, in English – her pockets are stuffed with them! Let's have her choose a good one.

Lucette: If you wish, I'll sing my arietta. It's no problem choosing, since I only know one. But it's better than a lot of others, since it's precisely the one Her Ladyship sings!

Dowager: I'm really happy to see you all agree on this now. It's nice to see people admit they've been wrong. And just the thought of us all getting together, as our folks used to do in the good old days! – Oh! how sorry I am they've gone – as far as good *ragoûts* and pastry-making goes, those were the days! My, how things have changed and gone downhill since then! – In any case, all you have to do is tell me what day you've chosen for the party, and I assure you I'll do the honours as well as anyone. Don't forget, now!

Mr Primenbourg: We won't, Mother, and you can count on us to let you know.

Dowager: Splendid. I'll see you then.

SCENE XII
Mr Primenbourg, Mrs Primenbourg, The Colonel, Lucette

Mr Primenbourg: I'm really happy to be able to invite both my sister and my aunt! You know, there's nothing like a good get-together, without fuss or bother!

Colonel: Well, as far as I'm concerned, from now on I'll go along with everything. Go ahead and follow the old ways, or the new fashions – it's of as little importance to me as to a village rustic! I know what my opinion is – but everyone to his own tastes! As the saying goes, you've got to run with the pack. But it's getting late – they've already sounded evening tattoo, and tonight I'm invited to a reception for the most refined society. I'll be back in a couple of days. Good evening, father-in-law; and to you, Madame Primenbourg.

Mr Primenbourg: What! You're leaving already?

Colonel: Yes, I really can't stay – I've overdone it, as it is! But you may count on me for the party, and I'll invite the Governor tomorrow, without fail!

Mr Primenbourg: (*running towards the door*) Tell him the family will be there!

Colonel: As you wish. But I still say: Hurrah for English style!

Mr Primenbourg: He won't budge an inch! – But he's gone. Now, my dear, we have to start getting things ready for the big day. And as for you, Lucette, tune up your vocal chords to sing that arietta. I expect your boyfriend will be there too, so ... no false notes!

Lucette: I'll do my best, Papa.

II

The Status Quo Comedies

INTRODUCTION

1. Political and Historical Context

The five satirical playlets we know as the *Comédies du statu quo* (*Status Quo Comedies*) are the clearest examples of what was an unusually vigorous theatrical vein in nineteenth-century Quebec: political theatre. More precisely, the texts presented here belong to a subgenre often labelled 'political paratheatre' because, like the majority of such texts, they were not intended for, or capable of, performance. They represent a tradition with roots going back to the French Régime in Canada, but which came into particular favour after the establishment of the first newspapers in the 1760s. And unlike the other French-language plays visible or available before the 1830s, political theatre was written by native Canadians for Canadians.

When the first of the *Status Quo Comedies* appeared in John Neilson's *Gazette de Québec* on 26 April 1834, it represented a real escalation in current political tension. At the moment, conflict centred around the reformist Ninety-Two Resolutions drawn up by the largely French-Canadian Patriote party and passed in the House of Assembly that spring. Those who supported these far-ranging resolutions were derisively labelled *résolutionnaires* by their opponents, and the latter were in turn branded 'supporters of the status quo' by the Patriotes. Writing in the *Quebec Mercury*, a journal allied with the *Gazette* in the anti-'Resolutionaries' cause, the editor, William Kemble, remarked, on 3 May 1834:

We wish we could translate, or successfully imitate, the admirable *petite Comédie* published in a late number of Mr. Neilson's French *Gazette* which brings on the scene several of the puppets employed by the master showman [i.e., Louis-Joseph Papineau] in getting up his resolutory, or more properly speaking *revolutionary*, exhibitions in this city. But the manner and phraseology of these *notables* is not translatable, and the humour can only be felt by those who are conversant with the French language, and who are acquainted with the parties presented.[1]

The importance of this playlet (and of the four others that followed it over the next few weeks) in the evolution of French-Canadian drama has long been conceded by scholars working in the field. But to date, Kemble's assessment of their untranslatability has been borne out. This is their first published translation.

There was no real tradition of French-Canadian dramaturgy to speak of by 1834. Demographic dispersal, opposition from the Roman Catholic hierarchy, the absence of printing-presses, and the impermanence of the social and economic class upon which theatrical activity depended, all had militated against theatre in most of its public manifestations in New France. After the Conquest, dialogues and paradramas had begun to appear in newspapers as soon as printing-presses were established in the new British colony. They were published in the early 1790s in pamphlet form, and with obvious political intent: they were functional, wooden dialogues and were most probably intended to be read aloud at public political assemblies for the benefit of the vast majority of the francophone population that remained illiterate in the absence of a general educational system. These markedly political and increasingly theatrical dialogues were the unlikely antecedents for an enduring dramatic strain that would eventually emerge in French Canada, a strain that is by no means extinct today.

This minor genre had reached a first, modest apogee of sorts after the founding in 1806 of *Le Canadien*, the first newspaper established by and for native francophones and their causes. The effectiveness of the original *Canadien*'s paradramatic dialogues – most of them directed against the *vendus*, people like Pierre-Amable de Bonne, who were perceived as traitors to French-Canadian interests[2] – may be deduced, in good part, from the suppression of the journal in 1810 by the colonial administration for the 'libellous' nature of articles like the dialogues, which were frequently directed against that administration.

Between 1810 and 1834 the only indigenous drama published in Lower Canada consisted, with one exception,[3] of scattered, dramatized dialogues in newspapers. Canadian politics, on the other hand, took a more and more dramatic turn in this period, as relations worsened between, on the one hand, the colonial governor, his officers and appointees, and his Executive Council, and, on the other, the House of Assembly, conscious now of its potential role and increasingly vocal in its demands for a share in government policies and the expenditures that implemented them. The session of the Assembly that ended in the spring of 1834 was an especially stormy one, highlighted by the introduction by the Patriote members of the famous Ninety-Two Resolutions.

The text of the resolutions had been composed mainly by Papineau and his friend Augustin-Norbert Morin, and they had been introduced in the House of Assembly (of which Papineau was the speaker) by Elzéar Bédard on 17 February 1834. They were passed by that body five days later, after intense and heated debate, by a vote of fifty-six to thirty-three. With the closing of the session and a general election called for the fall of that year, the drama shifted to another forum: the columns of opposing newspapers in the capital.

Louis-Joseph Papineau and John Neilson, formerly firm political allies, disagreed radically on the nature of this reform project, and the rift between the two would continue to widen. Neilson's newspaper had for some time been carrying well-written satirical attacks in the form of letters, not playlets, that were directed against the 'Resolutionaries' and their cause and signed, mockingly, 'A Friend of the Status Quo.' *Le Canadien* had responded in kind, but its responses, also generally pseudonymous though coming from different and often disparate pens, had been more moderate and less effective, or at least they appear to be so to the modern reader.

2. Sequence and Timing of the Playlets

The First Comedy

The first *Status Quo Comedy* is also signed 'A Friend of the Status Quo,' and it purports to represent a meeting of the principal members of the 'Resolutionaries' resident in Quebec City. It caricatures their speech, ridicules their political knowledge, and accuses them of pursuing base personal interests in their 'resolutionary/revolutionary' campaign. The scene is set in the library of the Legislature, with Étienne Parent, official librarian of the House of Assembly and editor of *Le Canadien*, as protagonist and principal target. The others lampooned in this first comedy are Elzéar Bédard, Hector-Simon Huot, Charles Deguise, Louis Fiset, Félix-Xavier Garneau, Pierre Winter, and Étienne Martel, all of them lawyers or notaries, young (twenty-five to thirty-six years old), and active in the Patriote cause.[4] This first play seems to have caught the opposition entirely by surprise, much to the delight of the editor of the *Mercury*, whose comments are quoted above.

The Second Comedy

Four days later (30 April) the 'Friend of the Status Quo' struck again with another playlet in *La Gazette de Québec* that purported to be a continuation of the first. In this 'Second Act' Parent, Bédard, Huot, and Garneau reappear, along with two new and even more amusing victims, the notary Louis-Théodore Besserer and the young Doctor Jean-Baptiste Grenier. The six scheme and squabble, revealing base motives and shallow minds as they seek to respond to the allegations against them that were appearing in *La Gazette*. This is often considered the funniest, best-structured, and most effective of the five playlets, a judgment that is certainly open to question. As their opponents chortled, the Patriote side fumed ineffectually, relying still on letters and editorials in *Le Canadien*.

The Third Comedy

On 12 May there appeared in *Le Canadien* a more appropriate riposte from the 'Resolutionaries,' couched in dramatic form and signed 'Une Autre Fois' ('Another Time'). This time it was the 'Friends of the Status Quo' who were taken by surprise, for the Patriotes' little playlet represented a further, important escalation. As mentioned, the transparent dramatic pretext underlying the first two comedies was that they represented conversations overheard and transcribed during meetings of the 'Resolutionaries.' The third comedy makes the same claim, but this time it is not pretextual: the author (or authors) and, indeed, the editor of *Le Canadien*, affirm instead that the text represents *actual* dialogue between two specific and named individuals who were overheard at a specific place and time, and they give all the necessary circumstantial detail. Jean-François-Joseph ('Johnny') Duval, member of the House for Upper Town (Quebec City), and Thomas Amiot, a local lawyer, the pair whose conversation is reported in this third playlet, were devastated, and both responded with poorly composed letters in the public press protesting not so much their innocence as the fact that a private conversation (in Duval's law office) had been overheard and made public by an eavesdropper.

Le Canadien published Duval's indignant letter on 14 May, in which he denied any involvement with the 'Friend of the Status Quo' texts, insulted Étienne Parent himself, and demanded to know who the author of the third playlet was. But Duval did his cause little good when he admitted, in the same letter, that he had indeed read aloud in his office the recent article by the 'Friend' *before* its publication in *La Gazette* (this being the central accusation made in the third comedy, from which fact the author or authors deduced that Duval was responsible for the written attacks on the Patriotes signed 'A Friend of the Status Quo'). Parent published Duval's letter, preceding it with his own editorial comment:

Mr Duval has addressed the following letter to us, in which he denies he is the author of the *Status Quo* writings. Judging from his letter, one would believe he is right: the 'Friend of the Status Quo' has frequently displayed wit, but this letter has not the slightest trace of it. According to Mr Duval, we have 'sold out our pen and our conscience to people of ambition'; yet when we took over the management of this newspaper Mr Duval was one of the people most interested in the undertaking and contributed a certain sum of money to encourage it. As to our own talents, they are paltry, to be sure, but they will never be for sale, and will always be free from outside interference.

The incident caused Parent to abandon for a time the relatively moderate stance *Le Canadien* had hitherto adopted in its editorials. In an open letter on the same page he included a much more detailed attack upon Duval, assailing him in particular for the duplicity he had shown in this reported conversation with Amiot on the subject of the creation of Parent's post as paid librarian, quoting chapter and verse of the proceedings in the House that showed Duval had spoken and voted in favour of this appointment.

The Patriotes' comedy, Duval's letter, and Parent's response led to open conflict with the *Mercury*. On 15 May the editor of the latter journal quoted at length – unusually, in French – from Duval's letter and followed it with a translation into English. Proof that the third comedy had struck home comes in Kemble's commentary on that letter, accusing whoever had overheard the conversation between Duval and Amiot of a criminal action ('There is an offence recognized by the English Law, called EVESDROPPING [*sic*]'). Quoting from Blackstone's *Commentaries* to prove his point, the editor of the *Mercury* concluded:

Of all creatures your radical Democrat is indeed the lowest. – But dangerous only from the stealthiness of his attack, which, like that of the Cobra Capella, is inflicted from under your pillow, when you are stretched in repose, in fancied security, and unconscious of the presence of the venomous reptile that is about to give the mortal wound. Happily, in the instance we allude to, the Viper has attacked a file!

Thomas Amiot, in his letter in *La Gazette* on 13 May, had identified Elzéar Bédard as the Patriote who had been in Duval's outer office and overheard the incriminating conversation. Two days later *La Gazette* published a detailed response from Bédard, admitting that it was in fact he, explaining how he had visited Duval's office on legitimate business and had inadvertently heard both the discussion and the reading of the 'Status Quo' article. Accusations and counter-accusations continued in Quebec's newspapers, their tone enlivened by the appearance of the next playlet – by far the shortest – in *Le Canadien* on 19 May, entitled 'A Little Dialogue between Two Friends of the Status Quo.'

The Fourth Comedy

There are only two interlocutors again in this fourth comedy, Thomas Amiot and a highly placed individual who would become the main target of the fifth and last playlet, Advocate-General André-Rémi Hamel. Hamel chastises Amiot for betraying their cause, and threatens to have Amiot reprimanded officially at the next meeting of the Friends of the Status Quo – an interesting bit of irony, since Hamel, in one of the most memorable incidents in the history of the House of Assembly to that point, had been formally reprimanded by the speaker on 19 February 1834 for his intervention in the electoral process. Whether because of the prominence of the individuals now being attacked or the more and more immoderate language being used on both sides, the editors of *Le Canadien* and *La Gazette* seem at this point to have reached a tacit agreement to let tempers cool. Apart from a few sputtering protests by Amiot in the latter journal, a more restrained tone returned to both papers, with even the 'Friend of the Status Quo' toning down, then ceasing his articles by the end of June. This development is not really surprising, for Parent, Neilson, Duval, and Bédard were normally temperate men. As a consequence, the last – and most adversarial – of the *Status Quo Comedies* was published separately in pamphlet form, with the imprint 'United States: Plattsburgh, N.Y., June, 1834,' although like the first Patriote playlet it was signed 'Une Autre Fois.'

The Fifth and Last Comedy

This Parthian shot is entitled *La Déroute du statu quo* (*The Rout of the Status Quo*), and indeed the grapeshot it discharges must have daunted the opposition, although there is no echo of this in the newspapers. The New York imprint is obviously a false one, and there is little doubt that the sixteen-page pamphlet was in fact a product of *Le Canadien*'s presses. This last comedy, unlike the two preceding it, is very close in format to the two written by the 'Friend of the Status Quo,' with its multiplicity of characters, each entering in turn and revealing his reprehensible motives, amoral self-interest, and stupidity. Although perhaps not as amusing as the second comedy, it is tightly structured and wields a well-honed knife against the ringleaders of the Status Quo party. The opening monologue by Advocate-General Hamel, principal target of the piece, has nice overtones of Shakespearean parody, something not found in the preceding texts, and new conspirators are introduced: Édouard Glackemeyer, Jacques Crémazie (brother of the poet Octave), and Louis-David Roy, with Hamel, Thomas Amiot, and Johnny Duval returning from the third and fourth comedies. There is a fine auto-refractory dimension to this last play as well when the Status Quo conspirators impose upon Duval and Amiot, in words and tone directly derivative of the formal reprimand administered to Hamel by Speaker Papineau in the House, a farcical censure for their blunder in allowing themselves to be caught.

Writing about the only three of these playlets he appears to have discovered (those we identify as first, second, and fifth), the conservative Narcisse-Eutrope Dionne gave his preference, seventy-five years after they were written, to the first two, judging the last to be decidedly inferior. Unfortunately, that opinion and in fact his very words have usually been echoed in subsequent references to these texts.[5] I believe any dispassionate reading will reveal that the productions from the 'Resolutionaries' are at least as witty and as well constructed as those written by the opposition.

3. Authorship

Who composed these five playlets? On the Status Quo side, it seems reasonably certain that the authors were Louis-David Roy, then a twenty-seven-year-old lawyer, later to become a respected man of letters and a judge, and Georges-Barthélémi Faribault,[6] at forty-four one of the oldest active participants in the literary battle of the Ninety-Two Resolutions, a lawyer also, a translator for the House of Assembly, and later to become an important archivist and historian. From Roy's appearance in the last comedy, it would appear that his involvement was indeed suspected by the 'Resolutionaries,' who, unsure of their prey, cast a rather wide net. Faribault would have had a particular interest in ensuring that his role was unknown, not only because of his position within the House but also because of his antiquarian interests that brought him into close collaboration with Étienne Parent (Faribault was honorary librarian of the Literary and Historical Society of Quebec and an adviser to the official librarian of the House of Assembly, Parent). One must emphasize, however, that attribution to Roy or Faribault or both, although reasonable, is far from established, despite authoritative-sounding asseverations to the contrary.[7] Others suspected as writers or collaborators are, in decreasing order of probability, Jacques Crémazie, Hamel, Duval, and the unfortunate Amiot.

On the other side, authorship is more complicated and more uncertain, the names most often proposed being those of François-Réal Angers and Elzéar Bédard. It is inevitable that Bédard should be suspected, given his admitted and direct involvement with the incident on which the third and fourth comedies are based. It was well known that the principal 'Resolutionaries' had met regularly at his home through the spring of 1834. He had been attacked mercilessly in the first comedy, jeered at as a 'poor displanted mayor' (he had been defeated, on 31 March 1834, in his attempt at re-election as mayor of Quebec, having been the first person to occupy that post), and depicted as a self-important and shallow blunderer. Bédard, thirty-four years old, had helped re-establish Le Canadien in 1831, was currently member of the House for the riding of Montmorency, and an honest, dedicated, and widely respected man who was generally regarded as the leader of the moderate element within the Patriote party (his unexpected acceptance of the position of judge of the Court of King's Bench in 1836 deprived the Patriotes of a sorely needed voice of moderation). Even if his authorship is uncertain, there is little doubt that he supplied information that was essential to the last three comedies. F.-R. Angers is the name most often accepted by historians. Only twenty-one at the time, a budding poet just beginning his law studies (he was working in the office of H.-S. Huot, who was attacked in the first comedy), Angers was later to demonstrate the literary awareness one notices in the fifth comedy.[8] But there is no conclusive proof, despite reiterated statements by some critics and historians that Angers was directly involved. Certainly the Status Quo side seems never to have suspected him. On the other hand, we must remember as well that all those involved in the composition of these texts had sound reasons for ensuring that their participation remained unknown to the general public and particularly to the opposition. In the spring and summer of 1834, neither side knew who was writing anonymously for the other; it is hardly surprising that we are still not entirely sure today.

What these men and nearly all those whose names appear in the five comedies had in common was their education at the Séminaire de Québec, an institution where paradramatic teaching methods remained much in vogue.[9] As graduates of that system, they would have considered drama primarily as a vehicle for adversative argument and debate, as it had been in the pages of newspapers in preceding decades and in the dramatized dialogues in pamphlet form to which we have referred above. No doubt they had also read classic French dramatists, and perhaps some English authors as well (the Ducis adaptations of Shakespeare had appeared in Canada by this time, *Hamlet* having been performed in Montreal by Firmin Prud'homme as early as 1832). But their acquaintance with live theatre would have been minimal.

4. Political Theatre in Quebec after 1834

One must be careful also not to exaggerate the importance of the *Status Quo Comedies* in the evolution of mainstream drama in Quebec. Armchair political theatre of this sort remained a vigorous but very much a secondary genre in the nineteenth century, with predictable, cyclical apogees and eclipses. Unlike mainstream theatre, polemical drama is very much a mirror of its time or, more specifically, of the political events of its day. In Quebec, especially before Confederation, it regularly reflected the grit and slime of partisan politics. In the decade following the *Status Quo Comedies*, political tension centred briefly on the return of the rebels of 1837–8, the birth of the radical Rouge party, and its struggle to reinterpret the past in order the better to confront the present. It was at this point that the anonymous *Tuque Bleue* comedies appeared in the Rouge party's newspaper (1848), cruelly lampooning George-Étienne Cartier and his cohorts, in a form very close to that of the playlets of 1834. Similarly, the ministerial crises of the 1850s brought the delightful *La Dégringolade* playlets (1856), expertly pillorying John A. Macdonald and his cabinet, their major improvement upon the *Status Quo Comedies* being the introduction of satirical drinking songs directed against federal ministers and their bibulous leader. The Confederation debates naturally brought a recrudescence of the genre, but its real summit came after union was a *fait accompli*, in Elzéar Labelle's lively operetta, *La Conversion d'un pêcheur de la Nouvelle-Écosse*.[10] This is the first full conjoining of political with mainstream theatre (Labelle's play attracted large audiences to the very end of the century), and – not incidentally – the first in the long tradition to include the author's name.

It signals the end of armchair journalistic drama as well, for Labelle's is the first *non-partisan* political theatre in Quebec. With the legal identity of French Canada now settled for the foreseeable future, with defined political parties and a traditional parliamentary opposition in place, there was no viable role left for anonymous, adversarial, and often libellous dramas of the type I translate here.

But the genre did not die: it kept mutating to meet different environments. Satiric attacks upon individuals, parties, and platforms became a central part of the revue, of burlesque, and of monologue; though without the acrimony and passion of 1834, 1848, or 1856, Gratien Gélinas' *Fridolinades* of the 1930s and 1940s share many of the aims and some of the strategies of the political dramas of the nineteenth century. When preoccupation with a national political identity again became central in the 1960s, political theatre, predictably, reappeared, sometimes in a shape surprisingly close to that of its distant predecessors. Robert Gurik's *Hamlet, Prince du Québec* (1968), for example, is frequently and startlingly similar in style, structure, diction, and intent to *La Dégringolade* (and, therefore, to the *Status Quo Comedies*). But it must be stressed that there is no *direct* filiation. Gurik had not read *La Dégringolade*: the form he chose was a natural one, a function of the partisan political intent of his text,[11] just as it was natural in nineteenth-century English Canada.[12]

5. Language

This translation, as with the others in this volume, seeks to remain as close as possible to the literal sense of the texts, but to convey as well the colloquial, often slangy flavour which separates them from most of the French published in newspapers in Canada to that time. In the notes that follow the translations I point out some of the peculiarities of language used by individual characters, and provide historical and biographical information for readers unfamiliar with the politics of the period, so that they may follow the numerous allusions to contemporary individuals and events.

The First Status Quo Comedy

Dear Editor,

    Since the riddle has finally been solved, and I am nothing but 'a comic servant in some sort of play,' I shall, true to my role, pass along to you a little patriotic playlet I had occasion to see enacted recently. I dare delude myself that the banter herein will not fail to amuse your readers.

SCENE I

The scene is the Library of the Legislature. Actors: Messrs P ... t, B ... d, H ... t, D ... e, F ... t, G ... u, W ... r, and M ... l.[13] Mr P., *librarian, editor of* Le C[anadien] *is seated at one end of a long table, in the middle of the room. He is profoundly absorbed in meditation over a work entitled 'Essay on the Resolutions.' He is looking for inspiration to finish a nice, pompous editorial for his newspaper, which is due to come out in two hours. A young printer's devil stands at the other end of the table, waiting impatiently for the editorial and mumbling to himself, 'Mister, they're waitin' for your copy!' MR B[ÉDARD] enters.*

Mr B.: Well, good day, Citizen Editor! How's it going, then?

Mr P.: All right, all right ... But look here, I'm rather busy. I'm finishing off an article that should demolish that damned 'Status Quo' rabble.

B.: For my part, I've come to show you a new piece on ... thingamabob ... er ... uh ...

P.: Hey look, my paper's coming out this evening, and I don't have time to listen to your prattle, B. You people think the rest of us have lots of spare time, like you!

B.: Come now, Citizen, you mustn't be angry. – It's actually in your paper's interest that I've come to talk to you. You see, that piece I gave you yesterday just *has* to appear in this evening's paper, otherwise we'll have missed our chance. What do you think of it? Isn't it well argued, eh? When B. decides to get involved in something ...

P.: Humbug! I didn't even read it. You know, it's funny, it's curious how you people are all the same! You take three days and three nights to write thirty lines or so that have absolutely nothing to say. But to listen to you, they're masterpieces of style. You don't worry about me, bloody damn! – and I have to rewrite reams, like the lowest hack, to correct your drivel! Not to mention all the contradictions you make me utter. But that's the way you are, all of you!

B.: But Citizen, you must admit I've given you some good stuff. Shall I remind you? Like the one on ... er ... uh ...

P.: Aw, enough of that!

SCENE II

(The door opens and H[uot] *enters.)*

P.: What! Another unwelcome intruder. Well, well, it's H.! So, how's our Eternal and Universal Secretary?

B.: And *banal*!

H.: Hey, don't pin that ugly name on me – it's already been applied in true and due form to J[acques] V[ige]r![14] Everyone's entitled to his own property!

P.: Well, what's the news, H.?

H.: Everything's going off marvellously! I've just had word from Pointe-aux-Trembles that our Resolutions went through with no problems there. I've had news, too, from all the schoolmasters (as you know, I go round and visit them every summer), and I can assure you that all is going well. It's amazing, the number of children's signatures we're going to get. They're coming by the hundreds, by the thousands! I'll draw up a chart for you ... for us, I mean.

P.: It's my editorials – in two, three, or four columns – that are responsible for that. And just wait 'till you get signatures from all the kids making their First Communion ... I've suggested that as a matter of policy in our issue for the 14th of this month. And after all that, bloody damn! and when all is said and done, you're letting me starve to death. That's how you people are!

H.: Come now, P., I know what you're hinting at. But is that my fault? Haven't I done everything I could, right from the beginning to the end of the session, to get money for you? Didn't I get cross with Papineau? Didn't I take responsibility – as I do every session – for all contingent accounts? Didn't we work out together – surely you remember – you, schemes for reports and speeches, and me, motions to be proposed, to get you money? But the clique[15] – yes, the clique – wouldn't listen to me. You should be happy you got the contract from the Assembly to print the journal of its proceedings and everything else. And who do you owe that to, if not me?

B.: He's right on that point, Citizen P. I can testify as to how much H. has done for *Le Canadien*. He schemed as well as he could with every member of the Assembly. I was involved in the thing as well, but Laf[ontaine],[16] Rod[ier],[17] and the others kept asking us, 'Does *La Minerve*[18] need a printing-contract from the Legislature to keep afloat? And what's your editor of *Le Canadien* got to complain about, after all? Didn't they take the job of librarian away from the son of the man who had served the Assembly longest – the job was only worth £30 to £40 then – and give it your Mr P. at a rate of £200, and then ...'

P.: Those wretches! How can they treat me like that, after I had buttered up the whole clique for two years before they gave me the job! To refuse me my back-pay now ...!

B.: Courage, Citizen Editor! Patience! I venture to say I shall have your arrears and the interest on them, plus a bonus, paid to you on the very second day of the next session!

P.: You poor defeated mayor,[19] you'd better make sure you get elected in your own riding first – have you thought about that?

B.: Oh, that's a different question altogether. Let's change the subject – here comes someone.

SCENE III

(Mr D[eguise] *enters.*)

P.: Well, look what we have here!

D.: Hello P., hello B., hello H., hello Mr ... oh I see, it's the little printer's devil for *Le Canadien*. So what are you all up to?

All: Politics, that's what we're up to!

D.: Aha, politics! That's what I'm into, too!

H.: Indeed! And what do you do for that, then, Deguise?

D.: I read the newspaper!

All: (*laughing*) He reads the newspaper! He reads the newspaper! ...

D.: Yes, I do, and I read things there ...

H.: ... that you don't really understand – right, Deguise?

D.: Now look here, don't insult me, you, Huot, and the rest of you, 'cause I know that ... that's how you all are, all of you. You figure, you imagine that others aren't so bright, or as well informed, that other people don't understand. But I can tell you that as far as I'm concerned, I can understand everything that's to be understood, as long as it's expressed in some way, shape or form that's self-explanatory, without further explanation – there you have it!

SCENE IV

(Mr F[iset] *enters.*)

F.: Well, done, well done, D.! Defend yourself, don't let them pull the wool over your ears![20] Let's not forget, gentlemen, that Mr D. was re-elected alderman for the ward of ... I can't actually recall the actual ward, at the moment ...

D.: Yes, and *unanimously*, at that!

H.: Because no one else offered.

D.: What?

H.: He says you defeated someone else in the election.

D.: Right! Actually, I think he said something else, but no matter. If they insult me, my mind's made up:
  I abandon Papineau
  And join the Status Quo!

F.: What a poet he is, our dear Mr D.!

D.: We all know what a joker you are, F., and ...

B.: Enough, let's put an end to this! Why, here's Mr G., one of the secretaries of our Constitutional Committee.

H.: And former secretary in the mission of the Right Honourable D.-B. V[iger],[21] our ambassador to the Court in London, residing at the London Coffee House on Ludgate Hill ...

F.: Where there wasn't a farthing to earn,
   So G. did quickly return!

P.: Hold on, H., you should say 'Citizen V.' That sounds a lot more republican, doesn't it, B.? Try to get used to using the term little by little. All you lot can think about is 'honourable' people.

F.: Right! Whereas *we* want to put the boot to all of them!

G.: 'Honourable'? – Bah! If you had been to London and Paris as I have, gentlemen (excuse me, I meant to say, 'citizens'), you would have seen what little fuss they make about 'honourables,' about marquesses, dukes, princes, or even kings there! There, in those great cities, dustmen are treated with the utmost respect, for they belong to the people, they make up the proletariat. In London I saw common people who sought to rebel (quite properly, of course) against established authority. And how wonderful, how grand that was! And in Paris I saw, near the Austerlitz Monument, mass assemblies of fine patriots (they call them sansculottes also, and in fact some of them *did have* no trousers – but that's because of government tyranny), and strangely enough the police, Louis-Philippe's notorious armed police, chased them from street to street, from bank to bank, like sheep!

F.: You certainly seem to have seen a lot in your distant travels, Mr G. But I bet you've never seen a foreign patriot capable of doing what one of ours is ready to do when the situation calls for it!

G.: And what's that? Tell me, because I've seen a lot of things, I assure you, especially when it comes to anecdotes!

F.: Well, Mr G., you should know that we have a patriot amongst us – or a sansculotte, as they say in Paris – who is capable of devouring a Scotsman right raw!

G.: Merciful heavens! What are you telling me? He's got to be a descendant of one of those terrible Iroquois who used to pillage this country when it was first being founded. Lord, how horrible!

F.: I haven't time to tell you anything else: here he comes right now. Just look at that ring of long hair around his face, look at his beaverskin coat – or is it bearskin? – oh, excuse me, he's only wearing a cloth coat. But look at his proud and imposing demeanour! Tremble, ye inhabitants of Caledonia, especially those of you who wear the kilt!²²

G.: But, but – it's my friend W.! What a jester you are, Mr F.!

W.: How frightened you all look, Citizens! Is it a case of revolution, of war? I so wish; we so wish it. I am ready; we are ready. Come, man the cannons! Fix bayonets! I'm the one who will lead you through the gunfire – don't you know I carry a Napoleon on my chest? ²³

F.: I'd prefer to have one in my pocket ...

SCENE V

(Mr M[artel] *enters and announces solemnly.*)

Citizens! The Constitutional Committee is now assembling. As secretary of the Committee, and by order of its chairman, I call upon you to present yourselves at that meeting forthwith, that we may deliberate on matters pertaining to the welfare of our homeland!

P.: Listen, Citizen M., would you try and see if your Constitutional Committee could find some way of paying me even a partial instalment?

M.: I must tell you, Citizen Editor, that we have no funds whatsoever. We operate and act under warranty of the Ninety-First Resolution, which guarantees that the next session [of the Assembly] – or 'Convention'²⁴ – will amply refund all our expenditures. I refer you to the text of said resolution, which should have the full force of law for us. And you know from experience that the Legislature never fails to keep promises of this sort, especially when they're given to those who have to stand by it in its blunders!

(*They all leave the room.*)

P.: And I say you can go to blazes, all of you! Bunch of b ... s, you've kept me here for two hours! All right, let's finish off this damned editorial. Here, boy, take this to the printers right away. Oh my – if some informer were to report the farce that's just been played here to the 'Friend of the Status Quo,' we'd be in a fine pickle!

Admit it, Mr P., wouldn't you be tempted to believe, on reading the above, that there was indeed an informer amongst you? Well, think about it – and, if you can, look at each other without bursting out laughing, like Louis-Philippe and Talleyrand, those most decent folk on the other side of the water!

A FRIEND OF THE STATUS QUO
Quebec, 25 April 1834

The Second Status Quo Comedy

Dear Editor,

I hasten to send you the second act which I alluded to in my last communication. By so doing, I keep my word – something the Patriotes don't always do! Now where's M. and his 'six falsehoods and three misstatements'?[25] I've been waiting for him for a month!

SCENE I
Messrs P[arent], B[esserer], H[uot], *and* G[renier][26]

Scene: the Library of the Legislature. Mr P. strides back and forth across the room, holding in his hand an extract from Mr Stanley's report dated ... [27] *He utters the following monologue.*

Oh, Stanley, Stanley! You must give up, you *must* give up, bloody damn! We'll make you cough it up! Come on – give us what belongs to us, right away! Especially our £300,000 that you withdrew from our coffers without our permission, do you hear? And be quick about it, Stanley, because ... we move fast, here in Canada!

(*During this monologue* B ... r *enters on tiptoe.*)

B.: Pardon me for disturbing you, Citizen Editor, but when those ringing words 'hundred thousand pounds' struck my eardrums I was quite concerned and came running. You were probably referring to my superb report on the receiver-general's misappropriation of funds? Quite a piece of writing that was – structure, style, logic, and ...

P.: All I have to say is that I was no more thinking about your report or about yourself than I was about ... the last shirt I wore. Do you actually believe that in *my* position I have time to think about your bloody stupid reports or about your sorry complaints? I have a lot more important things to worry about! At the moment I'm concerned, absorbed, and entirely immersed in the most serious political problem. It's a question of our nationhood, our very existence, bloody damn! Just look at this damned despatch from Stanley I'm holding – that's what I've been preoccupied with for the past two hours: it's been bedevilling me no end!

B.: Oh, I see. So it wasn't my report you were talking about?

P.: Do I have to repeat it again and again, bloody damn!

B.: Oh no, no, certainly not. Yes indeed, this despatch is upsetting, it's demoralizing. I intend to write a commentary on it, with a glossary, notes and all the rest. If others are going to poke their noses into things like that, we're quite capable of doing the same.

P.: Nonsense! Enough, let's put an end to this – I hear someone on the stairway.

SCENE II

(Mr H[uot] *and* Dr G[renier] *enter.*)

H.: Good day, P.

P.: Hello, H. Well, well, who's this you've brought with you?

H.: I've brought Dr G. here, an outstanding Patriote if there ever was one!

P.: And my cousin, to boot. So – here you are mixed up in politics too, dear Doctor, most learned Doctor!

G.: Yes indeed, by thunder! They've dragged me into it, and now I'm in it up to my ears!

P.: Don't worry, we'll drag you out of it as well as we can.

H.: But that's not the reason I've brought Dr G. to you, P., but rather so that you can write a letter for him in reply to the latest attack from that damned Friend of the Status Quo, who has the nerve and the gall to ask him for an affidavit concerning the meeting that took place at Château-Richer on a certain date ...

G.: Yes, yes, the meeting – No use denying it, no such meeting ever took place there, any more than it did on the back of my hand!

H.: (*elbowing him*) Come on, let me finish! It's true enough that I got a bunch of papers from B[édar]d, and badly written at that, but as to a meeting, may the devil take me if ...

P.: Come now, cousin, control yourself: this is no way to behave! All right, I'll compose a little letter of explanation, with some well-chosen words. But tell me, H., why didn't you take him to B[édar]d? He's the one who's at the bottom of this. You come and bother me, who haven't a moment to call my own, bloody damn!

H.: All right, I can tell you I did take him to B. who wrote up, as usual, a bunch of garbage such that the devil himself couldn't make head or tail of it. The doctor got angry and said to him, 'Listen, B., you've made me do a lot of stupid things, so I'm going to put my whole faith in Mr H., since I know he's a busybody and a schemer. Let's go to the library and find cousin P., he'll write me a letter that *says* something, at least.' That's why we're here So you see what must be done, and no time to waste!

P.: But why couldn't you write the letter yourself, Doctor?

G.: Oh, if only they'd let me! I'd start out, 'You goddam Status Quo, you rascal, with the only lancet I have left, I'd like to ... '

P.: Hey, hey, take it easy! Here, you take a little stroll around the library with these gentlemen while I write something that'll satisfy you.

G.: Write the letter any way you want, but by thunder! (*he pounds the table with his fist, knocking over the ink-well and a dozen books*) the word 'rascal' has to be included or else nothing doing, I won't sign it!

H.: Okay, okay, 'rascal' it will be, but ...

P.: All right, all right, let me write it!

(B ... r, G., *and* H. *walk back and forth together.*)

B.: For a little chap, you certainly seem like a shrewd one, Doctor.

G.: Well, don't forget,
My German friend, this you should know:
From tiny pots fine ointments flow!

B.: That's true, I'm German and a descendant of the ancient Teutons.

G.: You people have a nice library here.

H.: Yes, lots of books.

G.: Do you have medical books, too? I'd like to check on one of my cases ...

P.: Hey, Doctor, forget about your cases and come here. (*He reads aloud the follow-ing letter.*)
Dear Editor,
    What has happened to the *Gazette*'s informers? What, are you now brought so low that you ask for affidavits on what took place only five or six leagues away from your informers, on something the whole county is aware of? This is unbelievable. Perhaps there's been mass defection among your brethren?
    Do you appreciate the sheer audacity – nay, the nonsensicality of the pro-posal you have made me, Mr Friend of the Status Quo, that I should repeat

under oath the statements I've already made in my own name, as well as other facts I'm prepared to attest to in the same way, at the request of any gentleman? Yes, gentleman, for I do not know if I am dealing with a *rascal* or a person of quality; and neither the tone nor the manners of the Friend of the Status Quo are such as to assuage my doubts in that respect. Do as I do, Friend: don't be ashamed of your own name. Or rather, write in such a way that you aren't ashamed to sign it at the end of what you write. Do that, and I'm ready to meet you. As a man of honour, I would have satisfied you, if your conduct had not been utterly insulting; but I must remain silent as long as you don't identify yourself publicly with the same sense of responsibility as I have done.

Château-Richer, 18 April 1834

* * *, M.D.[28]

P.: Now would you sign this right away, Doctor?

G.: Hold on a moment – there's a mistake here: you put the address as 'Château-Richer,' and I'm here in Quebec City. I'll just cross out 'Château ... '

P.: No, no! Don't you see, that's to make people believe you wrote the letter yourself, from Château-Richer!

H.: It's all right, I think he understands that now.

G.: Oh, for heaven's sake, put 'Château-Richer' or 'Château Saint-Louis' if you want, it makes no difference to me (though I'd prefer to live at the latter address).[29] All right, I'll sign it. but on second thought, I'd like to add a little *post-rectum* ...

P.: The word's *postscriptum*, bloody damn! You're going to make me lose my temper, if you keep this up!

G.: All right, all right, 'postscriptum' if you say so. But I want you to add that if I meet Master Status Quo on some street corner, and as long as he's not bigger than me, I've got a lancet and I'll ...

P.: Easy now – be careful you don't wind up with a good thrashing, and you very well might, if his fist is as good as his pen! But let's put an end to this: we've had enough of you today. Come back and see me tomorrow in case we have need of your shining talents.

G.: Would you just listen to this man! Do you think you're going to keep me travelling back and forth on that road to Château-Richer? Remember, this is the fourth time in ten days I've made the trip for this bit of business. I've got a patient I was supposed to pull four teeth for, day before yesterday. Now, because of the delay, I may have to yank out a chunk of his jaw as well!

H.: Don't worry about it, doctor – I'll have you put on the supplementary pay list.

G.: That's more like it! Goodbye to you then!

All three: Good day! Good day!

G.: (*coming back*) Oh, while I think of it, I wanted to look up a word in the dictionary of the French Academy, to make sure I used it properly on a certificate I drew up to dispense a witness from appearing in court. Why, I can't find it! What does that mean?

P.: Perhaps you misspelled it?

G.: By thunder, so I did! Would you believe it, I wanted to write that he had a gall-bladder problem, and I wrote 'Gaul'-bladder! Really, I don't know where my head is, these days!

P.: It's probably not the first or the last mistake you've made.

G.: Anyway, what's done is done. (*He leaves.*)

P.: Well, what do you think?

B.: I think we've sunk pretty low, if we've got to use people like him!

P.: True enough. But when you think about it ... it's quantity, not quality we're looking for, when it comes to signatures.

B.: Yes, that's true – just like the people who voted for the Ninety-Two Resolutions.

P.: This whole Château-Richer foul-up is B[édar]d's fault, I can assure you. First, he took three or four trips, one right after the other, to that place, which attracted people's attention right away. Then he went around speechifying to people who just laughed at him. And finally, for an undertaking that required all sorts of skill, cunning, scheming, and secrecy, he handed over responsibility to ... Well, you can see from that sorry excuse for a man who just left, how the thing was going to turn out, and how it *did* in fact turn out, to our shame, bloody damn! I make no bones about it ...

The two others: Quite so! Only too true!

H.: You saw how I arranged things at Pointe-aux-Trembles, in my own riding of Portneuf? I had everything worked out in advance. I was sure of my people's support. I wasn't so foolish as to go there myself – I sent an *alter ego* (I'll tell you some other time who it was). And didn't everything go splendidly? No hitches whatsoever; you didn't hear any objections, and I hope there won't be any.

B.: So you didn't use your local clique?

H.: What! That old bunch can only sit around and scratch their heads. A fine mess they would have made of things!

B.: I do admire your skill, especially the business of scratching or erasing that bill ... Yes, indeed, that one!

H.: Do you see anything to criticize about that? Wasn't it well conceived and well arranged? When I think about it ...

B.: Oh yes, that was really wonderful!

H.: I could tell you a lot more, if I had time. But there's something afoot, and I must leave you and find out what's going on. Goodbye. (*He leaves.*)

SCENE III

B.: We have a real treasure there, in H. Really, he's got some wonderful schemes. I can't help giving him his due, even though he used the same tricks to stop me from being elected.

P.: Yes, but with all his capacity for scheming, for skulduggery and all, bloody damn! he didn't get me a so much as a penny in pay, last session!

(*A servant enters and gives a message to* P.)

P.: (*after reading the message*) It's a note from B[édar]d informing me there's to be a meeting at his place in fifteen minutes to discuss urgent business. Let's go: we'll find a few sound heads there, and we should be able to come to some decisions.

B.: I'll be glad to come with you.

P.: Hold on − I've got to bring my favourite book with me.

B.: Which one's that?

P.: This one: *Essay on the Resolutions*.

B.: Indeed, that's very appropriate at this stage. I read it every day, religiously, and expound it to my suburban neighbours. You should see how they gape at certain passages in it! They can already imagine themselves in charge of everything in the new social order. In fact, just between the two of us, they wouldn't have much of a share of power! After we're all properly taken care of there wouldn't be much for them!

P.: Quite true, actually, but let's make sure they never find that out till the time comes!

B.: It's already been pointed out, by that Status Quo chap in the *Gazette*.

P.: I'd like to see him in hell, Master Status Quo!

B.: You must admit he's been giving us a hard time for the last while, and it doesn't look like he wants to leave things as they are!

P.: We'll find him out, and he'll have reason to remember us. Yes, that's it − try to catch that chap, the 'Friend of the Status Quo!'

A FRIEND OF THE STATUS QUO
Quebec, 1 May 1834

The Third Status Quo Comedy

A Dedicatory Letter to the 'Friend of the Status Quo'

Worthy Friend,

By dedicating to you this first product of a novice's pen, I pay well-deserved homage to your talents, homage those talents have earned by their superior brilliance in the field of dramatic composition; and what is even more significant for me, I hereby gain, from the use of your name, a degree of fame to which I would never otherwise have hoped to attain. But of course you are used to enjoying the glorified status of a man of genius. You have managed to nurture and develop to its greatest potential that blessed disposition which Nature had implanted in you. The interest you exhibit in the prosperity of others, without thought to your own; the boundless generosity you display towards budding talent, as if you had none of your own; and finally, your admirable proclivity for indulgent acceptance of the feeble efforts of those who would try their skills in the same sphere as you, as if you had not already surpassed all others in that sphere – all these represent, for me, more than sufficient reason to aspire to the honour of your magnanimous protection. In truth, great talents and mean-spiritedness have never gone together, and the three Graces were sisters. If on occasion Satire has handed you her full quiver and allowed you full use of her shafts; if you have been obliged to wield sarcasm or irony, I know this has never been at the expense of Friendship or Truth. I therefore pray, worthy Friend of the Status Quo, that you will deign to look favourably upon the following dialogue, and hope you will be able to recognize the characters in it.

U.A.F.[30]

The action takes place on Rue Saint-Louis, on the 5th of May.

Thomas A ... t[31]: (*he paces back and forth nervously, looking this way and that, staring out at a low-built house now resplendent with a few new shingles that have recently replaced the moss growing around the windows of the garret*) No doubt about it, people like me are a wretched lot! For example, the fact that I can't hold my head up when I walk, and have to squint at people out of the corner of one eye.[32] A single word is enough to terrify me and make me run away, and yet that word's the one that's ringing in my ears. I can hardly take a step without hearing it. What, is 'INFORMER' spelled out on my very face? Alas! to ply such a trade and – worse still – to do it for nothing! If there were even a job as secretary, or associate, or even head clerk in some attorney's office! But nobody wants me anywhere, not even the newspaper I serve so well. There's not even the least little deal to be struck – a loan to arrange, a frock-coat to barter. Here I am reduced to spending the plentiful leisure my lack of clientele affords me, wandering around snooping, spying, and serving as stool-pigeon and errand-boy for the Friend of the Status Quo and his paper! No matter – any day now some opportunity may arise, and I can take my chances as I would at roulette or at an auction sale. And since I've jumped or was pushed into this role of slandering ... Hmm – no one's watching, I believe – let's go in! (*He runs hurriedly up the stairway to the garret, the door of which is open.*)

SCENE II

Thomas A ... t: (*he notices* Johnny D ... l,[33] *who is staring at him*) (*aside*) Doesn't he indeed have a body that resembles the soul within? Socrates was right: a beautiful body is the outward sign of a beautiful soul. (*Aloud to* Johnny D ... l.) Here I am! Anything you need done this morning?

Johnny D ... l: You seem quite rattled. Did someone see you?

Thomas A ... t: I don't think so, but I'm starting to get fed up with this job.

Johnny D ... l: (*staring at him again, his face twisted in a grimace*) Because it doesn't pay?

Thomas A ... t: That's not such a bad reason, and these are hard times. All right for you – you'll get all the glory and the profit from the game we're playing, while I'll get nothing but dishonour – my conscience is beginning to trouble me –

Johnny D ... l: Bah, your conscience! I thought it was for sale, that only the price was in question!

Thomas A ... t: How you mock me!

Johnny D ... l: But it's only in fun – I'm only talking 'politically.'

Thomas A ... t: That's all right, then. But my conscience is still bothering me for allowing myself to be used by you like ...

Johnny D ... l: (*he mutters, aside*) Yes, like the cat uses its paw to pull the chestnuts out of the fire! (*Aloud.*) Buck up – you've nothing to be afraid of!

Thomas A ... t: No, except being found out one of these days. Then I'd just be background in the overall picture: you'd be the part that would stick out.

Johnny D ... l: We have to be very careful, especially where I'm concerned, because I'm under suspicion. They'd call you an informer and me a traitor, like my friend M[ondele]t.[34]

Thomas A ... t: And, you might add, a liar. I'm speaking 'politically' as well, because, just between the two of us, your 'Friend of the Status Quo' for tomorrow doesn't do you much credit as far as the truth is concerned.

Johnny D ... l: So what, as long as it achieves its purpose? So what, as long as I can denigrate all those schemers I had vowed to lead, to control? The whole machine was supposed to roll when M[ondele]t and I wanted it to. We were supposed to be at a higher level than [Denis-Benjamin] Viger, the Assembly's agent, and Papineau, the speaker. The plot was all arranged, and seemed to be on the verge of success. And then Papineau puts the run to M[ondele]t, my plans vanish into thin air, and people start thinking and acting without me, in spite of me, and who knows, perhaps *against* me! But I shall have my revenge, I shall discharge the bile that Papineau has made me store up, and I'll vomit it out on our fine friends P., V., H., B., P., and B.[35] No need to be straightforward with people who won't listen to me! What does Truth matter, after all, if I can ruin the reputation of the clique in the minds of *that lot of gallows-bait, the electors of the Upper City of Quebec*?

Thomas A ... t: Nicely said, but there's the Gordian knot! Say, have you put the last touches on your Status Quo article for tomorrow?

(*While* Johnny D ... l *is rummaging in his hat, a noise is heard at the outside door.* Johnny *drops his hat and takes to his heels. The noise stops.*)

Thomas A ... t: It's nothing – come on back! You're quite the general, aren't you: You put everybody else in front of you, and ensure a safe retreat for yourself!

Johnny D ... l: Is there no one there? (*He gathers up the scattered papers that have fallen from his hat.*) I was afraid we'd be found out and identified.

Thomas A ... t: And afraid, because of that, to see your name in the clique's newspapers! Up to now you've had the advantage of waging war without being recognized. You've been covered by the cloak of anonymity. I pity you if you're found out: you'd wind up being the target, just like the people you're attacking now! The role you play in the House wouldn't exactly be consistent with what you've been writing!

Johnny D ... l: That's why if there are any grounds for suspecting me you've got to assume full responsibility for what the Friend of the Status Quo has written.

Thomas A ... t: I guess so. You've got to make an outward show of being serious-minded and truthful ... (*aside*) ... that I don't believe in for a moment!

Johnny D ... l: So it's up to you to make a good show of it, and to keep denying, in every circumstance, that I've done any of the writing. Pretend you're the one who did it.

Thomas A ... t: But no one will believe me, even if I offer as many affidavits as you keep demanding from other people!

Johnny D ... l: Here's a way to do it. If anyone sees you leaving here, pretend you were here on business. Nothing could be more normal. And you've got time to deliver the 'Friend of the Status Quo' that's due to appear in tomorrow's paper. I'll give you the text of it, you'll rewrite it in your own hand and give it to the printer. That's enough to allow you to say you're the author. Surely you realize that if the official librarian of the House identified me as the 'Friend of the Status Quo' there'd be no respite for me! I'd have to face the anger of all the Patriotes from Montreal for having attacked their leader, Mr Papineau, and the official agent of the Assembly, Mr

Viger; and the anger of the Patriotes from Quebec City as well, because of my attacks against my friends and constituents. All I'd hear would be reference to 'Status Quo' and 'Gallows Bait,' and my election would be in jeopardy!

Thomas A ... t: That's a clever dodge – I wouldn't have thought of it myself! But speaking of electors, I thought I heard you say, a few days ago, that since you're assured of support from the 'English Party,' as you termed it, and counting on the division you can cause in the enemies' ranks, you would be able to do without the voters in Faubourg-Saint-Jean, and were thus pretty certain of being elected.

Johnny D ... l: That's right, but that's no reason to go around letting them know what pretty compliments I'm paying them and their representatives! They certainly wouldn't forgive me for that ...

Thomas A ... t: (*mutters, aside*) 'Little ... Vulcan,'[36] they'd say, like when the House was in session!

Johnny D ... l: (*continues*) Any election is doubtful, and doubt could easily turn into the sort of certainty I wouldn't much like!

Thomas A ... t: So you mightn't win, in fact, but you'll have your revenge in advance! But be patient, now – you couldn't be treated any worse than I was in three different ridings where the voters weren't willing to let my good looks serve as pledge for future good services. And yet I hadn't done anything, either for or against them!

Johnny D ... l: (*laughing*) Oh yes, and especially on the Île d'Orléans, right? Where someone who used to work as a summons-server for me had more luck than you, since he garnered a *few* votes!

Thomas A ... t: (*offended*) Yeah – just like the first member of the Patriote clique on the scene will get more votes than you in Upper Town, if he does what the voters want! (*D ... l's face contorts in a grimace.*) But take heart: you'll share the fate of many of your friends, and then you can take consolation in composing epigrams. And anyway, we'll divert all our election expenses to our own use. We have to be as philosophic about this as our friend H ... l[37] was. You remember what happened to his allowance for election expenses on the Île d'Orléans?

Johnny D ... l: Oh, don't talk to me about that well-scolded lawyer – he's a real nincompoop!

Thomas A ... t: What! You say that in spite of the letter he wrote in English to the returning officer?[38] In spite of his articles against Papineau and the House? And in spite of his masterpiece, 'Voyez-vous ...'?

Johnny D ... l: He's not the one who wrote that. All he did was stitch together words that he got from a source we all know ...

Thomas A ... t: *(aside)* That's what we often do!

Johnny D ... l: ... and anyway, Master Thomas, he should never have lowered his dignity by allowing himself to be scolded publicly.

Thomas A ... t: But he was afraid of going to jail – I heard that from a good source!

Johnny D ... l: He would have been better off going to jail!

Thomas A ... t: You never would've gotten him to agree to that. He wouldn't even hear of it! After all, he who's scolded isn't beaten!

Johnny D ... l: And it was such a pretty sight! My, how puffed up he was! *(he laughs)*
When he raised his whole body, short, fat, and dense
The Bar of the House groaned from his corpulence![39]

Thomas A ... t: My, how you murder Boileau, Master Johnny!

Johnny D ... l: Just like he murders English! Any way you look at it, he put the executive branch in jeopardy with his actions, and let himself be scolded in public.

Thomas A ... t: But at that point he wasn't wearing any of the formal accoutrement of his office – robe, bands ...

Johnny D ... l: Is he the one who came up with that excuse? It's the only one he could find. The governor should never have appointed him.

Thomas A ... t: Maybe so. The official robes would have looked better on you, Master Johnny! But enough on that topic – save your wisecracks for your own constituents. I still have information I must glean before noon, errands to run, several people to spy on, articles to pick up for the *Gazette*. After I leave here, I'm going to our friend Gl ... k ... r's.[40]

Johnny D ... l: As far as *he's* concerned, he should learn the language properly or else give up writing and bragging about it afterwards, and continually saying 'Hello for funny!' – that's become a real mania with him. Just the same, he's not as bad as he used to be. A few years ago, he had been spoiled by his own crowd, and given a really comical degree of importance. They nearly made him lose his head ...

Thomas A ... t: 'Hello for funny!' – but he's right!

Johnny D ... l: He thought all the wisdom in the world was right under his own bonnet. He was the boring, banal speechmonger at every meeting. He even went so far as to call for an elected Legislative Council, as Goderich[41] did.

Thomas A ... t: But he changed his mind on that one!

Johnny D ... l: We dragged him back into the Status Quo, and that's where he'll have to stay till he croaks!

Thomas A ... t: Here I am wasting my time, listening to you show off how much you know. Is your text ready?

Johnny D ... l: Hold on, we have to read it. Let's go into this room.

(*They both enter the small adjacent room, closing its door but forgetting to close the doors leading to the street.*)

SCENE III

(*Various clients keep entering the first room, and then leaving when they see no one is there.*)

Thomas A ... t: There wouldn't be anyone in the attic?

Johnny D ... l: Let's have a look ... no. (*He reads aloud.*) 'To the Editor of *Le Canadien*, paid librarian of the House of Assembly: It's with great pleasure that ... bla, bla, bla ... because, I assume, you had too much modesty.' (*To Thomas.*) I guess this will make Master *Canadien* shut his trap!

Thomas A ... t: Shouldn't you drop that word 'modesty'? Someone could recognize it – you use it so much. Every day, you quote the lines,

Forgive him ...
He's committed a rhyme out of sheer *modesty* ...

Johnny D ... l: Oh, no – that's one of my witty sayings! And the word 'modesty' could be on anyone else's lips as well as mine.

Thomas A ... t: (*aside*) If only he had a bit of it in his heart, nobody would regret the change!

Johnny D ... l: (*continues to read*) 'Among the public officials of this country I find one whose name is rather similar to yours, and who is paid no less than 800 piasters ... '

Thomas A ... t: You should count in francs – the number would be much more impressive. That would come to 4,800 francs, the interest on which, at ten per cent, would come to 480 francs 20 centimes a year ...

Johnny D ... l: Simple Thomas, trying to prove himself smarter than his master![42] When *Le Canadien* published a 'Comparative Account of the Salaries of State Governors in the USA,' it was given in piasters. Don't we have to pay them back in the same coin? Let's read on. 'Eight hundred piasters a year as librarian of the House of Assembly for ... ' Hell, I don't know what for ...!

Thomas A ... t: (*interrupting*) Oh, don't swear – you know very well what for!

Johnny D ... l: ... or rather, I know only too well what for, and dare not say ...

Thomas A ... t: That's more like it! You'd do well to be discreet, since you were one of the ones who helped to create the position of librarian. You were a member of the committee that proposed it, you spoke in favour of it, and voted for it.

Johnny D ... l: That needn't prevent me from criticizing it now, if I'm sure not to be found out. (*He continues to read.*) Hold on a moment – let me finish off with a question. (*He reads as he writes.*) 'What do you think, Mr Parant [*sic*]? Isn't there some truth in the foregoing?' (*He signs.*) 'A Friend of the Status Quo.' (*To* Thomas.) Here you go, my friend Thomas. Take this right away to Mr N[eilso]n. I must say, his newspaper has become a lot more interesting since I've begun contributing to it! A few years ago it was pitiful – the poor chap just couldn't do the job. We, his friends, just had to tell him so! But tell him not to foul things up again, and to be careful not to shuck off all his editorial responsibility on me, and not play on me the type of trick he did on Lord Dalhousie's secretary, Cochran.[43] It's no skin off his nose if he's found out – he was paid to write, but I'm not!

Thomas A ... t: (*aside*) True – for absolutely nothing you say stupid things to everybody! (*He exits, taking with him the 'Friend of the Status Quo' article for the following day's 'Gazette.'*)

SCENE IV

But that's enough of this for now – a play should have either three or five acts ...

Well now, what do you thing of that, MR JOHN DUVAL, ESQUIRE, MEMBER OF THE HOUSE OF ASSEMBLY, REPRESENTING THE RIDING OF QUEBEC CITY (UPPER TOWN), WORTHY FRIEND OF THE STATUS QUO? *Isn't there some truth in the foregoing?*
You've tried your hand at poetry in your writings; well, then, sing this now:
Now we've got this wild thing's nest,
With two, three, four young in it;
We've been trying to catch you for so long,
Poor birds, and now you're captured![44]
Before daring to deny it, just remember this: last Monday, between 9:30 and 10 a.m., you were behind closed doors in the room adjoining your office. At which time you – yes, you, JOHN DUVAL, Esquire, M.P.P., were reading aloud, in a loud and intelligible voice, the document that appeared the following Tuesday, addressed to 'The Editor of *Le Canadien*, Paid Librarian of the House of Assembly,' and signed 'A Friend of the Status Quo.' Don't trouble to deny it, for the text in question, read by you, JOHN DUVAL, Esq., M.P.P., was so clearly heard and so well understood that more than one person knew, on *Monday*, that the text would appear *the next day*, in Tuesday's *Gazette*, and they knew what its contents would be.

You must admit, if the authority of a name as imposing as that of JOHN DUVAL, Esquire, M.P.P., could add any weight to a document lacking one essential ingredient – truth – 'A Friend of the Status Quo,' in order to be believed, was long in need of your clearly written signature. You should have revealed your identity sooner, but I suppose you have *too much modesty* to set yourself up as an example! So, until

ANOTHER TIME

PS. Sorry, Mr Thomas, but we haven't time to waste dealing with ... informers!

A.T.

The Fourth Status Quo Comedy

A Little Dialogue between Two Friends of the Status Quo

[Thomas Amiot, André-Rémi Hamel]

A.: Good day, Mr Chairman. What news?

H.: (*grumpily*) That's quite a mess you people have made – the Status Quo is a lost cause!

A.: How so? I thought things were improving for us. Didn't you see how we treated Bédard,[45] on whom we've heaped full blame for reporting on the reading incident in Duval's office? Do you think they can get out of that one? They kept accusing us of being informers, and now we can turn it back on them. Isn't that priceless?

H.: You poor young man! You would have been better off sticking to the role we had assigned you. You youngsters should have confined your activities to spying, digging for news, pumping people for information, and peddling our writings. All of a sudden you thought you were big guns, you decided to turn your hand to writing, and now you've ruined everything!

A.: For heaven's sake, explain what you mean – you're frightening me!

H.: All right, you numbskull, here's what I mean: Bédard's the last man you should have tried to cast suspicion upon. He's one of the people who've been most severely mishandled in our writings, so how do you expect him to keep a secret in this case? It was fair game for him to make use of what he discovered, and it's unreasonable of you to criticize him for that!

A.: True enough. But what would you have had us do? We were found out, we had to say something, and the only way out was to talk of shame and dishonour – to put up a smokescreen, so to speak!

H.: That's probably what had to be done, all right, but wouldn't it have been better just to deny the whole thing?

A.: Deny? – Yes, but if they had come up with proof, we would have been shown to be liars.

H.: Bah! Would it have been the first time? What would one more lie have mattered? At least you were lucky that no one else came by first.

A.: Probably so. But if they had decided to ask us for an affidavit, as we did with Dr Grenier, we would have been up a tree.

H.: In that case, you should have decided to cover up, to make up cock-and-bull stories, as we so often do. You should, for example, have said that they paid someone to spy on us. At least that would've given us something to build on. But it was a gross blunder to criticize someone for blowing the whistle on you when you had been attacking him and his friends by name for two months, in every issue of *La Gazette*. Just wait till the next meeting of our committee: you're going to be admonished!

A.: Easy, easy now, sir! I'm not like ... you know who! I'd tell the committee to go to hell first!

BONJOUR

The Fifth Status Quo Comedy

Dedicatory Letter to the Friends of the Status Quo:

Gentlemen,

The success of a certain first production, success due largely to the good grace with which you know how to take bantering of that sort, and due especially to the outstanding reputation of the actors in it, induces me to return a second time to the stage and to dedicate to you, in all *modesty*, a new offering in the literary genre of which you are the inventors. Following in your footsteps, I cannot fail to keep to the right path. My foolish presumption is such that I refuse to concede to you in quantity of compositions, and so I shall endeavour to produce as many pale imitations as you have produced masterpieces in the genre. I flatter myself that the number and importance of the characters I bring on stage this time will, even with only part of their natural brilliance, make up for whatever deficiencies I may have and will sustain me in a competition where it is so difficult to win the prize twice. May your patronage and your kindness – qualities you demonstrated brilliantly in your attitude towards my first play – continue to favour me and help me to avoid the cool reception and undeserved distaste that greeted your own second masterpiece! Moreover, I suspect you will be all the more grateful to me for this when you learn that I hastened to do everything I could to enliven your sorrow and dissipate your melancholy humour after discovering, with sorrow, that an unfortunate contretemps had troubled your precious existence. Such indeed is my goal. I do hope I shall not fail to achieve it and thus contribute in my own way to your amusement!

ANOTHER TIME

THE ROUT OF THE STATUS QUO

United States
Plattsburgh, N.Y.

June 1834

*The scene is a procurator's office, Rue Sainte-Anne, Quebec City, in the house
next to the sign of the Turtle.*

I call things by their name; my mind's an open book;
I call a spade a spade, and ... a crook![46]

SCENE I

Hamel: (*alone, pacing back and forth in his office*) Oh! What a lovely thing, to hold
high honours! How glorious it is to be a statesman, to see oneself, in the most
demanding situations, act as counsellor to him who governs! For that's the position
I now enjoy, the office to which I have risen. Good heavens! When I think about it,
I nearly lose my self-control! My heart skips a beat, my head swims. I can hardly
believe it's true. Is all this but a dream? Am I not just imagining this? Am I really
king's counsel? What a disappointment if it were indeed only a dream! But no, it's
not: I feel full well that I'm a great, great man. Great thoughts, great plans, great
opinions[47] keep churning in my head!

Alas! cruel memory! That summons to the Bar of the House, the censure,
the speaker's discourtesy: how heavily they weigh upon this heart of mine! Oh
no, I shall never forget that incident! ... How cruel, how humiliating for me! The
first time the governor solicited my help, and I was so proud of it, had taken it as
a point of honour, worked day and night on that damned *opinion* that I wrote –
and look how the whole thing turned out! How could I have been so weak as
to give in? I, king's counsel, let myself be scolded in public view! How could the
government have decided to let one of its foremost officers be insulted like that?
Why didn't I have the courage to resign my post, to retire from the whole world,
to go bury myself on my island![48] No, no! – better to stay on! I must have vengeance, I must vilify these Patriotes, I must persecute them. The Friends of the
Status Quo are to meet here this evening. I swear, I shall have my revenge, my
revenge ...

SCENE II

Glackemeyer: (*rushing in*) What's all the commotion, Mr King's Counsel? Why are you carrying on so? I could hear you from the middle of the Place d'Armes! It's not wise to shout so loudly! Was some Patriote trying to attack you? Perhaps you discovered some plot, some treachery?

Hamel: (*pretending to be calm*) Oh no – I'm not at all suspicious ...

Glackemeyer: You don't have to be, to keep a sharp eye on everybody. But I say, what's the matter? Did some sergeant at arms perhaps ... (*He laughs loudly.*) Hello fer funny! ... Let me have my little joke, sir, that's a weakness of mine, as you know. But tell me, what was going on?

Hamel: Oh no, sir, I cannot: it's an official secret.

Glackemeyer: Some official secret, if all the neighbours heard it! No matter – I've just had a great idea. Let's spread the rumour that the Patriotes paid someone to assassinate you. That could be the topic of a good article for the Status Quo side, and we could get marvellous mileage out of words like 'revolutionaries,' 'sansculottes' and 'terrorists.' Wouldn't that be a scream?

Hamel: It might be for you gentlemen, but not for me! Can't you see that I would be the laughing stock in that case? It would be the last straw if people thought that I had been beaten, after having been scolded!

Glackemeyer: Indeed, you're right. Quite so, quite so – I withdraw my suggestion. But let's talk about today's news. What do you think of the situation we're in at the moment? Critical, isn't it? Don't you think our little Vulcan and that foul Thersites,[49] his informant, have brought us to a fine pass? It will be no easy challenge to emerge from this one unscathed because we've been found out – the jig's up! If, however, I could chair this evening's committee meeting, I'd find ways, interesting ways ...

Hamel: Take it easy, Mr Glackemeyer – I won't be shunted aside like that! We're not back in the old days when you used to make so much noise at meetings.

Glackemeyer: All right, we'll see ... But why aren't the others here? What are they up to? Probably re-reading *Le Canadien*'s piece – they have such a starring role in it! At least it's some consolation to me that they didn't dare attack me directly. They barely touched me. But you, Mr King's Counsel, did you see what a drubbing they've given you? Hello fer funny!

Hamel: All they do is call me 'that well-scolded lawyer.' As Thomas says, 'he who's scolded isn't beaten!'

Glackemeyer: True enough. But those two lines:
When he raised his whole body, short, fat, and dense
The Bar of the House groaned from his corpulence!

Hamel: (*offended*) Don't you push me too far, Mr Alderman, or I might say a lot of things for them! They spared you all right, but ...

Glackemeyer: Let them say what they want, they won't stop me from being re-elected for Lower Town in the upcoming election. Rest assured, Sir, that *I* won't lose the money *I* spend on deposit and election expenses, My, it was a scream to see you lose both the island and your deposit!

Hamel: (*angrily*) Oh yes, I know you're a candidate. And as things stand, you're sure to win. The women will be all for you. They can't vote, but they'll work behind the scenes for you ...

Glackemeyer: (*offended also*) Are you really the one to be poking fun at others, Mr Cujas?[50] Aren't you forgetting the accusation of ignorance the speaker levelled at you? And yet there you went and received your reprimand as if it were some triumph! And we had a hard time convincing you not to show up in your silk robes! Too bad we did, actually – the Patriotes would have made something really funny out of that!

Hamel: I came out of the whole thing rather well. People were impressed with my composure, my graceful poise, my stately manner when I appeared before the Bar of the House. Didn't all the members of the legal profession come to my defence? In a case like that, would they have come to yours?

Glackemeyer: You know very well that the members of the Bar did *not* support you!

Hamel: I bet you would have done a lot, if you had been there instead of me – Notary!

SCENE III

Johnny Duval: (*entering*) Gentlemen, gentlemen! You're making enough noise to give us all away, and to corroborate that damned comedy printed in *Le Canadien*! Everything you said could be heard on the street, loud and clear. The printer's devil from *Le Canadien* was going by just now, and I wouldn't be surprised if he heard the whole thing. If you keep this up, it's going to be hard to smooth this whole thing over!

Hamel: It's hardly *your* place, mister wordsmith, to criticize us, after what your fine words have done to us!

Johnny Duval: What I did was ... was ... well, I have no idea how it happened. I really don't know who in hell could have heard us. Those really were our very words, to the letter! But they're going to pay for that!

Glackemeyer: Isn't there some way we could get out of this mess with some good, inventive article ...

Johnny Duval: That's why we're meeting here this evening, and we'll come up with something of that sort, seeing you're here! But it's a real shame: this thing means the end of my chances for election. And they did it on purpose!

Hamel: But what are your spies doing? They all seem to be braggarts. Have they been scared off by the clique's first offensive? We've been attacking them for three months, and this is our only set-back.

Johnny Duval: Yes, but it's a serious one. Facts, facts – they're hard to swallow!

Glackemeyer: Quite so – the truth can come as a shock. But what were you doing anyway, reading aloud at the top of your lungs in that little office? Why didn't you tell us you had spoken in favour of, and voted for, giving that job to the Patriote Parent?

Johnny Duval: You're closing the barn door after the horse is out. I had no idea he would find out, and you know it. I was enjoying myself attacking the librarian, and I was sure no one would come up the stairs without my hearing him, for I'm used to keeping an ear on things. But it just occurred to me: perhaps Thomas sold me out in exchange for some 'bargain'?

Hamel: Not very likely: He was the one who was treated worst of all!

Johnny Duval: But who knows? What does an insult matter, if one's well paid in exchange?

Glackemeyer: He gets around a lot with the Patriotes – I'm afraid he may be up to more than just spying for us. Oh – here he comes!

SCENE IV

(Thomas Amiot, J[acques] Crémazi[e], *and* David Roy *enter together*.)[51]

Thomas Amiot: At your service, gentlemen! We've brought a quorum, I believe. Tonight we must write, and write, and write. Don't you think it's cruel of them to have stuck the term 'usurer' on me?

Johnny Duval: Ah yes, the term ... (*He sings.*) 'That one, and many more with it ...'

Crémazie: So this is the home of the Status Quo, terror of the Patriotes, the ... uh ...

Johnny Duval: None of your pompous phrases, Mister Pedant!

Others: It's time to begin! Hamel – chair the meeting! Hamel – chair the meeting!

Glackemeyer: Perhaps someone else ...

Others: Hamel, Hamel! (Hamel *takes the chair.*)

Glackemeyer: (*mutters, aside*) The idiot! He doesn't even see that they're making fun of his vanity!

Hamel: (*pompously*) Gentlemen of the Status Quo, and you also, our valued spies ...

Johnny Duval: (*aside*) Now he's going to be officious!

Hamel: ... I hereby assume the chair for the twenty-sixth time since the closure of the last session, but I must confess I have never assumed it in more difficult or more alarming circumstances. Until today, I have had only successful operations to report to you; today, however, it's quite different. Two of our number have been the victims of great contumely; even your chairman has not been spared. To whom do we owe this? To you, gentlemen (*turning to* Duval *and* Amiot), to you two, who were incompetent enough to get caught in the act. You are the ones who brought on our heads that damned dialogue printed in *Le Canadien*! For having compromised us all with your bumbling, you richly deserve my censure.

Others: They must be reprimanded! They must be reprimanded!

Hamel: As chairman of this committee it is incumbent upon me to take the floor and to make an example of you. I assume full responsibility. Step forward, gentlemen, that I may impose a formal act of admonition upon you.

Johnny Duval: (*his whole face contorted in a grimace*) Well! You certainly must know the style and the formula for that!

Thomas Amiot: How cruel, to be rebuked by one's enemies, and then by one's allies! I shan't submit to this!

Others: Submit! Submit to our chairman's authority, or we shall denounce you!

Glackemeyer: That's right!

Thomas Amiot: But there hasn't even been a formal motion to regularize these proceedings!

Johnny Duval: Let him get on with it – he's going to say something impressive, in French and in English!

Hamel: (*pompous and imposing*) You, Johnny Duval, Esquire, Barrister, Member of the Provincial Parliament, Friend of the Status Quo, and Editor of our Writings; and you who peddle them, Sire Thomas Amiot, Barrister also, and Stool-Pigeon:
   WHEREAS on the 5th of May inst., in the full light of day, although your orders were to act only at night and by stealth, you did compose, did read, and did deliver a certain text addressed 'To the Salaried Librarian of the House of Assembly';

AND WHEREAS in so doing, you allowed yourselves to be caught red-handed, and did thus cause us all to be betrayed ...

Duval: He's going to have a hard time finishing off this sentence!

Hamel: THEREFORE, I repeat, my duty obliges me to reprimand and to censure you. This occasion is all the more painful, because you were the ones we most counted upon ...

Duval: (*aside*) Ah! he's talking like the speaker![52]

Hamel: ... and who demonstrated the most zeal against the Patriotes;
    WHEREFORE, to preserve our honour, and to make an example of you, I hereby censure and scold you; and you are herewith censured and scolded.

Glackemeyer: That's right! – yes, yes, that's the way! Indeed, this is quite satisfactory as far as we are concerned. But we need something more for public consumption, something from the members of this present committee. To deprive these gentlemen of the honour of being taken for the authors of the 'Status Quo' texts, it would be a good idea to make them sign a letter – I've written one for each of them – which we'll have published in the newspapers.

Johnny Duval: Another of your fine proposals, from a proposer of trite propositions!

Glackemeyer: Hold on – let me finish my explanation! You, Thomas Amiot, will sign a letter insulting some Patriote (who will then rake you over the coals more expertly than we could do), and in this letter you'll deny categorically that Mr Johnny Duval ever wrote anything for us. And you, Mr Duval, will sign another letter that will express your fears about your chances in the coming election, state that you're wounded and outraged, and end with nasty insults against the librarian of the House of Assembly.[53]

Johnny Duval: Now that's a fine justification! Seems to me I could have written that myself, without relying on *your* pen!

Glackemeyer: True, that's right, but ...

Hamel: Let's hear the two letters, at least. (Glackemeyer *reads the letters.*)

Johnny Duval: Sir! you're admitting things that could be the ruin of all of us! You accept as a basis for argument that the conversation really took place; and the 'honest living'[54] of Amiot will make everyone laugh out loud!

Glackemeyer: Indeed, I think you're right. I would be willing ...

Others: No, no! It's fine just as it is! Let them sign, let them sign!

Hamel: Division! I call for a division!

(*Those present divide. FOR publication of the letters:* Roy, Crémazie, Amiot; *AGAINST:* Duval, Glackemeyer.)

Johnny Duval: (*signing*) I would have put money on it that Glackemeyer was going to do as he did on the Quebec Municipal Council in the McKenzie case, when he moved a motion and then voted against it! He's satisfied as long as he can propose *something*. I don't give a fig about this whole thing: with this letter, thank God, I'll have no trouble convincing people that I don't belong to the Status Quo!

(Thomas Amiot *signs after him.*)

Hamel: Now, gentlemen, we must take our revenge on the Patriotes. We must write some little piece with the signature, 'A Friend of the Status Quo.'

Johnny Duval: Anyone who wants to can go ahead and write. As far as I'm concerned I've done my bit, and paid for it too!

Glackemeyer: As for me, I've prepared a nice little article that's such a scream! I nearly die laughing every time I read it. But I'll save it for some other time. What about you, Mr Crémazie – you've generally got some fine phrases prepared for us ...

Crémazie: Oh, no more than anyone else! As you know, I was the one who wrote the article signed 'Another,' on the subject of the meeting held on the 20th, and in it I threw a lot of insults at the residents of Faubourg-Saint-Jean. It's a pity our editor cut that one up on me. As you're also aware, it was I who wrote the one about 'la graine de Perlimpinpinette ... '[55]

Glackemeyer: That was a funny one – hello fer funny!

Crémazie: I also wrote another lovely little piece that I gave Roy for our printer.

That's the one your committee, in its generosity, decided to suppress one day, keeping the contents for its own uses!

Johnny Duval: You should have shouted 'thief' and 'plagiarist'! But don't tell me you're going to recount in detail all the masterpieces you've written, Mr Crémazie. Spare us, spare us please!

Crémazie: All right, let's get down to business. For this evening I've put together a nice collection of strong, sonorous words I've borrowed from the Memorial on the French Revolution.[56] We can lard our writings with them. Here they are: 'resolutionaries, revolutionaries, revolution, dissolution, Maratism, Robespierrism, liberals, assassins, reformists, terrorists, Jacobins, canines ...'

Johnny Duval: I've never heard so many words expended on one simple ploy. Why didn't you bring along a rhyming dictionary?

Glackemeyer: We could really do something funny with those words. Say, I could make a fine tirade in verse. Hold on a moment, while I think. (*He rubs his brow.*)
   People who are resolutionaries
   Are at heart revolutionaries.
   They all want revolution
   So they can profit from our dissolution.
   They'll create a hideous Maratism
   Along with dire Robespierrism!
   That's the way these liberals stand:
   They'll assassinate their own land!
   Don't trust any reformists,
   Proud schemers, vile terrorists,
   Brigands, bandits, Jacobin swine,
   Cliquish crooks with morals canine!

Johnny Duval: No doubt this is one of your 'improvisations,' composed at leisure?

Roy: Lord, what a fine piece! It's quite similar to a few nice pieces I've read in *L'Ami du peuple*.[57]

Glackemeyer: But it *is* an improvisation!

Crémazie: An improvisation, sir? Hold on a minute – you and I have been working on it for a week!

Johnny Duval: (*aside*) Ha! I would've put money on that!

Glackemeyer: Didn't we agree ...?

Crémazie: But you're taking all the glory for yourself. I deserve credit for having supplied all the rhymes.

Glackemeyer: But I contributed the thought and the poetry!

Johnny Duval: And I, thank heavens, deserve credit for having contributed nothing to it. As for you, Mr Crémazie, you obviously want to play a role in the comedies they're writing. That would make you more important. Take consolation – we shall all be immortalized together!

Hamel: All well and good, but this fine prattle isn't producing an article for Mr Neilson. If we didn't send him one for the first time in two months, everybody would say that the play published in *Le Canadien* put us on the run! Mr Crémazie, go out and see if you can't dig up a few bits of material for us. (*Crémazie exits.*)

Johnny Duval: As far as I'm concerned, I couldn't write a single decent line tonight, and anyway I don't want to. Let's drop the whole thing – we've come to the end of the line. These Patriote swine are giving us a problem now, it's true, but if I manage to get re-elected we'll get our own back. You first of all, Mr Glackemeyer, in return for all your scheming and epigram-writing, we'll get you the job you want so much: clerk of the court.

Glackemeyer: (*aside*) Fair enough!

Johnny Duval: And you, Mr Jacques Crémazie (*turning on his heel*) – oh, he's left – Well, he won't have the job of assistant translator that he's lobbied so much for: he massacres the English language (but don't tell him I said so!) By the way, how come his boss doesn't come to see us any more? Maybe he doesn't want to be given a role in a comedy!

Glackemeyer: Ha! That'd sure be a scream!

Johnny Duval: As for you, Mr Thomas, we'll try to remove Mr Parent and make you librarian ...

Amiot: I certainly deserve to be!

Johnny Duval: ... at a salary of 4,800 francs, with which you can make 480 pounds sterling a year. That's enough to let you carry on your 'honest living' comfortably so you can give up all those retail sales of yours – especially the frock-coats, which have caused you so much embarrassment. That's not all: you know those 400 *louis* they refused to grant the king's counsel? I'm going to make that the subject of a bill, and I promise I'll get it approved. As far as I'm concerned, I'll be happy enough making a lot of noise, duping the electors in my riding, and being head of a clique!

Glackemeyer: But what about poor Mr Neilson – aren't you going to give him anything? It would only be fair ...

Johnny Duval: Him? He's a great spendthrift, and he's only in this for the money. Well, all right – he can have the printing contract for the Assembly, but at the old rate. There you have it, gentlemen: you work for my election and I'll work for your pocketbooks! But I'm still worried about that damned Faubourg Saint-Jean. The voters there are so ... And you know, that thing about the 'gallows-bait' is going to hurt me, no matter what you say ...

Hamel: Yes indeed, and I'm very much afraid you won't be able to keep all these promises! As for Mr Neilson, we have to try to win him over again. Maybe there's some way of making him editor of the official gazette. I'm king's counsel, after all ... and there's already been some talk of that.

Johnny Duval: That wouldn't be a bad thing. That way, we could be sure where he'd stand in his politics, and that he wouldn't shift around on us!

Hamel: Just the same, we still have to prepare an article on the Status Quo for him –

Glackemeyer: It's gotta be something comical!

All: Yes, oh yes!

Glackemeyer: Gotta be comical! (*All laugh.*)

SCENE V

Crémazie: (*enters, distraught*) The time for laughing's over, gentlemen: the jig's finally up!

All: What! What do you mean?

Crémazie: The secret's out, gentlemen.

Hamel: Say what you mean!

Crémazie: Well first off, Master Neilson himself has blundered into an admission that the Patriotes had indeed hit upon the editor and peddler of our writings. And Neilson is worried about subscriptions to his paper ...

Johnny Duval: The ungrateful wretch – he's betrayed us? Who's been filling up his paper for him, for the past two months? His own father was right when he said you should never trust a Scotsman!

Crémazie: That's not the worst of it. What have *you* been up to, Roy? It seems they've discovered on your desk and in your own handwriting that article commenting on the sentence, 'We admit that on this occasion, Mr Papineau was wrong ...'

Hamel: (*to* Roy) What! The one I had dictated to you? That will be grounds for another formal censure by me, in the proper time and place!

Crémazie: But what about yourself, Mr Hamel?

Hamel: What do you mean, me?

Crémazie: Yes, you. What sort of racket were you making here anyway, before we arrived, that they heard you so clearly on the street? Everybody knew we were to meet here this evening, long before we got here! They posted spies and all the Patriotes are already talking about what went on here this evening – it's the topic of every conversation!

Glackemeyer: There you go, Mr Chairman. Didn't I tell you so?

Johnny Duval: Well, Mr Chairman, we shall have to formally censure you ...

Glackemeyer: It's only right – at the next meeting!

Roy: But what if they went out and wrote another play about this whole thing?

Thomas Amiot: This is not a good place to be – I'm leaving. If we were caught in committee session, that would be a fine kettle of fish! Anyway, I'm in a hurry to send off a certain article that I understand is in great demand in Montreal – and I'll make a nice profit on it! Good night!

Johnny Duval: It's good night from me too, gentlemen: once bitten, twice shy ... Try to get out of this one as best you can! (*They leave.*)

Glackemeyer: (*follows them, muttering to himself*) Hello fer funny! But by golly, it's hard to be a member of the Status Quo ...!

SCENE VI

Hamel: Now that's what the Friends of the Status Quo are like! As long as they were under cover, they were brave and flung insults with both hands. But at the least hitch, they all scatter. You'd have to say they're ashamed of what they've done! No one wants to assume any responsibility. They run off and leave me to deal with the whole mess – leaving me holding the bag for their blunders! What can we do in the predicament we're in? Just accept our misfortunes? It must be so! But just think – Mr Neilson won't have anything from the Friend of the Status Quo this evening ... What will the clique say about that? Well, fellow spies, I can see we'll have to change tactics. It certainly looks as if the signature, 'Friend of the Status Quo,' won't get anywhere from now on, as long as we have anything to do with it. So be prepared to write on, under a thousand different names! You go suggest this plan to our friends who've just left. As for me, I'll continue my operations as well. We must seek revenge, revenge! Strike, strike hard, and especially against Papineau!

Crémazie: (*mutters, ruefully*) Oh, yes:
  You've shamed the Bar, but who's to know?
  Who's fault's it, then? Why, Papineau! [58]

Crémazie and Roy: At your service, sir! (*They leave.*)

SCENE VII

Hamel: So there we are: our secret's out! Good Lord, what will the public think? They'll say it was just the fact that I was scolded that's made me spit out all those insults against the Patriotes. But let's not be discouraged – let's write something. *He goes into an adjoining room, where he can be heard mumbling a few disjointed phrases. And so, the last of the Friends of the Status Quo disappears! We shall see them*

ANOTHER TIME

PS. Well now, gentlemen of the Status Quo, if you manage to meet together again, have a good look at yourselves – I won't say, without laughing at yourselves, but at least without blushing from shame and spite!

A.T.

III

The Donation

INTRODUCTION

1. The Play and Its Author

The audience assembled on the evening of 16 November 1842 for the first performance of *La Donation* (*The Donation*) was probably unaware of the lasting significance of the occasion. In the modest auditorium of the Prince de Galles/Prince of Wales Hotel, situated on busy Rue Saint-Jean in Quebec City's Upper Town, the curtain would rise on the first play by a native French Canadian to be written, performed, and *and* published in this country. The author, Pierre Petitclair, was virtually unknown. Three of his poems and two of his short stories had already appeared in various newspapers, but with his name omitted or disguised. More significantly perhaps, his first work (published five years earlier), *Griphon, ou la vengeance d'un valet*, had been (apart from numerous political playlets never intended for performance, such as the *Status Quo Comedies* included in this volume) the first play published by a native Québécois, and, though it was never performed, it had obviously been *intended* for performance. But the appearance of *Griphon* had gone unnoticed, in the first year of the Patriote rebellion.[1] In the interval the author had resigned his position as clerk-copyist in a legal office in Quebec and lived for more than four years on the remote North Shore and in the Labrador area employed as tutor to the numerous children of a prosperous trading family. His visits to Quebec City remained infrequent for the rest of his life and it is not known if he was present for the opening of *The Donation*.

Petitclair's roots in French Canada ran deep. He had been born in the tiny farming community of Saint-Augustin-de-Portneuf, some twenty kilometres west of Quebec City, on 12 October 1813. His parents were illiterate, according to the parish register which records his baptism on 13 October. Their ancestors had settled in Canada in the last third of the seventeenth century and had apparently remained wedded to the land. Pierre was able to break the tradition of illiteracy, however, and attended a newly established local primary school in the Faubourg Saint-Louis, just outside the walls of Quebec City, to which his family had moved by the time he reached school age. His intelligence attracted attention and led to his acceptance into the prestigious Petit Séminaire de Québec in 1825. Four years later he withdrew, apparently for economic reasons, since his academic performance there had been more than satisfactory. It was at this point, at the age of sixteen, that his formal education ended and his career as a legal clerk and notary's copyist began,[2] while nominally he continued to study law. Painfully shy, according to his principal biographer,[3] he was obviously unsuited for the legal profession, but at least found time to read omnivorously, to learn English, and, probably, to attend theatre in Quebec City.

His introduction to the stage would have come about at the Séminaire. Even before the death of Joseph-Octave Plessis – bishop of Quebec and the most redoubtable opponent of theatre Canada had seen since Bishop Saint-Vallier in the 1690s – in the very year that Petitclair entered that institution, educational theatre had been quietly making a comeback in the rapidly expanding system of *collèges classiques*. (The 1830s and 1840s would witness an explosion of such activity, highlighted in the latter decade by the performance and publication of Antoine Gérin-Lajoie's *Le Jeune Latour* in 1844, activity that continued into the decade of the 1860s with *Archibald Cameron of Locheill*, which is included in this volume.) Thus it is not surprising that the principal defects of Petitclair's first play are those of the college stage.[4] But in the interval between his departure from the Séminaire and the performance of *The Donation*, Petitclair would have had ample opportunity to read, and occasionally to see performed, more varied and more modern theatrical fare, especially in English, a language in which he apparently felt quite at home.

2. Theatre in French Canada in the 1830s and 1840s

Montreal, with the opening of the Theatre Royal in 1825, had begun to take precedence over the capital in stage arts – at least as far as imported works were concerned. The next decade would accelerate that trend, aided on the francophone side by the arrival of expatriates from France after the political turmoil of 1830, notably Firmin Prud'homme and Hyacinthe Leblanc de Marconnay.[5] But Quebec too had seen a sudden renascence of theatrical activity in French after the Patriote rebellion, activity due in large part to the seminal troupe, Les Amateurs Typographes, founded by Swiss-born Napoléon Aubin in 1839. Indeed, the most memorable theatrical event of the generation, as far as the capital was concerned, was the performance by the Typographes in October 1839 of Voltaire's *La Mort de Jules César*, which had led to serious confrontation with the authorities and the temporary closing of the theatre. Aubin, after all, had been imprisoned in January of that year because of the 'seditious tone' of his newspaper, *Le Fantasque*.[6] And it was the same troupe, with the same leader, that was to perform Petitclair's *The Donation*!

3. Social and Political Context of the Play

Jean-Claude Noël, whose doctoral thesis is the most complete and useful survey so far of the life and works of Petitclair, alludes frequently to what he perceives as the political neutrality, if not apathy, of the playwright.[7] Baudoin Burger, focusing on Petitclair's choice of William Cowan, who was favourable to the British administration, as the editor for his *Griphon* in 1837, sees the author's political commitment to French Canada as suspect.[8] The conclusions of these two theatre historians have been adopted by all others who have written on Petitclair. Closer analysis of his scattered works and his sketchy biography makes it difficult to accept these conclusions, however, as I shall attempt to show.

The arguments external to *The Donation* will be dealt with first. Then as now, there are reasons other than political for choosing a publisher, especially for a first book by an unknown writer. Petitclair had in fact *first* turned to the pages of the newspaper *Le Canadien*, closely identified with the Patriote cause; in November 1836, inserting a prospectus and seeking financial support for publication of another play, 'Qui trop embrasse mal étreint.'[9] It seems legitimate to assume that the funds he needed were not forthcoming from *Le Canadien*'s readers or its hard-pressed management, and that he then sought another source. If the choice of William Cowan for *Griphon* is significant, then the choice of *Le Canadien* for a prospectus is at least as much so. Furthermore, in the interval between *Griphon* and *The Donation*, the three works Petitclair published (two poems and a short story) all appeared in the pages of *Le Fantasque*, the irreverent, anti-administration periodical edited by Napoléon Aubin, and in the reformist *L'Artisan*, vigorously opposed to all 'ennemis de la nationalité canadienne [i.e., canadienne-française].'[10] Much more indicative than these facts, however, was the choice of Aubin's Amateurs Typographes for the performance of *The Donation*. It would have been impossible for any intelligent French Canadian to remain unaware, in 1842, of the political profile of Aimé-Nicolas ('Napoléon') Aubin, whose satirical barbs were directed almost exclusively against the colonial administration and its supporters. And the choice was conscious: the advertisements for the première of *The Donation* that began to appear in *L'Artisan* on 7 November 1842 state that the play had been written *specifically for* the Amateurs Typographes. Finally, as concerns arguments external to the play itself, even the choice of *L'Artisan* for advertising contradicts any conclusion based on the choice of Cowan in 1837, for this short-lived newspaper (it had been founded the previous month by James Huston and Charles Bertrand, and would cease publication in July 1843), was at least as sympathetic to the French-Canadian cause as Cowan's firm and the periodicals it published were opposed. (By no coincidence, it was in the pages of *L'Artisan* that *The Donation* was first published, a few weeks after its première, to reappear six years later in Huston's famous *Répertoire*.)[11]

Internal evidence against the purported political apathy (or worse) of Pierre Petitclair is even more striking. When, in act 2 scene 9, the most active and admirable character in the play, the maidservant Susette, characterizes the villain, Bellire, as 'that tyrant, that Sydenham' ('c'est c'tyran, ce Sydenham de Bellire qu'est la cause de tout ça!'), she is invoking Charles Edward Poulett Thomson, 1st Baron Sydenham, governor of Canada (1839–41), a firm opponent of responsible government for the colony and a major proponent of the anglicization of French Canada. 'Chicken' ('Poulet') Sydenham had been the favourite target of Aubin's vitriolic humour in *Le Fantasque* until the governor's death, scarcely a year before this performance of *The Donation*, in a riding accident in Kingston. Susette's reference is as clear and as hostile as it is topical. An example just as direct comes from the mouth of the loyal, simple *Canadien*, Nicodème, when he is asked by his master where Auguste is staying in Quebec – in Rue Champlain? Nicodème responds, 'Oh no, sir: it's just in front o' that there square that stands for Canada, 'cause there's chains all 'round it. How do they call it? Ah, yes: the Place d'Armes.' (2, 17). To any French-Canadian spectator or reader in 1842, acutely aware how his or her province had just been forced into an unfair and unequal union with Upper Canada, such an allusion could not suggest apathy. It is in this context as well that one should interpret remarks like those made by Delorval in his monologue (2, 8), when he wonders aloud whether his treatment of Auguste may have been unjust: 'It's terribly unfair to discover you've been condemned with no hearing. It's true that sort of thing seems to be happening a lot these days, but I can't quite get used to it!' The imprisonment, execution, and exile of so many Patriote activists would still be fresh in any French Canadian's memory. From evidence such as this, one deduces that if Pierre Petitclair had ever been apathetic, then there had been considerable evolution in his political awareness since *Griphon*, a play which, it is true, could more realistically have been set in the France of the *ancien régime* than in Canada, and in which, despite valiant efforts at symbolic analysis of its plot by certain recent critics, one discovers not the slightest echo of contemporary politics.

4. Sources and Structure

The Donation is a curious hybrid, a comedy of intrigue adhering resolutely to the classical unities of time (half a day, at most), place (a sort of antechamber), and action, but with a heavy overlay of melodrama. As to the play itself, Jean-Claude

Noël has pointed out borrowings from Molière, Regnard, Beaümarchais, and Scribe, concluding that 'in the final analysis, there is virtually nothing left in the play ascribable to Petitclair himself. The only recognition we might grant him now should be for his skill in reconciling all these different borrowings.'[12] To its derivativeness should be added the inconsistent level of speech used by the servants, the inadvertent anglicisms, and the glaring mistakes in plot preparation.

Examples of these mistakes follow. It is not until act 2, scene 8 that Petitclair seems to realize that the expulsion of Auguste without his being told why he has been fired needs some explanation, but Delorval's brief monologue, referring to the 'promise he had made to Auguste' (he *must* mean, 'to Bellire') not to reveal the reason for this action only serves to heighten our confusion. A similar problem arises in act 2, scene 12, where Martel explains (through Bellire, to the audience and reader) how he has prepared the false documents incriminating Auguste. Again, why would Delorval not confront Auguste with the 'evidence'? Bellire responds, 'Oh, I have no worries on that point. He swore he would show the documents to no one but his niece. And as I say, personal honour comes first and foremost with him.' This is a curiously unconvincing conception of 'honour,' but one that simplifies plot control. At a more basic level, there are problems of motivational credibility. How could a successful businessman like Delorval be so gullible, so naïve? Why would he choose to donate his wealth to a stranger, not to his beloved niece? Why do Auguste and Caroline, if their love for each other is so strong that Delorval fears she may die when he banishes Auguste, never exhibit the slightest interest in each other when they are together, even after Delorval has revealed to each the other's love and informed them they are to be married? They are a curiously bloodless pair of lovers, even for the squeamish nineteenth-century French-Canadian stage! Other deficiencies are those characteristic of contemporary melodrama, chiefly the abuse of soliloquy (twelve scenes are monologues) and asides, and gross oversimplification of character: Auguste is the noblest of youths, animated by his pure, unspoken love for Caroline; Delorval is an honest, generous, well-intentioned man led astray by a cunning scoundrel; and the latter is a two-faced, leering villain whose every entrance must have been accompanied by hisses and boos from the audience.

Yet despite all this, one suspects that *The Donation* plays well, a suspicion corroborated by its stage history, for it was performed at least half a dozen times before the author's death in 1860. Certainly the basic structure is dramatically sound: Petitclair has established a parallel development in the play's two acts, the first ending with a direct threat to the happiness of the young lovers and to the wealth they would inherit, the second ending with an even more dramatic *coup de théâtre* (for we do not know that Bellire and Martel have been overheard discussing their scheme), and the full dissolution of that threat in the third after its dramatic suspense has been exploited to the utmost. Thus one is not surprised to learn, in the issue of *L'Artisan* for 17 November (the day after the première), that the play had enjoyed considerable success: 'Mr P. Petitclair's play was very well received. The outbursts of explosive laughter that erupted frequently among the audience are proof of its success, and an encouragement for the author.' Melodrama, already well established on European stages, was a new phenomenon for French Canada – or at least, for Quebec City in 1842. Among its other significant 'firsts,' *The Donation*, is the first and one of the clearest examples of the influence of the melodramatic tradition on French-Canadian dramaturgy.[13]

In literature, Petitclair remained a dilettante for the rest of his life, writing occasional poems, songs, and stories, painting, and composing and performing music when his duties as tutor left him free time or when he felt so inclined. Only one other play of his survives, and it is his best: *A Country Outing*, an amusing satire of anglophile excesses among certain *Québécois*, the translation of which follows *The Donation* in this volume. The titles of two others are known, 'Qui trop embrasse mal étreint,' already referred to, and 'Le Brigand,' the date of composition of which is unknown. In this respect he is typical of every French-Canadian playwright until the very end of the century: dramaturgy is an avocation, an amusing diversion from more 'appropriate' pursuits. Only the writers – and they are generally anonymous – of political dialogues and partisan playlets represent an exception to that rule.

5. Language

The French spoken by Delorval, Caroline, Auguste, Bellire, and Martel is 'standard,' 'correct,' and virtually indistinguishable. Delorval and Caroline commit blatant anglicisms which must be imputed to Petitclair himself (for example, Delorval at act 2, scene 5: 'il doit même m'introduire un de ses amis,' and, in the same scene, Caroline's response, 'Je ne suis pas de votre opinion'). Susette and Nicodème speak a comic, non-standard French, strongly Norman in flavour, and obviously much indebted to the popular speech of many of Molière's peasant characters, but with recognizable *québécois* elements as well. I have sought a contemporary, colloquial, 'non-standard' English to render their speech, including Nicodème's frequent malapropisms ('pardon ... si j'interromps la laine de votre conservation' [1, 2], instead of 'le *fil* de votre *conversation*'). There is an obvious attempt by the author to individualize Villomont's speech, most audibly with the expression that is his signature, 'corbleu!' – still a rather forceful expletive at the time, and which I render, 'bloody hell!'

My translation is based on the text of the play that appeared serially in *L'Artisan*, on 15, 19, 22, 26, 29 December 1842. Differences between this version and the one appearing in both editions of James Huston's *Répertoire national* (1848, 2:

234–70; and 1893, 2: 262–304) are inconsequential: typographical errors are corrected (and, incidentally, others introduced), punctuation is adjusted, and there are a few minor attenuations of the dialectal forms used by the servants (in 2, 15, for example, Nicodème says, in *L'Artisan*: 'Queu diable de vacarme nous cries-tu donc, toi?' whereas the *Répertoire* (both editions) has 'Que diable de vacarne [*sic*] ...'). The information on actors' entrances and exits appended to the version in *L'Artisan*[14] does not appear in the other editions.

PIERRE PETITCLAIR

The Donation

A PLAY IN TWO ACTS

First performed at Quebec City by the
Troupe of the Amateurs Typographes
16 November 1842

CHARACTERS

Delorval, an aging businessman
Bellire, a swindler
Auguste, Delorval's assistant
Caroline, Delorval's niece
Martel, friend of Bellire
Villomont, a notary
Nicodème, a servant
Susette, a servant

ACT ONE

Setting: *A room with at least four chairs and a table on which an ink-well, quill pens, and paper are visible. In the background, to the audience's left, a screen.*

SCENE I
Caroline, *about to leave*; Susette, *dusting furniture*

Susette: Oh, Miz Car'line, Miz Car'line, I can see you wanna keep it secret, but I figured out what's makin' you so worried!

Caroline: (*turning back, surprised*) Pardon? *What* have you 'figured out,' Susette?

Susette: Breaks me heart to see you drownin' in sadness like that, y'know! You don't eat no more, you don't sleep, an' I see you day-dreamin' all the time. Sometimes you don't say nothin' at all, just starin' at stuff that ain't there. You don't even open your pretty li'l mouth to laugh no more, like you used to. Oh, I know what's behind it all!

Caroline: Say what you mean, Susette!

Susette: In one word, you're in love with Monsieur Auguste, your uncle's head clerk.

Caroline: (*surprised*) Susette!

Susette: Oh c'mon now, I know what I'm talkin' about!

Caroline: Wherever did you get that idea?

Susette: As if it was hard to guess! Every time he comes in here, don't I see you blushin' so hard your eyes water, an' all of a sudden you look down like you was lookin' for somethin' on the ground when there ain't nothin' to look for. Ain't that so?

Caroline: (*aside*) She makes me feel ashamed of myself. (*Aloud*) Is that all?

Susette: It's enough, I reckon! And another thing: your uncle knows, too.

Caroline: (*surprised*) He knows, you say?

Susette: Sure, he knows. He's pretty happy about it, too!

Caroline: Just where are you getting all this information?

Susette: You'll find out. I ...

Caroline: Shh! Someone's coming!

SCENE II
Actors, *as before*; Nicodème, *entering stage right*

Nicodème: Do excuse me, ladies, for breakin' the yarn o' your conservation. I, uh – y'know – uh ... I got a couple o' words to say to Miz Car'line, me missus ...

Caroline: What is it, Nicodème?

Nicodème: I wanted to tell you, private-like. (*He comes close to* Caroline, *but speaks as loud as he can*) Monsieur Delorval, your uncle, sent me to tell you he's got serious stuff he wants to talk to you about, in his rooms! There you have it.

Caroline: I'll go see him right away. (*She exits.* Nicodème *crosses the stage, and is about to exit left.*)

SCENE III
Susette, Nicodème

Susette: (*running towards him*) Nico! Nico! D'you know why he wants to see her?

Nicodème: No, I don't. Anyways, what business is it o' mine?

Susette: *I* know why!

Nicodème: Well, then?

Susette: Ha! You think I'm just gonna tell you straight out? Not me, Nico, no sirree bob!

Nicodème: Fine an' dandy, then. I know somethin' that's bein' cooked up too, an' not too far from here ...

Susette: Like what?

Nicodème: 'Ha! You think I'm just gonna tell you straight out? Not me, Susette, no siree bob!'

Susette: What a tease you are! All right, fair 'nough: if you promise to tell me your secret, I'll tell you mine.

Nicodème: Fine secrets you got, sweetie-pie! D'you think I don't know he called her in to chat with her about her weddin' to Monsieur Bellire? What a lot o' dough Bellire's goin' to get – Monsieur Delorval is as rich as a born Jew!

Susette: (*laughing*) Ha, ha! – Monsieur Bellire!

Nicodème: 'Ha, ha?' Look at her laughin' in me face, would you! Yes, Monsieur Bellire I say, Monsieur Delorval's friend, who he loves more than I love you. An' there you have it!

Susette: Monsieur Bellire! Monsieur Delorval's friend! You mean, 'friend of Monsieur Delorval's money!' You can't be serious, Nicodème. I thought they were headin' to get married too, but that's all broke off now. Miz Car'line can't stand the sight o' Monsieur Bellire. I dunno, I don't think I could take him neither. An' you know Monsieur Delorval's so nice he wouldn't force his niece into nothin', so he's marryin' her off to ...

Nicodème: Aha! I can guess! (*He whispers in her ear, and* Susette *nods in agreement.*) Fine an' dandy then, I'm happy for him, 'pon me soul! Best chunk o' young manhood I ever seen, that lad. Ain't at all like Monsieur Bellire. I can't figure out what Monsieur Delorval sees in Bellire – he's got such a holt on him!

Susette: (*flirting*) Well, you know, sometimes it's the worst kinda men that're the most attractive. 'Twas the Serpent that first charmed Woman, after all! Present company excepted! (*She laughs.*)

Nicodème: You're just tryin' to pull me leg, I think, you little scamp. I'm leavin'. (*He starts to exit.*)

Susette: Hey, wait up! I tole you what I know: you gotta tell me what *you* know!

Nicodème: (*pauses*) Oh, yeah, that's right, I forgot. It was ... (*He scratches his* *head*.) It was ... Y'know, it was nothin' at all! There you have it! (*He runs off,* Susette *after him.*)

Susette: (*returning*) Oh, here's Monsieur Delorval!

SCENE IV
Susette, Delorval

Delorval: Well, everything's going nicely. (*To* Susette.) Susette, go down and tell Auguste I'd like to see him for a minute. Quickly! (*She exits.*)

SCENE V
Delorval, *alone*

Well, I'm really pleased with what I've done. The poor young thing's not too unhappy either, I'm sure! I agreed to be responsible for her, and I'll see to it that she's happy. She's my only heir as well. That's why ...

SCENE VI
Delorval, Caroline

Caroline: Is Susette not here, uncle?

Delorval: She'll be back in a moment, niece. I'll send her to you.

Caroline: Thank you, uncle. (*She exits.*)

SCENE VII
Delorval, *alone*

I've been wanting to talk to her about this for a long time, and I've finally done so!

SCENE VIII
Delorval, Susette, Auguste

Delorval: Well, good morning, Auguste!

Auguste: What can I do for you, sir?

Delorval: Susette, your mistress needs you. (Susette *exits in the direction of* Caroline's *room.*)

SCENE IX
Delorval, Auguste

Delorval: (*in a serious tone*) Auguste, I've just heard some strange things about you! I certainly didn't expect this sort of news about you, after I had had so much confidence in you, looking upon you as one of my own! People are so ungrateful nowadays! (*Even more serious.*) My! how coolly you return my stare! Aren't you afraid of me? You should be trembling with fear!

Auguste: (*with dignity*) Sir, as you know very well from experience, only the guilty tremble. But I'd like to know ...

Delorval: (*smiling and patting him on the back*) Come, come, Auguste, don't you see I'm joking? This strange bit of news I've heard is that you're in love with my niece. (Auguste *appears surprised.*) And I can tell you that your love is returned. No use pretending – I know all about it! You've been in love with her, and never breathed a word to her about it. But you confided in someone who told me. And she has loved you too, in secret – I've just heard it from her own lips. In a word, you love her, don't you?

Auguste: My dear sir, I cannot deny that I adore Miss Caroline, and would long ago have declared my love, if one unsurmountable obstacle hadn't stood between her and me.

Delorval: What's this obstacle, then?

Auguste: Your niece is rich, and I'm, I'm ...

Delorval: Ugh! Money! Listen, no more talk about 'obstacles,' understand? You've been working for me for many years now, and I can't help noticing – can't help *admiring* the regularity of your conduct, your energy, your honesty, your love of honour, in short. For all that you have my sincere congratulations. Thus I am particularly pleased to find in you a means of making my niece happy as well. That's why I want you to take her as your wife. Are you happy with that?

Auguste: Sir, how can I ever repay you for your generosity? Marriage to her is what I most desire! My only regret is that I may not be worthy of a wife like her ...

Delorval: Tut, tut! Your wedding will be next Tuesday. You may as well start preparing for it.

Auguste: As you wish, sir. (*He exits.*)

SCENE X

Delorval, *alone*

(*Consulting his watch.*) Now what's keeping Bellire this morning? He seems rather late to me – I'm starting to get bored. Funny thing, that: I'm never in a good mood when he's not around. He's such a likeable person! I know some people say I'm getting on in years, but that doesn't mean I don't enjoy young people and good times. Besides, he's so devoted to me, so sincere in his friendship that I can't ... well, let's just say I can't live without him! (*He exits.*)

SCENE XI

Bellire, *alone*

Aha! There's the fellow now, going into his study. He didn't see me. I wonder if he's thought about the donation, the old fool! As long as I can get my hands on the money, I can do very nicely without his niece, all the more so since she doesn't seem particularly fond of me! She's forbidden me to utter a word to her, in fact. But what if he were to make the donation to someone else – his assistant, Auguste Richard, for example? He thinks highly of him, and it's true Auguste deserves it. No, that mustn't happen! I'd like to see that chap Auguste a long way from here, just the same ... But with nerve, patience, and, most importantly, impudence, you can succeed in anything. Which reminds me: tomorrow's outing, and me without a carriage or horses (never have owned either, in fact). Ah, but this guy's an easy mark ... and here he comes! Let's laugh it up a bit, to put him in a good mood.

SCENE XII

Bellire, Delorval

Bellire: (*laughing*) Ha, ha! Ho, ho!

Delorval: My dear friend! Dear Bellire! (*He takes his hand and holds it.*)

Bellire: (*continues to laugh*) Ha, ha! Ho, ho!

Delorval: I wonder what's set him off again this morning?

Bellire: (*still laughing*) Ha, ha! Ho, ho!

Delorval: My word, whatever he has is catching! (*Both laugh together.*)

Bellire: Just a joke, my friend, a very funny one! Ha, ha, ha!

Delorval: Well I hope you're going to tell me, then!

Bellire: Yes, yes, I'll tell you. But how are you today, my dear friend, my best friend, the friend for whom I'd lay down my life, if need be? (*They shake hands again,* Delorval *beaming with good humour.*) How happy I am to see you this morning, glowing with health, so frisky and young looking! Upon my word, age has no effect on you, I say it with no intent to flatter! (*They sit down at opposite ends of the table.*)

Delorval: Age, did you say? I'm not really that old, Bellire. I was sixty ... sixty ... *four*, the day before Saint-Jean-Baptiste Day, June 23rd. Surely you wouldn't call sixty-four being old!

Bellire: Not at all, dear friend. What I mean is, no one would ever guess you were that age. The very best judge of faces would be stumped by yours. As far as I'm concerned, I see nothing but the full bloom of mature manhood!

Delorval: I believe you, Bellire. But there are some people, you know, who insist on calling me an 'old timer.' Isn't that terrible? 'Old timer!'

Bellire: (*laughs*) Ha, ha, ha!

Delorval: What! Surely *you* don't believe ...

Bellire: I'm still laughing at that joke of mine.

Delorval: 'Old timer,' Bellire!

Bellire: Blockheads, that's what people like that are! It's not the number of years that makes one old, Monsieur Delorval. It's not the years, for sure, its – (*Aside.*) I don't know what in hell to say next! (*Aloud.*) You know yourself, Monsieur Delorval, a young man may in fact be an old one. It's one's appearance that makes a person seem old. You don't look like an old man, so you're *not* an old man. That's what you might call logical reasoning. The people you're talking about haven't learned logic, that's all!

Delorval: (*aside*) He's witty too, the rascal!

Bellire: Say, I haven't had the pleasure of seeing your niece this morning. I do hope she's in the best of health?

Delorval: Better than ever, my friend.

Bellire: I'm delighted to hear that. (*He appears thoughtful.*)

Delorval: (*after a moment's silence*) What's wrong, Bellire? Now you seem distracted.

Bellire: Well, yes, there *is* something I've been fretting about. You see, my dear Monsieur Delorval, several of my friends are planning an excursion tomorrow, to Lac Calvaire.[15] You know the place?

Delorval: Of course I know it!

Bellire: Lovely spot, isn't it? Well, I've been invited to go along ...

Delorval: So? There's nothing about that to make you sad, Bellire!

Bellire: You'll see what I mean. Would you believe it, the other day my fine dapple-grey, a horse that's mettlesome as all get-out, panicked and wrecked my carriage, so badly I can't even use it!

Delorval: Good heavens, is that all! I own a carriage, don't I? Why the devil didn't you speak up? My carriage is as much yours as it is mine! Everything I own is at your disposal. Just look at him, would you – there he was, worrying about a mere trifle! I'll send my carriage and pair around to you tomorrow morning, at whatever time you wish.

Bellire: Dear Delorval! Really, you're too kind! Perhaps now you're going to think I brought the subject up in order to ... but ...

Delorval: What! What an idea!

Bellire: It wasn't that at all, I assure you. (*He laughs.*) Ha, ha, ha! I can't get that darned joke out of my mind!

Delorval: Good! Now I see you laughing, and it makes me happy, too!

Bellire: I'd be even happier if I knew you'd thought about what I've been telling you for the last while.

Delorval: I've thought about it, Bellire.

Bellire: You understand, dear Monsieur Delorval, the advice I've been giving you is strictly in your own interest. Although, as I was just saying, your appearance certainly doesn't betray it, you know very well you're not exactly a youth anymore. I mean, you can't devote as much energy as a young man could to all the different things that demand your attention. Besides, as you know, when you're rich you can never be entirely carefree.

Delorval: That's true.

Bellire: So, as I've explained, a legal donation in favour of someone, some friend ... You must understand, it would have to be some friend, someone you could really trust. I repeat, a donation like that would be the answer for you. All your worries, all your problems would disappear. Your every wish would be attended to by faithful, attentive, *honest* servants. Friends of your own choosing would help you spend each day pleasantly, when you weren't off on some delightful little trip or other. To sum up, you'd have exactly the same social advantages you have now, minus the cares and worries, and that's no small matter!

Delorval: I'm much indebted to you, Bellire, for your sound advice. And on serious reflection, I've finally decided to follow it. And you know, Bellire, I've noticed, just as you say, that I'm starting to get tired of business problems.

Bellire: That's the sort of problems I'd like to spare you. They could be fatal, at your age – not that I think you're an old man, but you're not exactly a youngster any more ...

Delorval: That's right! So I'm going to arrange a legal donation *inter vivos* of my entire wealth and property, Bellire.

Bellire: Well, since everything that concerns you is of concern to me, my dear Monsieur Delorval, could I ask, without appearing indiscreet, who the person is to whom the donation is to be made?

Delorval: A friend, a young man in whom I have the utmost confidence. And he's not far from here right now. There, I'm practically giving it away! I'm sure you'll approve of my choice!

Bellire: How should I know? Maybe it's that fine musician I saw here the other day, who prefers a jig to one of Rossini's operas? He'd make your money dance – right into his own pocket!

Delorval: He's not the one.

Bellire: Then I bet it's that little doctor who, when he pulls a tooth, yanks out three or four, and part of your jaw too, just to be sure he gets the right one. You certainly wouldn't last long with him!

Delorval: (*laughing*) Ha, ha, ha! No, not him, not him! You mean you can't guess? I tell you he's not far from here, right now. It's –

Bellire: Upon my word, I don't know. (*Aside*) Well, here it comes!

Delorval: Auguste Richard. (*Both stand. Bellire is **dumbfounded**.*) As you can see, someone whose decency and honesty I can count on. He'll soon be my nephew-in-law as well, and that's what made me decide to arrange the donation in his favour. Otherwise, my dear Bellire, you can be sure that you and no other would have been the recipient. But you won't be left out – I'll see to it that there's a clause inserted in your favour. Now then, isn't that the way to do it?

Bellire: Auguste!

Delorval: Yes, Auguste, my chief assistant. Wasn't I right in saying he's not too far from here? Downstairs, in the shop!

Bellire: Auguste!

Delorval: Yes, Auguste. You mean you don't approve of my choice?

Bellire: Auguste! Monsieur Delorval, didn't he come in late, this morning?

Delorval: What do you mean, come in late?

Bellire: Well you see ... No, I won't say a thing. I hate scandalmongering ...

Delorval: What do you mean?

Bellire: Well, you know, he *was* seen in a certain establishment ...

Delorval: (*angry*) Auguste?

Bellire: Yes, Auguste, your assistant.

Delorval: In a certain establishment, you say? What kind of 'establishment'?

Bellire: Well, it's – no, it just goes against my principles to meddle in other people's affairs! Unless someone like you is involved, my dear Delorval, someone whose welfare concerns me ...

Delorval: That's why you must tell me everything you know about him, Bellire. I beg you to do so. Where was he seen?

Bellire: Well, if I *must* tell you, it was a certain establishment on Rue Champlain.[16] Seems he's well known in that spot: they call him 'the Hypocrite,' because he really knows how to put on a show of virtue in the presence of – but I guess the word 'hypocrite' says it all. Unfortunately, there's another name for him as well ...

Delorval: What sort of name? Quick!

Bellire: Oh, it's none of my business – why should I tell on him?

Delorval: Dear Bellire, I beg of you!

Bellire: They call him a libertine and a rake.

Delorval: Auguste a hypocrite, a rake! But what was he doing in this establishment? Quick, dear Bellire!

Bellire: Aw, how do *I* know? ...

Delorval: Come on, don't make me drag it out of you!

Bellire: Well, he was doing what he usually does when he goes there.

Delorval: He goes there often?

Bellire: Every day, I understand.

Delorval: No, that's impossible, Bellire, because I'd know about it!

Bellire: I can't swear that he's there *every* evening, but I do know he spent all of last night there, along with half a dozen young, rosy-cheeked, purple-nosed dandies!

Delorval: And how did they spend their time?

Bellire: Oh, gambling, drinking, singing, carousing ...

Delorval: And what about him?

Bellire: He kept his end up.

Delorval: This is dreadful, Bellire! When was that?

Bellire: Last night.

Delorval: Last night? (*He rubs his brow.*) That can't be: you're wrong, Bellire – Auguste spent the whole night putting account-books in order.

Bellire: Must have been the night before last, then. What does it matter to me, anyway!

Delorval: (*thoughtful*) Night before last. No, you must be wrong again. He came and spent that night with me, waking poor dead Biron!

Bellire: Night before last?

Delorval: Night before last.

Bellire: Think about it: you might be mistaken!

Delorval: No, I'm as sure as anyone can be. But tell me, Bellire, you yourself saw him in this establishment?

Bellire: Did I see him?

Delorval: Yes.

Bellire: With my own eyes?

Delorval: Yes.

Bellire: Are you serious, my dear Delorval? *Me*, hanging out in places like that? No, I didn't see him myself, but I have it on good authority.

Delorval: Oh, now I understand! He's not guilty, Bellire, he's not guilty, you can be sure of that. He's been mistaken for someone else, or perhaps some enemy of his is just spreading false rumours. Auguste is a decent man, you see, and decent men are rarely without enemies. Auguste is too fine a person to frequent the sort of spot you describe. Impossible, Bellire – I'd have to see it with my own eyes!

Bellire: As you wish, sir. But as far as I'm concerned, and just between the two of us, I don't like the looks of that chap. Despite all the honesty and decency you see in him, I believe he's just as liable to be circulating in fast and loose company as to – (*He shakes his head.*)

Delorval: Out with it!

Bellire: What's the use of telling you, if you don't even believe what I say? It's none of my business, anyway.

Delorval: Is it something really serious?

Bellire: More serious than you think. If you knew, you'd never want to set eyes on Auguste again!

Delorval: Come, come, Bellire, eh! This is a lot of nonsense. If you knew Auguste as I know him, you'd never dream of believing the slightest impropriety that people might attribute to him ...

Bellire: Perhaps you're about to learn a good deal more about him.

Delorval: (*laughing*) Ha, ha! What a joker you are! You like to tease me, you rascal! Come on, enough of that – there's something I want to talk to you about. If you'll be so good as to follow me into my study, I'll give you a good laugh. (*He exits.*)

SCENE XIII
Bellire, *alone*

Failed! I've failed completely. Oh, I was right to be afraid of that damned Auguste! No matter, you can't keep a good man like me down! The old fellow hasn't seen these two documents yet. (*He takes two papers from his pocket.*) It was a good thing I fortified my chances with them!

SCENE XIV
Bellire, Susette

Susette: Monsieur Delorval is waitin' for you, sir.

Bellire: I'm coming, little gal. (*He leaves.*)

SCENE XV
Susette, *alone*

'Little gal!' The oaf! 'Little gal!' Good job he didn't stay another minute! I woulda showed him it's better to be small on the outside than on the inside! By gum, I can't help hatin' him with all me heart, that turkey! 'Little gal,' he says. He always got some adjickive like that to throw in me face!

SCENE XVI
Susette, Caroline

Caroline: Susette, what's wrong? You seem disturbed.

Susette: I got a right to be! To think that clod, Monsieur Bellire, just insulted me with insults!

Caroline: Susette, Susette! You must speak more respectfully of people!

Susette: What d'you expect me to do, miz? It's frustratin' to have people treat you like that!

Caroline: What did he do?

Susette: 'Little gal,' he says! 'Little gal,' he calls me! The other day he called me his 'little nymph!' Now is that any name to stick on a decent girl?

Caroline: (*laughing*) Ha, ha, ha!

SCENE XVII
Actors, *as before; then* Auguste, *who enters bowing, hat in hand*

Auguste: Beg your pardon, Miss, I wanted to see if your uncle is in. I see that he isn't.

Caroline: He's in his study. Susette, go tell him Monsieur Auguste would like to see him. (Susette *starts to leave.*)

Auguste: Oh, no, don't! He may be busy, and it's nothing urgent.

SCENE XVIII
Actors, *as before*; Nicodème

Nicodème: (*to Auguste*) Sir, your tailor is downstairs, with your weddin' suit.

Auguste: Very good, Nicodème. I'll go see him right away.

SCENE XIX
Actors, *as before*, Delorval

Delorval: (*furious*) The wedding's off! (*To Auguste.*) And as for you, you impostor, out with you – I never want to see you again! And I'm not jesting this time! (*There is general consternation.*)

Auguste: But sir, surely you're at least going to tell me what I've done to deserve such treatment!

Delorval: Out of here this instant! (Delorval *and* Auguste *exit in different directions.* Caroline *is too weak to stand, while* Nicodème *and* Susette *are frozen in attitudes of surprise.*
Curtain.)

ACT TWO

SCENE I
As the curtain rises Nicodème *and* Susette *are seated on-stage*

Nicodème: No, Susette, you just don't understand this whole thing, that's all!

Susette: What do you mean?

Nicodème: Like why he put the run to Auguste like that, without tellin' him nothin'.

Susette: So tell me, Nico, why *did* he put the run to him like that?

Nicodème: Aha! There's the meat of it! So you don't know neither, eh? Well I'll tell you, I think it's awful the way he kicked him out, an' it makes me heart bleed, Susette – drivin' away Monsieur Auguste, a man everyone respecks! It's bewilderin', not to say perplexin'! Now you see, that's why I want to get you to do this – you've got a good tongue in your head.

Susette: Oh yes, thank heavens, I can hold me own when I want to. I done learned me grammar, you might say, Nico!

Nicodème: Fine an' dandy then, an' I can speechify pretty good too. So we're gonna stand right up to Monsieur Delorval an' ask his pardon for Monsieur Auguste. Surely he ain't gonna refuse us! That's it!

Susette: I'm with you all the way, Nico. You really think we got a chance to pull it off?

Nicodème: For sure!

Susette: But what if he had real reasons for runnin' him off?

Nicodème: What kind of reasons *could* he have, Susette? How could he ever have reasonable reasons for doin' that to a guy like him?

Susette: I don't think so neither, an' I even think I'd go so far as to swear to that!

Nicodème: Fine an' dandy then, we gotta take the plunge an' go an' talk to Monsieur Delorval face to face about this thing.

Susette: Which one of us is gonna do the talkin'? Or are we both gonna talk at once?

Nicodème: You'll be the one makin' the speeches, an' I'll slip you a word or two now an' then. You know how much a woman's tongue can do, with a tear or two to help things along. Can you cry?

Susette: What a question!

Nicodème: Fine an' dandy, then! As I was sayin', a woman, usin' tongue an' tears, can master the greatest master in the world. You can see that in any book of ancient history, modern an' future history. Say, here he comes! Let's be ready for him! (*They stand.*)

SCENE II
Actors, *as before*, Delorval

Delorval: (*aside*) The poor girl! This may be the death of her. (Nicodème *and* Susette *assume a respectful position in front of* Delorval.)

Nicodème: (*half aloud to* Susette, *pushing her forward*) Go ahead!

Susette: (*pushing* Nicodème) You go first!

Nicodème: (*pushing* Susette) No, no – the power of a woman's tears, remember?

Susette: (*pushing* Nicodème) I don't know how to cry!

Nicodème: Talk, then!

Delorval: What do you young people want? I take it there's something you want to tell me?

Nicodème: That's right, good master, somethin' bloody serious. Fine an' dandy, then, you'll see ... You see ... The way it is ... (*To* Susette.) Come on, say somethin'!

Delorval: Oh, I think I know. It's probably about your coming marriage. You may marry, my friends, as soon as you wish. I know you love each other, and I only hope Susette won't have an impostor like that chap Auguste for a husband.

Nicodème, Susette: (*together*) An impostor! Auguste!

Nicodème: It's him we wanted to talk to you about!

Delorval: That hooligan?

Nicodème: Oh, good master, that certainly ain't the right word for him. You know, I'd give me life's blood for Monsieur Auguste, an' it really hurts to hear him called anythin' like that. So fine an' dandy then, I says to myself and then I says to Susette: 'Monsieur Delorval is a fine, just, generous man. Let's talk to him, and beg him to forgive Monsieur Auguste if he thinks he's guilty of somethin.' Susette agreed right away. So here we are!

Susette: Yes sir, an' we beg you to pardon him, an' take him back. Monsieur Auguste is as innocent as a new-born babe, an' you can be sure of it!

Delorval: Innocent! Children, you have no idea what he's really like. I have absolute proof to the contrary!

Susette: But sir, he worked for you for fifteen years, an' you never seen him do the least bit o' wrong, or the least thing that wasn't right!

Delorval: That's true.

Susette: Nobody never said a single word against him.

Delorval: That's true: I've only heard good things about him.

Nicodème: Fine an' dandy then, good master: there's no way he could suddenly of jumped into an evil life of vice, like some despairin' desperado! Take me, now: I was in your service before you hired him. Is it possibly possible I wouldn't of spotted somethin' wrong with him, if there was somethin' wrong? Holy jumpin', he's the best person you could ever meet, in the whole universe of the world!

Susette: An' if you only knew all the good things he says about you! If you knew how devoted he is to you!

Nicodème: Fine an' dandy, then, dear master, here's a suggestion from my brains. (*He touches his forehead.*) Supposin' he *did* do somethin' wrong (but I don't believe it!) why wouldn't you forgive him this once, if he promised never to do nothin' wrong again?

Delorval: That's impossible! What he did is unpardonable. I know, young friends, that your intentions are good. You think he's innocent, and I don't blame you for interceding for him. But as far as I'm concerned, I'm convinced he's guilty. It was quite a struggle for me to treat him the way I did, but I had to do it. (Nicodème *and* Susette *throw themselves at* Delorval's *feet.*)

Nicodème: Oh, good master!

Susette: Oh, sir!

Delorval: It's no use. Susette, tell Caroline her uncle wants to see her. (*They stand, and* Susette *exits.*)

SCENE III

Nicodème: (*leaving*) Poor Monsieur Auguste! I'm sure his grievin' will lead him to the grave, that's what! (*He exits.*)

SCENE IV
Delorval, *alone*

(*Pulling two papers from his pocket.*) Here are the incriminating documents.

SCENE V
Delorval, Caroline

Delorval: Come here, my dear Caroline. I promised to tell you what made me drive him away, and I'll keep my promise. But for your part, you must swear not to breathe a word of it to anyone. Not one syllable, directly or indirectly!

Caroline: I swear I won't, uncle.

Delorval: (*handing her one of the papers*) Here, read this. (Caroline *reads*.) You're trembling! (Caroline *seems about to faint.* Delorval *helps her to sit, and sits down himself.*) You see? He already has a wife, and he would have married you!

Caroline: I must say, uncle, I don't believe a word of this!

Delorval: (*taking back the paper*) But isn't this a copy taken from the marriage register in the parish of Saint-Auban?

Caroline: It may be a forgery.

Delorval: I know that signature as well as I know my own! The *curé* of Saint-Auban was an old classmate of mine, so there's no doubt about it. (*He shows her the paper.*) You see the date of the wedding? 20 September 1841. That's precisely when he went to Saint-Auban, on business for me. And just to prove to you that his wife is still very much alive, here's a letter in her own handwriting, dated the 8th of this month (today's the 16th), in which she begs for financial help, since she has nothing to her name. Here's more proof of what she says: I've noticed him more than once enclosing banknotes in letters he was writing. The swine!

Caroline: Oh, uncle!

Delorval: I'm sorry, child – I'll never use that word again, in your presence.

Caroline: But this letter, this extract, how did they come into your possession?

Delorval: Well you see, my dear niece, it was the letter that led to the extract from the marriage register. This is how it happened. A friend of mine, whom you won't mind my mentioning, Monsieur Bellire, came across the letter lying around here somewhere. Seeing that it was unsealed, he decided to read it. Perhaps that wasn't very sensitive of him, but what he did afterward showed great sensitivity. Anyone else would have come running to show me the letter in triumph, especially since it incriminated a rival. But you have to admire his unselfishness: he says nothing until he has a chance to check into it. Meanwhile, he goes to Saint-Auban, and brings back the extract. He's even supposed to introduce me to one of his friends from Saint-Auban who knows Auguste's wife quite well. It wasn't until the very last moment that he showed me these documents. How deeply indebted to him we both are!

Caroline: (*standing up*) I don't agree with you, uncle. My, how tired I feel! I have a dreadful headache ...

Delorval: (*helping her to the door*) Go and lie down a bit, child, go lie down. (*She leaves.*)

SCENE VI
Delorval, *alone*

Whew! I don't know, I just don't feel as well as I did a while ago!

SCENE VII
Delorval, Bellire

Delorval: (*aside*) But here comes Bellire. (*To* Bellire) How grateful I am to you, my dear Bellire! (*He takes his hand.*) I shall never be able to ...

Bellire: Not at all, not at all, dear Delorval – my conscience, my sense of duty made me do what did. I swear, it was a very difficult thing for me to do. I knew that Auguste would have to pay for this, and the thought that I would be the cause of his downfall was real torture for me. But one's duty comes first, especially where a friend is concerned!

Delorval: What an unselfish young man you are!

Bellire: I'm really sorry, for Auguste's sake.

Delorval: Never mention his name again, I beg of you! Alas, I can see that what you were telling me this morning is only too true. If he's a hypocrite, he's quite capable of being a gambler and a rake as well. But let's change the subject. My dear friend, I've been thinking about you since this morning. I'm going to donate everything to you. But there's one thing –

Bellire: But sir! ...

Delorval: Oh no, I won't take no for an answer! All you've got to do is to go see my notary and ask him to come draw up the legal papers as soon as possible. There's just one thing ...

Bellire: Oh, you're too kind, Monsieur Delorval! ...

Delorval: Come, come, no compliments – it's settled! Just one thing I would ask of you: I would urge you to include, in the legal papers, a clause in Caroline's favour. Poor child! She's just my niece, but I love and cherish her as though she were my own daughter! So I wouldn't want her to be left out ...

Bellire: Quite so!

Delorval: Right. Hurry back with the notary, dear Bellire – I'm impatient to see this whole thing over and done with!

Bellire: As you wish!

SCENE VIII
Delorval, *alone*

What still bothers me is the promise I made [to Bellire][17] that I wouldn't tell Auguste why I fired him. It's terribly unfair to discover you've been condemned with no hearing. It's true that sort of thing seems to be happening a lot these days, but I can't quite get used to it!

SCENE IX
Delorval, Susette

Delorval: Well now, Susette, what's on your mind?

Susette: (*sadly*) Miz Car'line.

Delorval: Caroline?

Susette: Yes sir, Miz Car'line. All she does is cry an' cry, an it's really heart-wrenchin'. An' it's that tyrant, that Sydenham of a Bellire that's behind it all!

Delorval: Come, come now, Susette!

[Susette]:[18] Oh, pardon me, *please*! I mean t' say, that charmin' young man, so sensitive an' philersophic appearin', your own dear, your intimate friend, Monsieur

Bellire in short ... That he, I say, is the reason why poor mistress may be going' to
die of sorrow. Such a likeable young man he is, really! (*Aside*.) 'Little gal,' eh?

Delorval: Well, Susette, you *are* in a talkative mood, I must say! What do you
mean?

Susette: Oh, dear master, I'd be so sorry if I made you unhappy! I was just reactin'
emotional, you see. I mean, I've figured out who got Monsieur Auguste sacked ...

Delorval: And who 'got him sacked,' then?

Susette: Monsieur Bellire.

Delorval: (*astonished*) What makes you think that?

Susette: What I know about his characker.

Delorval: (*laughing*) Ha! And what, dear Susette, do *you* know about his character?

Susette: I know quite a lot, sir. Lemme just say that, when he don't know I'm
around, I often hear him sayin' a lot of things about you. Breaks me heart to hear
him say bad stuff about you the way he does. I get mad, I'm about to pop out and
tell him off an' run an' tell you all about it; but then I remember he's your friend.
You probably wouldn't believe me anyways, an' I'm sure he'd weasel his way out of
it better than me ... But anyways, since I put me foot in it now, I'll tell you your
friend is a false friend, and as far as I can figure, it ain't you that put the run to
Auguste, it was your 'dear friend.'

Delorval: What are you talking about, Susette? 'Lots of things about me,' you say?
What did he say?

Susette: He called you an old idiot, an old fool, a silly old crackpot. He said he
could make you swaller anythin' he wanted, an' lots o' stuff like that. An' what
really shocked me, right after that he was sayin' such nice things to you, an' anyone
else but me woulda believed he was tellin' you the absolute truth!

Delorval: Bellire said that!

Susette: Yes, Monsieur Bellire.

Delorval: When was this?

Susette: The other day, when he came here with that old dude that wears a wig.

Delorval: That's impossible, Susette – you're talking nonsense! Bellire criticizing me! Tut, tut, tut!

Susette: All right, all right! You're pokin' fun at me, but you might *have* to believe me, before too long! (*Aside.*) Poor Miz Car'line! (*Aloud.*) Please, sir, would you be so kind as to go an' cheer up mistress?

Delorval: I'll go right away. (*Aside, as he exits.*) 'Old idiot? Old fool?'

SCENE X
Susette, *alone*

He don't believe me, but it's the plain truth I just tole him! Hey, here comes that scoundrel hisself – along with one of his own kind, I 'magine!

SCENE XI
Susette, Bellire, Martel

Bellire: Well, little gal!

Susette: (*annoyed*) Sir, please! ...

Martel: She's a lovely little lass, indeed. What's her name, Bellire?

Bellire: Susette.

Martel: Soothette?[19]

Bellire: Or 'Soothette,' if you want, Martel.

Susette: (*annoyed*) Gentlemen, I ain't gonna stand ...

Bellire: (*interrupting*) Has Monsieur Delorval gone out, Susette?

Susette: (*pouting*) No, sir.

Bellire: Where is he?

Susette: (*pouting*) In Miz Car'line's rooms.

Bellire: Tell him I'm here with the gentleman I was supposed to introduce to him.

Susette: (*still pouting*) Yes, sir. (*She starts to leave.*)

Bellire: Hurry, little gal!

Susette: (*turns back, annoyed*) Sir!

Bellire: Come, get a move on! (Susette *exits.*)

SCENE XII
Bellire, Martel, *both pacing back and forth*

Bellire: Those damned notaries always make you wait! Well, as I was saying, the old fellow is an imbecile who believes everything you tell him. Just the same, he was a bit sceptical this morning when I was telling him that tale I made up about poor Auguste. But as I've said, my friend, the papers worked like a charm! (Susette *appears silently at stage left and listens while* Bellire *and* Martel *pace towards stage right.*) I can make him do whatever I want! (Susette *disappears.*) But you have to know what you're doing. You mustn't ever refer to him as an old man, for instance – that makes him mad as hell. Same thing with all older men, actually, and especially all older women! You have to be jolly with him, laugh, tell him tales you make up as you go along. That way, you can get whatever you want from him. What's more –

Martel: Excuse me for interrupting, Bellire, but I'm a bit surprised that he'd fire this assistant of his so quickly, since you told me he was so devoted to him, and the chap had been working for him for so many years. I would have expected him to wait a bit, check your statements, and the like ...

Bellire: Honour, Martel – he sacrifices everything to his sense of honour. And that extract from the marriage register, and the letter ...

Martel: (*laughing*) Ha, ha! ... So you see, Bellire, it's a good thing to hold on to letters!

Bellire: At this point, I'm more convinced than ever! I swear I don't know how I would have managed to get the old man to agree without your help!

Martel: I never let a single letter escape my clutches, I can tell you. That's why I can forge the signatures of over fifty of the leading businessmen in this town perfectly, I guarantee it! And that can sometimes be useful.

Bellire: (*laughing*) Ha, ha, ha! I can attest to the fact you're no slouch, since I saw how well you succeeded, making up those letters from that old *curé* in Saint-Auban! How long did you work as a tutor in that parish?

Martel: Just a few months. There's no money in that. The city's still the best place for living by one's wits!

Bellire: And he wrote to you frequently?

Martel: Every week!

Bellire: How long did it take you to forge the handwriting for the wife of Auguste Richard, the old fellow's assistant?

Martel: (*laughing*) Ha, ha! There never has been any such woman! But listen, Bellire, can you count on the old fellow's silence? I'm sure you realize this whole thing would be rather risky if Auguste learned about his own fictitious 'marriage.' Since that was the cause of his downfall, he wouldn't stand idly by, you can be sure of that!

Bellire: Oh, I have no worries on that point. He swore he would show the documents to no one but his niece. And as I say, personal honour comes first and foremost with him. He won't say anything about it, I'm sure!

Martel: But what about his niece? She's a woman after all, you know!

Bellire: She'd never utter a word that could harm her dear Auguste's reputation!

Martel: You're right, she'd never do that. But what if the old man decided to investigate? If he decided to write to the *curé* of Saint-Auban, for example?

Bellire: Impossible! He trusts me more than he trusts himself, and the letter would have been enough to do the trick. But including the extract made the thing doubly sure.

Martel: Impossible, you say? It's quite possible, Bellire – the old fellow could get suspicious, he *could* write to him. What would you do then?

Bellire: I swear I don't know. Some people would stick a pistol in their ear and – bang! it's all over! Why shouldn't I do the same? As Voltaire put it:
     When all is truly lost, when no more hope remains
     To live is a disgrace, to die becomes a duty.[20]

Martel: As far as I'm concerned, I prefer Louis Racine's attitude:
     It's cowardly to want to die; courageous to live on, if one can.[21]
So I'd be off to visit the Yankees!

Bellire: That's fine, my delicate friend – if they gave you time to make your get-away!

Martel: Certainly! That's one of the conditions I'd insist upon! (*Both laugh.*)

Bellire: All joking aside, we'd be in hot water! But let's not talk about that, let's think of the present. Besides, as I told you, I'm going to introduce you to old Delorval. You're supposed to have seen Madame Auguste Richard. You'll tell him she practically deafened you with her complaints about her husband. You'll describe her, her eyes ...

Martel: How should I describe her eyes?

Bellire: You know, women's eyes ... Surely the old fellow won't have any doubt left, after so much proof!

Martel: No problem – I'll play my role properly.

Bellire: I have no doubt about that, having seen the prologue to your play! As for me, I'll keep my side of the bargain: as soon as the papers are signed for the donation, you'll get the sum I promised you for your efforts.

Martel: I certainly hope so!

SCENE XIII
Actors, *as before*; Susette

Susette: Gentlemen, Monsieur Delorval is sorry, but he ain't able to see you right now. But if Monsieur Bellire would be so kind as to come back in a few minutes with the notary and the papers for the donation, he'll be glad to see you then.

Bellire: Well! I wonder what's wrong with the old fellow?

Martel: A touch of rheumatism, no doubt!

Bellire: (*looking at his watch*) Damn! It's getting late. Let's hurry over to the notary's office. Come on, Martel. (*He takes* Martel's *arm; both leave.*)

SCENE XIV
Susette, *alone*

Clapping her hands with joy: Well done! Well done! Bravo! Nicodème! Nicodème! Come quickly! I'm dyin' ... of happiness!

SCENE XV
Susette; Nicodème *rushes in, holding food in his hand*

Nicodème: Why the devil you makin' so much racket? Is that any way to disturb a man who's just followin' the dictations of nature that states 'swaller a bite, to keep on breathin'?

Susette: Listen, I'll tell you the whole thing. Stop eatin', so you can hear me right! I done it, Nicodème! I done it!

Nicodème: (*eating*) Whaddya mean, you done it?

Susette: He didn't wanna ...

Nicodème: (*continues to eat*) He didn't wanna?

Susette: No he didn't: I had to give him a push!

Nicodème: (*eating*) You pushed him?

Susette: Yes, you ninny!

Nicodème: And ninny to you, too: word for word, tit for tat!

Susette: He's gonna come back. We'll soon be seein' him again.

Nicodème: *Who?*

Susette: *Him!* My, you're thick-headed! No use tellin' you nothin', you don't remember no more than a bottle!

Nicodème: You're right there: when I've drunk *a* bottle, I don't usually try to take in two or three more!

Susette: Yes, he's comin' back. Oh, me heart! Me heart's dancin' for joy! (*She dances off.*)

SCENE XVI
Nicodème, *alone*

(*Looking off-stage where* Susette *has disappeared*). That all you got to tell me? Made me leave the table just for that? ... I think she's goin' off her rocker! 'I done it!' 'He didn't wanna!' 'Had to give him a push!' 'He's comin' back!' Quite a story, fer sure! If any of it was understandable, I coulda understood it; but I'd defy a supreme court judge to make out a word of it, no matter how much he scratched his head an' furrowed his brow! ... But here comes master himself: I must give him the message. (*He takes a letter from his pocket, puts what he was eating in the same pocket.*)

SCENE XVII
Nicodème; Delorval, *letter in hand*

Delorval: Nicodème, I need you to run an errand for me.

Nicodème: Dear master, even if it wasn't me job, it would be me greatest pleasure to do any errand you want, even if I had to go to the ends of the poles in the Torrible Zone!

Delorval: You must try to find out where Auguste is staying. I want this letter delivered to him.

Nicodème: (*leaping for joy*) Monsieur Auguste?

Delorval: Yes.

Nicodème: Your assistant? Oh, I know where he is!

Delorval: Where is he? Rue Champlain, I suppose?

Nicodème: Oh no, sir: it's just in front o' that there square that stands for Canada, 'cause there's chains all 'round it. How do they call it? Ah, yes: the Place d'Armes! Right in front of the Place d'Armes ... A big house on the corner ...

Delorval: Payne's Hotel?[22]

Nicodème: That's right, master.

Delorval: How do you know he's there?

Nicodème: 'Cause I saw him there an' talked to him, less than fifteen minutes ago!

Delorval: Oh! You go there often, then?

Nicodème: Oh no, that place is too grand for me. Ain't no use goin' there – they charge too much for their rum! But listen, I'll tell you straight out how it happened. I was just walkin' by the Place d'Armes, okay? All alone, thinkin' of nothin' at all. All of a sudden I sees, in one of the windows in that there big house, a head stickin' out, full of eyes that was all a-gogglin' at me. He beckoned me over with his finger, an' it was Monsieur Auguste, he wanted to talk to me. I hopped to it, I was that happy to see him! I run up the steps in such a hurry I knocked down a big gawk of a guy, an' he smacked me with his cane for me trouble. But I didn't feel nothin'. The door opens an' I sees Monsieur Auguste. 'How are you, Nicodème,' he says, shakin' me hand. Well, I can tell you, me heart was bustin', 'twas all I could do to answer, 'it's goin' alright with me, thanks.' 'And how are Monsieur Delorval and Mademoiselle Caroline?' he says to me. 'They're fine,' I says. 'Delighted to hear that,' he says without a smile. Then he starts pacin' up an' down the room, okay? holdin' his face in his hands an' coverin' his eyes. He walks back an' forth like that for a long time, not sayin' nothin' an' without seemin' to know I was even there. Finally he notices me. 'I'm not feelin' well,' he says. 'I can see that,' I says, 'you're a lot paler than I ever seen you,' an' for sure he was! A few minutes later he says to himself, 'oh, I'm so unhappy,' an' he keeps pacin' up an' down. Made me sad, 'cause I could see he was really hurtin'. So okay, he sits down at a table and starts to write. 'Twas no use, 'cause when he wanted to put some sand on the letter to blot it, he grabbed the ink instead, an' he stained his paper black like a black man from Africa! 'What an idiot I am,' he says, an' takes another page, an' writes another note – an' here it is! (*He hands* Delorval *a paper.*) There you have it. Probably his answer to the letter you got in your hand, I expect. (*During* Nico- dème's *speech* Delorval *frequently appears moved by what he hears.*)

Delorval: (*reads*) 'Dear Sir: My life is intolerable. The situation I am in is pure torture. Free me from it, I beg of you, by letting me know the reason for my mis- fortune, so that I may at least attempt to defend myself. Yours sincerely, Auguste Richard.' All right. Here, take this to him. Hurry! (*He gives him the letter he had in his hand on entering.*)

Nicodème: Okay sir, me feet have wings – an' I'm off! (*He exits, running.*)

SCENE XVIII
Delorval, *alone*

Well, Bellire should soon be here with the notary.

SCENE XIX
Delorval; Caroline, *sad*; Susette, *happy*

Susette: Lookit, sir – she won't crack a smile, no matter what funny faces I make!

Delorval: Tut, tut! You mustn't be like that. Sit down, Caroline – you mustn't go on being sad like this!

Caroline: Uncle, I'm sick and tired of the city, and would like to spend some time in the countryside. I don't feel at all well, and perhaps the country air would do me some good.

Delorval: Quite right, my dear. When would you like to leave?

Caroline: Right today, uncle, if it's all right with you.

Delorval: Why today? Why not at least wait until tomorrow?

Caroline: As you wish, uncle.

Delorval: Yes, wait until tomorrow because, you see ... Oh, here comes Bellire.

SCENE XX
Actors, *as before*; Bellire; Villomont

Bellire: (*smiling*) As you can see, sir, I'm as good as my word! Here's Monsieur Villomont, your notary.

Delorval: Ah, Villomont! (*Shaking his hand.*) Well, how are you?

Villomont: Well, bloody hell, just the way you see me!

Delorval: My word, it's been a while since I've seen you! You see, Bellire, this man was one of my classmates, along with the *curé* of Saint-Auban. We roomed side by side, in fact. (Villomont *bows.*)

Bellire: And I'm sure you never quarrelled, for Monsieur Delorval can't stand hypersensitive people who see only the gloomy side of things! From the chat I've just had with Monsieur Villomont, I can tell that his personality must be a perfect match for yours, Monsieur Delorval.

Villomont: Bloody hell! Monsieur Bellire will be happy with me on that score, I'm sure! (*He laughs.*) The donation.

Bellire: (*shaking his head*) Shhh!

Villomont: What held me up, my dear Delorval, was that I had to ... but first I should tell you my clients are awful, terrible, dreadful, not to say boring as hell. I work day and night. Bloody hell! And when I do grab a dozen hours' sleep or so, it certainly does me some good! I had to go out to the country for an estate inventory, an inventory, my friend, an inventory such as you've never drawn up in your life.

Delorval: Probably so, since I'm not a notary.

Villomont: Oh, an inventory as big as this. (*He gestures.*) Six quires of paper, would you believe it?

Delorval: Good heavens! A lot of money involved?

Villomont: Yes indeed!

Delorval: So what were the proceeds from the sale?

Villomont: Three pounds, six shillings thruppence farthing, sterling rate.

Delorval: Six quires of paper for that?

Villomont: Bloody hell, yes! A candle here, a broken mirror there, a cotton hand-kerchief full of holes, that had belonged to a gentleman, a pot with no bottom ... a scrap of paper here, a box of matches there ... And what caused a lot of work, it all had to be sold separately, item by item, rag by rag ... match by match!

Delorval: That must have been a lot of work, indeed! But you do have clerks and secretaries?

Villomont: Clerks? Bloody hell – I've got four of them, it's true. But which one of them could help me? One of them's a romantic and a dabbler in literature: instead of reading Justinian's *Institutes* or *Parisian Common Law* he whiles away his time reading *Jacob Faithful* or *La Cuisinière canadienne*.[23] The fool thinks he's a poet too, and he constructs verses without the slightest knowledge of the art of spelling! Verses as long as your arm – alexandrines with eighteen or twenty syllables, no problem at all for him! Then he's off pestering editors to publish what he believes, in his great modesty, to be poetic masterpieces. And after a lot of visits of that sort, he does manage to have a poem printed in some newspaper, as long as he pays the going rate for a commercial advertisement! Good grief, what prestige, eh! And that's what he spends his time at! My second clerk is only interested in horses, hounds, hunting, fishing, and the latest fashions: he never comes to the office. The third thinks he's an important chap, since he's a law student. That's the only thing he thinks about. He's no good for anything else, and just between the two of us, I'm a bit vexed with him. I've frequently noticed that he looks down on people that used to be his best friends because they're merely craftsmen, or because they're poor. Bloody hell, I don't like that sort of thing! The fourth fellow is mad about politics. He's interested in nothing but politics. 'Nowadays, in this materialistic society,' he often says to me, 'it's the only way to get prestige or a reputation. Literature, science, the arts – they're all useless!' And to prove his case, he points to that famous Institut Vattemare.[24] Not that his conclusions are wrong; but, bloody hell, I don't need politics in *my* office! So as you can see, I don't get much help from any of them. Not the way it was in our day, bloody hell! We *worked* – we didn't spend our time worrying about our looks or our lovely hairstyles, or thinking about *The Arabian Nights*! We spent our time on the profession we wanted to enter, bloody hell! But anyway, here's the legal form for the donation. (*He pulls a huge piece of paper from his pocket.*) If you're ready, gentlemen, we'll proceed!

Delorval: Oh indeed, indeed! (*They take seats around the table,* Bellire *on the audience's right, with his back turned to the door,* Villomont *facing the audience,* Delorval *on the audience's left.*) If the notary would be so kind as to read aloud ... we're listening!

Villomont: (*unfolds the paper and spreads it out on the table*) Gladly. (*He reads.*) 'This deposition in the presence of the undersigned, notary public for this region of the Province of Canada, lately the Province of Lower Canada. Present: Monsieur Hippolyte Delorval, merchant, resident of the City of Quebec in aforesaid province; who, by the present document, executes a donation *inter vivos*, purely, simply, and irrevocably, in the manner prescribed and approved for such donation, in favour of ...'

SCENE XXI
Actors, *as before*; Auguste *and* Nicodème *enter stage left and stand just on-stage, unseen by* Bellire

Nicodème: Sir, here's ...

Delorval: (*gesturing to* Nicodème *to remain silent*) Oh, there you are, Nicodème! All right – just wait a moment. (*To* Villomont.) Where were you again, Villomont? Would you please read those last few words again?

Villomont: (*reads*) 'Executes a donation *inter vivos*, purely, simply, and irrevocably, in the manner prescribed and approved for such donation, in favour of ...' (*To* Bellire.) Your given name, Monsieur Bellire?

Bellire: Alexandre, sir.

Delorval: How did you put it, 'simply and irrevocably ...'?

Villomont: Bloody hell! I thought I explained it clearly enough! Here, I'll read it again. (*Reads.*) '... by the present document, executes a donation *inter vivos*, purely, simply, and irrevocably, in the manner prescribed and approved for such donation, in favour of ...'

Delorval: (*loudly and distinctly*) 'Auguste Richard and his spouse, Caroline Delorval!' (Caroline *and* Bellire *stand up, surprised;* Bellire *turns around and is doubly surprised to see* Auguste *behind him.* Susette *and* Nicodème *have been chatting to each other in the background, and when* Delorval *says,* 'Auguste Richard and his spouse, Caroline Delorval,' Susette *claps her hands.* Delorval *continues.*) Well, what's wrong, my dear Bellire?

Bellire: That's quite enough. I can see this whole thing has been arranged in advance. I've got some secret enemy here.

Delorval: (*stands and points to the screen*) Yes, Bellire, and the screen there is your enemy! I'd advise you never to speak aloud when there's a screen present, or your schemes will never prosper! That's where Susette almost had to force me to hide – she almost had to *drag* me there, you might say! You and your friend couldn't see me, because there's a door behind the screen. And that's where, choking with rage, I was able to discover the wretched plot you and your friend had hatched. That's where I heard statements like 'You have to know how to go about it,' and 'He gets mad as hell at the term "old man" ...' That's where I learned that 'it's a good idea to keep letters, because forged signatures can be useful ...' In short, and unfortunately for me, that's where I finally learned a lot about people, which is an experience I would have preferred to avoid! Oh, Bellire! ... But you don't deserve a word, even in reproach. My only advice to you and your loathsome friend is to head off and 'visit the Yankees,' to use your friend's expression – and I'd do it as soon as possible!

Bellire: Sir! Is that the only reward my unselfish friendship deserves from you? Is that what you call gratitude?

Delorval: Out of my sight! It's my duty to inform the authorities, which is what I'm going to do right away!

Bellire: (*spitefully*) Go ahead, sir, innocence has nothing to fear. Let me give you some advice, in return: be a little more careful about what you say, or else a good libel suit could quickly make you even older than you are!

Delorval: How dare you! You impudent ... (*He strides towards* Bellire, *who exits.*)

SCENE XXII
Actors, *as before, except* Bellire

Delorval: (*goes to* Auguste *with hand extended*) Auguste! I don't know how to beg your forgiveness for having even for a moment suspected you of immorality and dishonesty! I was blind, but now as you can see my eyes have been opened. I'm happy for your sake, but displeased with myself. Today I can see much more clearly than before. I now see that self-interest is the characteristic of mankind! Oh, Auguste – try to forget the effects of my lack of experience with people!

Auguste: Sir, I must admit I've never suffered such mental anguish as I have today. But my present situation is ample reward for what's past. Just the same, I would like to know what ploy he used against me ...

Delorval: He forged an extract ... a letter ... I'll tell you all about it. (Villomont *stands up.*) Would the notary please be so kind as to wait to draw up the marriage contract, so we can take care of the donation at the same time? You'll be properly compensated for the trouble you've had here today.

Villomont: Bloody hell! As long as both parties agree!

Delorval: I'm most profoundly obliged to Susette for what she's done, and I want her marriage to Nicodème to be celebrated along with yours (*turning to* Auguste *and* Caroline). I'll take care of Susette's dowry.

Susette: Oh, sir!

Nicodème: (*ecstatic*) Okay, me dear master, me whole soul is overfloodin' with grattytude for your kindness! (*To* Susette.) Well, Susette, let's kiss on it! (*He attempts to kiss her.*)

Susette: Nicodème! ...

Delorval: (*to* Caroline) well now, Caroline, wasn't I right to say that fate is fickle? When are you leaving for the countryside?

Caroline: (*smiling*) I seem to feel a lot better now, uncle. I think I'll put if off for a while ...

Delorval: Well, children, both weddings will be next Tuesday. In the meantime,

I'm going to take a bit of a rest. I certainly need it, after the shocks and surprises I've just been through!

END OF THE SECOND AND LAST ACT

Note: *Actors' entrances and exits* [author's note]:[25] Delorval and Caroline always enter and exit on the audience's left. The same for Susette, except in act 1, scene 4, when she exits right, and in act 1, scene 8, when she enters from the right with Auguste. Nicodème enters and exits on the audience's right, except in act 1, scene 2, when he enters left and exits right. Bellire enters and exits right, except in act 1, scene 14, when he exits left. Martel, Auguste, and Villomont enter and exit on the audience's right.

IV

A Country Outing

INTRODUCTION

1. History of the Play and Its Performances

Une Partie de campagne (*A Country Outing*) is the third and last surviving play from the pen of Pierre Petitclair, French-Canada's first native dramatist – the first, that is, to have signed his name to what he wrote, as opposed to the numerous, anonymous political playlets that had preceded Petitclair's *Griphon, ou la vengeance d'un valet* (1837).[1] Composed, its editor tells us, in 1856, *A Country Outing* was first performed in Quebec City the following year by a troupe calling itself Les Amateurs Canadiens, an unrevealing, generic appellation dating back to the 1780s. Petitclair died in 1860; the play was published five years later by a relative of his, the printer and amateur impresario Joseph Savard. It has never been reprinted, and this is its first translation.

Perhaps the relative difficulty of locating copies of the text (it appears only sixty were printed) explains the otherwise curious lack of attention it has received. Perhaps also this neglect is due to the repeated and erroneous stance adopted by theatre historians – even very recent ones – who see this work as, at best, strongly influenced by, and at worst a mere re-working of the first play in this volume, Joseph Quesnel's *Anglomania, or Dinner, English-Style*, composed around 1803. It is time to lay that allegation to rest: it is most unlikely that Petitclair was even aware of the existence of Quesnel's text, since *Anglomania* remained unpublished until 1932. When Petitclair was finishing his play in 1856, Quesnel's piece had never been performed publicly (as it has not to this day), and its manuscript was in the possession of that inveterate collector of Canadiana (and first mayor of Montreal), Jacques Viger, who was to die two years later. It is highly improbable that Petitclair had had access to the manuscript.[2] In addition Petitclair had, by the time his play was completed, been living in Labrador and on Quebec's remote North Shore almost continuously for eighteen years. It is coincidence – and, I shall argue, in many ways a *predictable* coincidence – that he and Joseph Quesnel both chose a similar topic for the most 'Canadian' of their plays.[3]

The first performance of *A Country Outing* took place on 22 April 1857 at Quebec's Salle de Musique on Rue Saint-Louis, as part of an all-comic program including Desforges's *Le Sourd* and *La Sœur de Jocrisse*. A brief and, as usual, anonymous review in Quebec's *Le Canadien* reports that the play was much appreciated, having 'kept the audience in paroxysms of laughter.'[4] There is no further reference to a performance until April 1860, when advertisements began to appear in the *Journal de Québec*, *Le Courrier de Québec*, and *Le Canadien* announcing a 'Grande Soirée dramatique' to be held at the same place on the 28th of that month. The play would be performed by the Compagnie des Jeunes Amateurs Canadiens, this time under the distinguished patronage of the most active French-Canadian patriotic and cultural association, the Société Saint-Jean-Baptiste. And this time Petitclair's play would be the *pièce de résistance* in the program, preceded by the social comedy *Grandeur et décadence de M. Joseph Prudhomme* by Henry Monnier and Gustave Vaez, first performed in Paris in 1852.[5] Significantly, proceeds from the evening's entertainment would go towards erecting a monument to commemorate the centenary of the battle of Sainte-Foy, the last military victory of the French over the British in Canada (a topic explored in greater depth in the play *Archibald Cameron of Locheill*, also included in this volume).

2. French-Canadian Theatre in the 1850s and 1860s

Why did the organizers of the evening's entertainment turn to *A Country Outing* on this patriotic occasion? The obvious answer is that at the time there was no more appropriate French-Canadian dramatic text available. There existed in print, and to various degrees of accessibility, exactly five plays in 1860: Lescarbot's archaic and eccentric *Théâtre de Neptune en la Nouvelle-France*; Quesnel's *Colas et Colinette*, in many ways as dated as Lescarbot's text, and only vaguely Canadian in context; Antoine Gérin-Lajoie's scholastic verse-tragedy, *Le Jeune Latour*, unsuitable in format and tone for an occasion such as this; and Petitclair's own previous texts, *Griphon* and *The Donation*.[6] For this occasion, given the political climate of the two Canadas in the years immediately preceding Confederation, *A Country Outing* must have seemed by far the best choice available.

Its central theme, relations between anglophones and francophones, was of obvious concern to both provinces, but paramount in Lower Canada. It was therefore a natural subject for dramatic treatment, as it had been when Quesnel, during the Napoleonic Wars, had composed his satiric *Anglomania*, as it had continued to be in armchair political theatre, and as it has since continued to be in Canadian literature in general. There is no doubt that the topic was then much in the air: a scant two years later came the première of Louis-Honoré Fréchette's nationalistic *Félix Poutré* (which appears next in this volume), the most successful publicly performed play of the century, dealing for the first time on stage with the sensitive topic of the Patriote rebellion of 1837–8 and English-French relations at that troubled time; and the following year (1863) the most important novel of nineteenth-century Quebec, Philippe Aubert de Gaspé's *Les Anciens Canadiens*, dealing also with English-French relationships, would be published. Dramatized as *Archibald Cameron of Locheill* the latter was, within a decade, turned into the most successful college play of the century. *A Country Outing* is less nationalistic than these three other texts, but to a large extent it shares their focus. Moreover, by 1860 it was a proven play, whose enthusiastic reception three years earlier must still have been fresh in the minds of local amateurs, some of whom had no doubt appeared in the first production.

3. Analysis of the Play

In structure as in topicality, *A Country Outing* certainly represents a clear improvement over the author's two preceding plays. *Griphon*, I have proposed elsewhere, was at the time of its publication already an anachronism: an eighteenth-century situation comedy, grafted onto the main stock of a 'recipe'-farce.[7] The play has never even been performed, it appears, by amateur or college troupes. On the other hand, Petitclair's second dramatic text, *The Donation*, had been staged successfully on at least half a dozen occasions by 1860. Although it too is derivative to some extent, and although there are some structural deficiencies apparent in this work as well, its lively two acts represent a clear improvement upon *Griphon*'s repetitive, rapidly flagging three. Another significant development in *The Donation* was its Canadian topicality: the then very recent political confrontations of the late 1830s and early 1840s are directly alluded to in the play, in tones that make the author's own stance clear, and the setting (Quebec City, as for *Griphon*) is of direct importance to these allusions.

On all counts, *A Country Outing* represents a further evolution and general improvement. As with *The Donation*, there are two economical and nicely balanced acts, the first setting up the character of the antipathetic Anglomaniac William, whose exemplary castigation is then the natural focus of act 2. There is no repetition either of structures or comic ploys as there had been in *Griphon*, or of dramatic devices such as the *coups de théâtre* that end acts 1 and 2 of *The Donation*. An excellent introductory scene elucidates what will be the main plot and, in a tactic used so expertly by Molière among others, both readers and spectators get to know the character and motives of the protagonist long before his first appearance, which comes in 1.6, more than a quarter of the way through the play. The dialogue is much more natural, with few of the asides and monologues that had been the bane of *The Donation*. Subsidiary plots are well resolved and characters are shaded more noticeably than in the author's second play and are more carefully counterpoised to each other, notably the French-Canadian Anglomaniac William/Guillaume against the English-Canadian Francophiles Brown and Malvina.

A serious defect of *A Country Outing*, to my mind, is its depiction of character. Brown is prone to the same gratuitous and cruel practical joking that characterized the valets Citron and Boucau in *Griphon*; William's sudden infatuation in the course of a single year with all things English is too extreme to be credible, as is his complete change of personality;[8] Eugénie is all passive, pathetic charm; and Malvina's strange moral authority over William and her cruel treatment of him (especially in act 2, scene 17, where she laughs outright at his sincere marriage proposal, delivered on his knees) are not convincingly presented.

Simplistic depiction of character is also largely to blame for a serious thematic defect in this work: the trivialization of the central topic, English-French conflict. Instead of dealing with the increasingly serious social and cultural problems posed for French Canadians by the growing hegemony of English language, manners, and values, Petitclair here marginalizes the issue, dealing instead with the comic, almost farcically exaggerated effect of Anglophile excess on an exaggerated and ultimately incredible character. The general goodwill and *bonhomie* with which the play ends thus appear specious. Of course one must add that this is the atmosphere and tone one finds as well in other important works of the nineteenth century, from *Félix Poutré* through *Les Anciens Canadiens* (novel and play) to Fréchette's *Papineau* and Laurent-Olivier David's *Le Drapeau de Carillon*. But the play is not by that fact more convincing.

Further reflection reveals other serious unresolved problems, perhaps most significantly the cavalier treatment of religious differences in this play. Certainly it is fascinating to find, in the middle of the nineteenth century, rural Québécois as liberal-minded on the topic of religion as the Hunchback appears to be in act 2, scene 14:

Hunchback: [speaking of Brown and his sister, Malvina] ... Nice, fine people they is, no matter whatcha say!

Baptiste: Ain't it a shame they's Protestants! ...

Hunchback: Hush! That don't make no difference! That there's just fanuticalism, as them upper-class folks says ...

Baptiste: Yeah, but you know what the catty-kissem book says –

Hunchback: Aw, forgit yer catty-kissem – You wouldn't understand a real mystery, nohow! An' anyways, that ain't none o' our business.

But what about the Protestant Brown's sudden and unopposed decision to marry Catholic Eugénie – a marriage that is apparently to take place the very next day? Even in late twentieth-century Quebec, when such a rapid arrangement is impossible for purely bureaucratic reasons, the two French-Canadian Catholics, Flore and Baptiste, would be unable to arrange a *civil* marriage that quickly. In the play they too will marry the next day, with no delay caused by compulsory publication of banns and the other known formalities for marriage within the Catholic Church. And when one recalls the much less tolerant atmosphere of the 1850s, crystallized in the well-known, inflexible opposition of Bishop Bourget to public association by members of his flock with Protestants (particularly anglophone Protestants), the 'quick fix' for Petitclair's plot is simply incredible. Here as elsewhere he has merely sidestepped the problem, painting in a rosy resolution for what would be a major real-life dilemma.

Yet this is the most original of Petitclair's plays,[9] and decidedly the most Canadian. Indeed, then as now, the theme of cultural, linguistic, and legal coexistence with English-speakers is, for French-speakers in this country, *the* most 'Canadian' of topics. One can only regret that the subject is here treated so superficially by someone who was in a situation to deal with it at first-hand, having mastered the English language and spent most of his adult years in constant interaction with English speakers.

4. Language

Finally, the characters' speech is much more consistent and more credible than in any previous French-Canadian play. There are four distinguishable levels of French here: first, the 'correct,' standard French used by Louis, William, the convent-educated Eugénie and Flore (and, perhaps surprisingly, Malvina); next, the almost-standard speech of Louis' brother Joseph, a grammatically correct French seasoned with colourful and appropriate Canadianisms characteristic of the educated country-dweller; third, the picturesque, here purposely exaggerated speech of rural, illiterate Quebec used by Baptiste, the Musician, and the Hunchback; and finally, of course, the fractured, outlandish variant employed so hilariously by Brown. Moreover, as J.-C. Noël has pointed out, Petitclair seems to have taken to heart one of the principal lessons of this play, in that the inadvertent Anglicisms that mar his first two plays have virtually vanished in this one.[10] Appropriately, most of these Anglicisms appear in the speech of the anglophile William.

My translation seeks to reflect the varying levels of accent and diction audible in the characters' French, staying as close to the original as possible. Notes at the end are intended to clarify specific allusions in the text that might escape a modern reader. Within the text itself occasional editorial interventions appear in square brackets (to indicate, for example, in which language a response is spoken, where otherwise this might not be clear).

PIERRE PETITCLAIR

A Country Outing

A COMEDY IN TWO ACTS

First performed at Quebec City by the
Amateurs Canadiens, 22 April 1857 and by the
Compagnie des Jeunes Amateurs Canadiens, 28 April 1860

Quebec

Printed and published by Joseph Savard, Typographer

1865

Preface

Now that [French-]Canadian literature is beginning to be appreciated properly, with many readers finding in it edification, relaxation, and amusement amidst life's serious concerns, I believe this is the appropriate moment to offer the reading public a Canadian literary work penned by a writer whose untimely death was most unfortunate for the world of letters. I am referring to Mr P. Petitclair.

I have long been desirous of printing the present text, but have repeatedly been forced, by circumstances I beg the reader's leave not to describe, to postpone that task. Now that those obstacles no longer exist, I hasten to publish this Canadian comedy of manners.

Since I am related to the author's family, I shall merely say a few words about him and provide a few short quotations from distinguished writers who have devoted a few lines to him, leaving the rest to others more capable than I.

As the reader knows, Mr Petitclair is the author of a charming two-act play entitled *The Donation*, which has been performed several times in Quebec City, and of
various short compositions in verse and prose. His scattered texts were collected by
Mr J. Huston and published in his *Répertoire national*.

In the issue of *Le Canadien* for 27 August 1855 there appears a literary column
by Mr A. de Puibusque, an author of considerable standing,[11] wherein he comments on the literary merits of the novel *Charles Guérin*, written by the Honorable
P.-J.-O. Chauveau, superintendent of education.[12] Among other fine and elegant
remarks, Mr de Puibusque observes:

He [Mr Chauveau] portrayed Canada as it really is, with a Canadian brush. Even if one con-
siders his work merely as an innovation in a new domain, it deserves to be singled out for
distinction, and to receive the same acclaim as the witty compositions of Messrs De Gaspé,
Angers, De Boucherville, Petitclair, Eug. L'Écuyer, Doutre, Patrice Lacombe ...[13]

Obviously, this French writer did not forget the author of our play, Mr Petitclair,
placing him, rather, in very good company.

A Country Outing was written in 1856. The following year a troupe of intelligent
and very enterprising amateurs staged this play, with a good deal of success, at the
Salle de Musique. It was enthusiastically received by a very large and distinguished
audience that was unstinting in its applause. Unable to attend the performance himself, the editor of *Le Canadien* had arranged for someone to provide an account for
him. I quote from that correspondent's report, published on 27 April 1857:

But in speaking of the talent displayed by the young amateurs who performed in this play, I
must devote a word or two to the author of the comedy, which is entitled *A Country Outing*. This work, as a portrait of Canadian manners and customs, is a minor masterpiece. Its
plot is ingenious, and the composition as a whole does honour to Mr Petitclair.

Three years later another amateur troupe staged the play in the same venue. It
was again received very favourably. Before this performance, *Le Canadien*, on 27
April 1860, described the work as follows:

One of the plays, at least, is the work of Petitclair, a man who, in another land and at
another time, would perhaps have been his country's Molière.

The same paper states, in its issue of 30 April, in a review of the performance from
which I quote:

The two plays, but in particular the second one, were performed with genuine talent. We would certainly like to know how anyone could possibly criticize *A Country Outing* in any way ... Mr Petitclair's play, so full of verve, so realistic, and so relevant, kept the audience continually in stitches.

And finally, the *Journal de l'instruction publique* remarked, in its issue of December 1860, in the section entitled 'Literary News':

Mr Petitclair, the author of several short Canadian plays lacking neither in action nor originality, and author of a few scattered verse compositions that appear in M. Huston's *Répertoire national*, died some months ago.

The foregoing prove abundantly that this play was judged excellent when performed on stage. I dare hope it will please the Canadian readers to whom I have the honour to offer it, and that it will not fail to amuse them in their moments of leisure.

Mr Petitclair died at Pointe-aux-Peaux (Labrador),[14] on 15 August 1860, at the age of forty-seven.

JOSEPH SAVARD, Typographer
Quebec City, December 1865

CHARACTERS

Louis, a city dweller
Joseph, a villager, brother of Louis
William, son of Louis
Brown, friend of William and brother of Malvina
Flore, daughter of Joseph
Baptiste, Flore's boyfriend
Eugénie, friend of Flore
Malvina, sister of Brown
A Hunchback
A Musician
Village men and women

Setting: *The shores of Lac Calvaire,*[15] *not far from Quebec City*

ACT ONE

SCENE I

A living room, with a door at stage rear and open windows, through which can be seen trees, flowers, etc. Louis *and* Joseph *enter from opposite directions,* Louis *with hat and walking-stick.*

Joseph: Well, well, brother Louie – up and about already! And where have you been then, so early in the morning?

Louis: 'Up and about,' brother? Come now, who could ever stay in bed, when all of Nature is astir? I've already made the rounds of your property two or three times, and ...

Joseph: My, my – you certainly enjoy these cross-country jaunts!

Louis: Yes, I must say I've really enjoyed them. I love to watch the sun rise, hear the chirping of the birds, breathe the cool, fragrant morning air, walk in the dew and ...

Joseph: Oh, yes – you're just like all the city folk who come to places like this to relax. They love to spend the whole day staring at a flower, while we country folk don't make any more fuss about a flower than we do about a fly. I suppose that's because we see things like that every day ...

Louis: Precisely, Joseph. Those who own something don't know its real value!

Joseph: Quite so. And anything new or different attracts one's attention. Anyway, since you've come to the country to relax, no need for me to repeat it over and over: Do whatever you want. If you like fruit, my orchards and garden are yours. Break branches, pull things out, snap them off, plunder and pillage, by gum! Whatever you please! If you like fishing, you know where the lake is. If you like hunting, I've got guns and ammunition.

Louis: You're very generous.

Joseph: And you can tell the people who came with you to do the same. But who's the gentleman who's come with your son, Guillotte?

Louis: Oh, you mean William's friend?

Joseph: Come again?

Louis: My son's name is William, not Guillotte.

Joseph: You mean you're going to teach *me* what his name is now?

Louis: I know he used to be Guillaume, or Guillot, or Guillotte, as you say, when we used to live in this village. But right now, his name is William.

Joseph: Now that's a strange thing! William, eh? But – tarnation! – that's an *English* name!

Louis: That's why he's adopted it.

Joseph: Because it's English? That's even stranger! By golly, I just don't understand any more. Do English people take French names, then?

Louis: No, they don't do anything so ridiculous as that.

Joseph: Then has your son less common sense than an Englishman?

Louis: What do you expect me to do about it?

Joseph: And what's the name of Guillotte's friend (sorry – I can't help calling him by his right name). *He's* an Englishman,[16] eh?

Louis: Yes, a Mr Brown.

Joseph: And his sister, who's here with him?

Louis: Malvina.

Joseph: All right – I understand: she's the one Guillotte is courting!

Louis: Yes.

Joseph: Tarnation! Her brother seems like a great fellow to me! The guy is always laughing and looking to play a trick on someone. Yesterday he made me laugh so much I nearly choked!

Louis: How so?

Joseph: Well, try to imagine the situation: Jean-Marie Pierriche Tibeau's son Charlie[17] happened to be talking to me, leaning on a picket-fence. Our young Mr Brown was there with me, a cigar stuck in his mouth. I had noticed him moving around close to Charlie, but you know I never suspected a thing. Well anyway, we finished our conversation, the young man and I were heading back home quietly, and Charlie was doing the same. But our English prankster kept on looking back every now and then, and seemed to be having a hard time to keep from laughing. Then all of a sudden – bang! boom! bam! kapow! – and then one hell of a shout! So I turn around, and there's Charlie running off as fast as his legs can take him, with smoke and flames coming from him, and a second later – kersplash! – headfirst into a brook! When he came out, he looked like some kind of monster, with his face all covered with mud! And there's that danged Englishman, nearly killing himself laughing! Firecrackers, he said it was, that he had put on Charlie! ...

Louis: That wasn't a very nice thing to do. He shouldn't have –

Joseph: You're right, but wait till I finish. When that young man saw what had happened, he ran right up to Charlie and apologized to him, explaining that he just wanted to scare him, but didn't think he'd go and jump in the mud! And after he said that, he pulled out his wallet and gave him a lot of money, saying it was to help him buy new clothes, since he had ruined what he was wearing. But Louis, what he gave him was enough to buy *two* sets of clothes! And Charlie, who isn't too well off, poor guy, didn't take much coaxing as far as taking the money went. He washed his face, and he was in a pretty good mood when we left him. That's why I say this young man is no ruffian. Seems to me he's got a lot of class ...

Louis: Oh, he's a fine lad, I assure you, and a real gentleman. And as far as his sister is concerned, she was brought up in France, where she just came from a few days ago. Both of them are well off, since one of their uncles died and left them a fortune.

Joseph: Gosh! So that Guillotte of yours will be happy to marry a gal like that!

Louis: It seems she's got more than just her wealth to recommend her. They say she's quite an accomplished young woman.

Joseph: Has Guillotte been courting her for a long time?

Louis: Oh, ten days or so, at most.

Joseph: No more than that? Does she love him?

Louis: That I don't know. But I do know for certain that he's crazy about her.

Joseph: And now that he's finished his training ... What do you call what he was doing?

Louis: His clerkship in a legal office.

Joseph: Right, his clerkship. Since he's finished that, I guess he's going to get married pretty soon?

Louis: I think so.

Joseph: Well, your Guillotte is pretty well set up, that sly dog! Educated, and all! Only one thing I see in him that I don't like.

Louis: And what's that?

Joseph: What! You haven't noticed?

Louis: I'm not sure. Say what you mean.

Joseph: But what I want to say might ...

Louis: Oh, not at all! No need to worry ...

Joseph: All right. It seems to me he's a bit ... stuck-up. You know what I mean – a bit ... haughty, wouldn't you say?

Louis: Only too true, Joseph. His arrogance, his vanity, his anglomania are faults I've been trying to cure him of for a long time, with no success to this point.

Joseph: Well, he's young – with experience he'll probably change his ways.

Louis: One can only hope so!

SCENE II
Actors, *as before*; Flore; Eugénie

Flore: (*to* Joseph) Good morning, Papa. (*To* Louis.) Good morning, Uncle. (Eugénie *greets them as well.*)

Louis: (*to* Flore) Good morning, Flore. (*To* Joseph, *aside.*) Who is this other young woman?

Joseph: What! You don't remember her? It's Eugénie, daughter of poor Michon-José-Jean-Gnace. She's the one who was always with your son, when you used to live here.

Louis: Eugénie?

Joseph: Yes, the one your boy seemed to think so much of, back then – and the lass didn't exactly hate *him*, either! (*To* Eugénie.) Isn't that right, Eugénie? To the point that we all thought they were going to get hitched, before you moved to town. Really, you don't remember? Eugénie, *you* know ...!

Louis: Oh, heavens yes – I remember her now! How are you, my dear? (*He shakes* Eugénie's *hand.*)

Eugénie: Very well, sir, thank you. And you?

Louis: And your father and mother? Are they still the finest people in the whole world?

Eugénie: They haven't changed, sir. They're supposed to come over and see you today, and they wanted to have me wait and come with them. But I hadn't seen you for so long that I couldn't resist the urge to come running – especially when I found out that Guillaume ...

Joseph: You hear that, Louis? I've always said that Eugénie was the best little gal in the world ... after my own Flore, naturally!

Flore: Please, Father! ...

Joseph: And she's just about as smart as Flore, too – just gotten out of convent school, you know.

Louis: A charming girl! Look, you mustn't be surprised that I didn't remember you at first. The way you've changed, physically and otherwise, I just didn't recognize you! I'm sure William will be delighted to see you.

Eugénie: William?

Joseph: Yes, his son's name isn't Guillotte any more, it's William.

Eugénie: (*surprised*) Oh?

Joseph: But where the heck can he have disappeared to this morning – I don't see any sign of him.

Louis: It's not nine o'clock yet.

Joseph: What do you mean, nine o'clock?

Louis: He never gets up before then.

Eugénie: But he used to be such an early riser! Do you remember, sir – every morning, when the weather was fine, he used to bring me a bouquet or a garland of flowers, or sometimes a cup of raspberries or blueberries ... and then ...

Louis: I remember, Eugénie.

Eugénie: Dear heavens, how happy I was then! I wouldn't have traded those flowers or the fruit that he offered me with his own hand, for all the world's gold!

Joseph: By gosh, he really loved you, back then!

Eugénie: Come now – he still loves me! (*To* Louis.) Isn't that right, sir? He can't have forgotten me! And yet ...

Louis: (*aside*) What innocence!

Eugénie: ... and yet it's strange, he only wrote me once in the whole time he's been living in town, and that was just a few days after he left here. I know that letter by heart, from reading it over and over again ...

Joseph: Do you hear that?

Louis: You're a fine girl, Eugénie.

Joseph: Come on, Louis, help me wake him up. That lazybones sleeps too much. His friend is already off in the wilds somewhere with his gun, hunting. (Louis *and* Joseph *leave.*)

SCENE III
Eugénie, Flore

Flore: So you still love my cousin?

Eugénie: Yes, dear Flore. Lord, I can't wait to see him! Tell me, has he changed a lot?

Flore: Changed? You won't recognize him. Tall, well-built, handsome. In spite of which ... but you'll soon see for yourself.

Eugénie: What do you mean?

Flore: Nothing. You know I'm a bit scatter-brained ...

SCENE IV
Actors, *as before*; Baptiste, *in a bad mood*

Baptiste: (*to himself*) No way! Can't be. Ain't gonna happen, an' that's fer sure!

Flore: Well, well – here's Baptiste! You seem to be in a grumpy mood, my friend!

Baptiste: I should be, an' I is!

Flore: What's disturbing you, then?

Baptiste: Disturbin'? Disturbin'? Makin' me mad! Drivin' me crazy!

Eugénie: I'll leave you two. I'll be back shortly ...

Flore: No, no! Stay!

Eugénie: I'll be back. (*She leaves.*)

SCENE V
Flore, Baptiste

(Flore *stares at* Baptiste *and breaks out laughing.*)

Baptiste: (*mimicking her*) Ha, ha, ha! Okay, go ahead an' laugh, but you ain't gonna ever be *my* wife, Flore!

Flore: Oh! ... but ...!

Baptiste: No ohs and buts about it. I come straight here to tell you that.

Flore: Tell me what?

Baptiste: That you're never gonna be my wife. Nobody's gonna say Baptiste Latulipe's got relatives that's ashamed o' him!

Flore: I don't understand ...

Baptiste: It ain't hard to understand. Yesterday, when I was on me way back from cuttin' hay with two friends o' mine, we seen a nice city-style carriage with two gentlemen in it. I spotted one of 'em, right off – 'twas Guillotte, your cousin. I was so happy to see 'im, I stopped 'im – and me two pals was bug-eyed, seein' as how I knew a big shot like that! I comes up to 'im, happy like an' laughin' away. 'Well, hello there, Guillotte,' says I 'how's she goin', eh? By golly, am I ever glad to see you!' An' you can just imagine how dumb I felt when he don't say a word, sittin' there like a statue, an' then he pulls a penny out of his pocket and puts it in me hand! Crack! goes his buggy-whip, and in a second he's outa sight! If he had a punched me or slapped me in the face, he couldn't a hurt me any worse. And then I sees me own pals bustin' out laughin' – an' now they're teasin' me all the time, an' it's gettin' me down. One of 'em'll say, like, 'Hey Baptiste, you gonna see some big shot today?' An' someone else'll say, 'Poor Batoche – I never woulda thought you was as poor as that! Stoppin' carriages on the highway for a penny! Why the heck didn'tcha ask me, I woulda been glad to give you *two* ...,' an a lotta other insults like that!

Flore: He probably didn't recognize you.

Baptiste: Reco'nize me? Dang it all, he didn't *wanna* reco'nize me, an' that's what makes me mad! So I says to meself, 'When I'm married to Flore, he won't act any different – he'll insult me again.' So it's over. Imagine me with relatives that's ashamed of me! No way – it won't happen. I'll *never* be Flore's wife!

Flore: Well, that's for sure.

Baptiste: What do you mean?

Flore: You'll never be my *wife*, that's for sure!

Baptiste: Aw – anyone can make a mistake! (*Emotionally.*) Don't think of me no more, Flore, an' I'm gonna try an' forget you. Farewell, Flore! (*He starts to leave.*)

Flore: (*holding him back*) Baptiste, listen – here he comes now. Stay here, I'm going to speak to him.

Baptiste: (*trying to get away*) No, no – it's all over!

Flore: (*holding him back*) Stay here, I tell you!

Baptiste: But ...!

Flore: Do me a favour and stay here. He won't bite you!

Baptiste: What the heck ...

Flore: Here he comes.

Baptiste: What?

Flore: Here comes William.

Baptiste: Who?

Flore: William – or Guillotte, whichever you want.

SCENE VI
Actors, *as before*; William

William: (*aside, without noticing* Baptiste) Is there anything worse than that? Dragged out of bed, when you'd like to sleep a while longer! But my poor benighted uncle has no more respect for the rules and manners of proper society than a citizen of the Celestial Empire [of China] has for a 'barbarian'! It's so *common*, so stupid! And what am I supposed to do now? Twiddle my thumbs? (*He notices* Baptiste.) Damn! – there's that bore I ran into yesterday!

Flore: (*to* William) Looks as though my dear little cousin didn't sleep too well last night.

William: 'Dear little cousin?' – what do you mean by that, if you don't mind?

Flore: That's the way it looks to me. No need to get upset about it. It just seems to me ...

William: It seems to *me* you're rather too familiar this morning, Miss. 'Dear little cousin!' 'Don't get upset!' – indeed!

Flore: Oh, you're quite right, Mr William, my cousin. Please forgive me: I keep forgetting. It's natural enough, you see – I was so used to treating you familiarly in the past that I can't help doing so in the present. But I'm not doing it on purpose, I swear!

William: Who is this oaf here?

Flore: Pardon?

Baptiste: What? What'd he say? I guess he thinks he's some kinda big shot 'cause he lives in town.

William: [*in English*] What's his business here?

Flore: [*in French*] Come now – it's Baptiste!

William: I'm not asking you what his name is – what's he doing here?

Flore: He's come to see you, Mr William. You ran into him yesterday, but I'm convinced you didn't recognize him.

William: (*aside*) I recognized him well enough! (*To* Flore.) To see *me*? What in blazes have I got in common with *him*? Hardly a moment goes by that one isn't besieged and harassed by some booby like this ...

Baptiste: 'Booby'? By tarnation, I'm gonna tear'im to bits, Flore! (*He moves towards* William, *but* Flore *restrains him.*)

Flore: What do you say, sir? It's Baptiste, your old friend. Look what a handsome lad he's become! He hasn't forgotten *you*, that's for sure – he often talks about you.

William: (*aside*) Oh yes, a handsome lout, indeed!

Flore: (*to* Baptiste) Talk to him, Baptiste. Shake hands with him.

Baptiste: (*to* Flore) But ...!

Flore: (*to* Baptiste) Come on, don't make a fuss over it!

Baptiste: (*to* Flore) But he just called me a booby!

Flore: (*to* Baptiste) He meant nothing, really – he wasn't really awake yet.

Baptiste: (*to* Flore) Well okay, if that's what you want ... (*To* William, *offering his hand.*) Hullo there, Guillotte.

Flore: (*to* Baptiste) Shhh! Call him 'William'!

Baptiste: (*to* Flore) Eh?

Flore: (*to* Baptiste) Address him formally, say 'vous,' and call him 'William.'

Baptiste: (*to* Flore) You mean I gotta talk to him like you do?

Flore: That's right.

Baptiste: (*approaching* William *hesitantly*) Hullo there, Mr Gwillium ... (*To* Flore, *after a moment.*) There – okay?

Flore: Shake hands with him.

Baptiste: (*to* William) Pleased to meet you, sir. How's she goin', eh? Tarnation! am I ever glad t' see ya! ... Hey! don't you recognize Baptiste?

William: (*pushing him aside*) Who is this oaf? (Baptiste *looks at* Flore.)

Flore: Oh, William, now you've really hurt me! How can you possibly ignore the man who once risked his own life to save yours, pulling you out of the water when you certainly would have drowned? Is that the sort of gratitude you show him? Oh, shame on you, sir!

William: (*laughing*) Ha, ha, ha! Keep going, Miss – you're quite eloquent, really! You're going to bring tears to my eyes! Ho, ho, ho!

Baptiste: (*moving threateningly towards* William) By tarnation! let me clout'im a good one! (*Coming up to* William.) I'm not much fer fights, but when I gets into one, I gives me money's worth, I can tell ya! (*Moving closer.*) You betcha! (*Closer.*) An' I can tell *you* a thing or two, me Gwillium of a Guillotte!

Flore: (*restraining* Baptiste) Come on, Baptiste, he's not worth getting angry at! (*To* William) Oh, Guillot, how sad you make me! (Flore *and* Baptiste *leave.*)

SCENE VII
William, *alone*

Oh, I can't wait to get away from here! Surely it was some evil demon that gave Father the idea of inviting Brown and his sister to come to this village for a visit. All I find here is acute embarrassment from hicks who treat me with familiarity and call me 'Guillot' or even 'Guillotte,' who talk to me as if they were talking to their ignorant chums, and who torture me in countless other ways! It's true that Baptiste did drag me out of the water, as she says, but my social status has changed a great deal since then!

SCENE VIII
William *and* Flore

Flore: Now Baptiste won't listen to me, and it's all your fault, William!

William: Well now, that's certainly a great concern of *mine*!

Flore: No, you're no cousin of mine, from now on.

William: What a pity, now, really!

Flore: I'm going to tell that young English woman who came with you how you've been behaving, and if ...

William: Hold on! What do you mean?

Flore: ... And if she's at all like her brother, I'm sure she'll listen to me. *He's* not ashamed of us; *he* doesn't display contempt and snobbishness towards us of the kind that makes you appear so ridiculous. Yes, ridiculous, because you should know that all the good people in our village, far from respecting you, have just been laughing at you since you arrived. Far from admiring you, they detest you, while your friend Mr Brown is everybody's favourite!

William: Just what are you going to tell the 'young English woman,' as you call her?

Flore: What will I tell her? I know what I'll tell her, you ungrateful, snobbish, stuck-up ...

William: For God's sake, stop that! .... (Flore *leaves*.)

SCENE IX
William, *alone*

I'm very much afraid that little fool may be going to say something bad about me to Malvina or her brother. Why the hell did I ever agree to come here? Oh, Malvina, my love for you must indeed be strong, for me to have given in to your wishes and come with you to this God-forsaken spot! The country? The country! Oh, the joys of country living – how delicious they are! I can't imagine where in the world all our poets and novelists manage to discover all these 'joys'! As far as I'm concerned, everything I encounter here only makes me melancholy.[18] Good Lord – what uncultivated boors! You're no more likely to hear English – the *stylish* language – spoken here, than to see stylish clothes worn! Everything is topsy-turvy. Seems as though these rustics have adopted as their motto the English word 'unfashionable,' because *nothing* is in style!

SCENE X
William; Brown, *in hunting clothes, with gun, hunter's game bag with wildfowl showing, etc.*

Brown: (*humming*)
  En roulant, mon boule roulant,
  En roulant mon boule ...[19]
(*Taking off his hunting equipment.*) [*In French.*] Hullo, my pal! Is you have sleep good enough? Ah, you lazy-buns! If you come wander on meadow with me, you not be bore. Hoorah for the hunting! How fun she is, by gash! Now I think I eat three lunch without stop. I think to have, here in my ... pooch?

William: Game bag.

Brown: Yes, yes, in my gum-bag I got nice duck and two crowbird, big like eagle. Why you no like hunting, huh? You still bore, like yessirday?

William: [*in English*] More than ever!

Brown: Aha! I un-bore you pretty soon. By the by, I has greeting to give you ... A big old womans who limp. She is know you real good. She come see you quick.

William: (*aside*) Damned old woman! – I know who he means ...

Brown: I meet too one young man, he very anger – oh, anger like a big devil!

William: Really!

Brown: Yes, this nice-looker guy we meet yessirday. You give him sovereign – I mean, penny.

William: (*aside*) This joker seems to know everyone here, already! (*Aloud.*) What did he say to you?

Brown: Oh, many little thing ...

William: (*aside*) He probably told him everything.

Brown: Me and him now best friend in world. Is true, what he say?

William: What did he say?

Brown: Him say he save you life.

William: (*aside*) He knows everything. (*Aloud.*) It's not so.

Brown: Well! This funny thing! But you know him?

William: [*in English*] Not at all! [*In French.*] I don't know anyone here. [*In English.*] I don't know anybody in this infernal part of the country!

Brown: No body ... But I just meet many peoples who says he know you good! You is not born in this village?

William: Good grief! ... In *this* village? No – at least I don't think so ...

Brown: (*laughing*) Ha, ha, ha! You not know where you born? Ha, ha, ha! You not know your mother?

William: (*aside*) This god-damned countryside!

Brown: But have you see mine sister?

William: Miss Malvina? No. Where is she? Perhaps she's gone out already?

Brown: Is probable – I just see her, and now I see her again time, because here she come with your cousin!

SCENE XI
Actors, *as before*; Malvina; Flore

William: (*advancing to greet her*) [*in English*] Miss Malvina! (*He takes her hand.*)

Malvina: Mr William!

William: [*in English*] I hope you had a pleasant morning walk.

Malvina: [*in English*] Extremely pleasant, sir. The country looks so beautiful! But why don't you speak French, Mr William? [*In French.*] Why don't you speak French to me? You know I'm terribly fond of that language.

Brown: (*imitating his sister*) 'You know I terrible found' – My sister he talk gooder French than me, I think. But I learn soon. 'You know I terrible found,' eh?

Malvina: (*to* Flore) I think your cousin would prefer to forget his own language, Miss.

Flore: There are a lot of other things he'd like to forget as well, and indeed he has managed to forget quite a few of them.

William: (*to* Malvina) In your presence, Miss, I forget everything, and am reduced to admiration of you, angel that you are ... And in any case, as you know, English is more fashionable.

Malvina: (*laughing*) Ha, ha, ha! – 'Fashionable' to scorn one's own language! And here I thought it was only certain members of the Legislative Assembly who had that privilege!

William: You're just as sharp-tongued as ever.

Flore: It is also 'fashionable' to have no human sentiments. (William *stares at her sternly.*) Please come with me, Miss. I'll show you the flowers I was talking about.

Malvina: (*following* Flore) Much obliged, Miss. (*To* William *and* Brown.) I'll see you shortly. (William *and* Brown *bow, and* Malvina *and* Flore *exit rear.*)

SCENE XII
William, *pensive*; Brown

Brown: Hey – you come to fish with me, after lunching. There is many fishes in the little lake: catfishes, crappy-fishes, and percherons too. But you too much lazy-buns – you die of lazybunning! We go lunching first, and after, out on water! Let's go! (*He drags* William *off, singing*)
    En roulant, mon boule roulant
    En roulant mon boule!

ACT TWO
Setting: same as for first act

SCENE I
Flore *and* Eugénie

Flore: There's no use being so sad about this, my dear Eugénie ...

Eugénie: Oh, why can't I forget him! Just erase him from my mind forever! Oh ... (*holding her hand to her heart*) oh, Flore, I feel as if I'm going to die!

Flore: Where did you meet him?

Eugénie: On the pathway leading to the grove over here.

Flore: Was he alone?

Eugénie: No, Flore – a pretty young woman was holding his arm ... His fiancée, according to what they've just told me! (*Aside.*) Oh, Guillaume, I thought about you night and day! I loved you as I love life itself!

Flore: What did he say when he saw you?

Eugénie: Nothing at all, Flore! In fact, as I came up to him, to greet him and welcome him home, he turned his head away. But the young woman, noticing that I had stopped as though I wanted to talk to him, called me to his attention. Then he whispered something to her that I couldn't catch, and continued on his way. How wretched I am, Flore!

Flore: Not as much as you're inclined to believe, Eugénie. My cousin isn't the same person he was. He's not the Guillot he used to be. He refuses to recognize anyone in the village any more. He's even forgotten his relatives. And Uncle tells me that even back in the city he won't stop for a second to speak to a common workman in the street. That would be lowering himself, demeaning himself. So you can see you're not the only one he scorns because of his own vanity!

Eugénie: Could he have changed *that* much?

Flore: Changed, my dear? He won't even recognize Baptiste any more – imagine that!

Eugénie: How can that be possible?

Flore: Very possible, my dear, to the point that Baptiste started a quarrel with me because of it, and left me in a sulk!

Eugénie: You're the lucky one: Baptiste loves you. But tell me, Flore, what should I do? Give me some advice, I beg of you ...

Flore: Forget him.

Eugénie: That's easy to say. But how do I go about forgetting? I'm afraid I'll never manage that!

Flore: Never? Oh, Eugénie, a love like yours only occurs in novels – it's out of style these days! Never, you say? That's a bit too long. Especially since I happen to know someone who might very well be able to help you forget my stupid cousin rather quickly ...

Eugénie: Who's that?

Flore: Oh, another handsome gentleman from the city ...

Eugénie: Oh, Flore, don't make it even harder for me, with your teasing!

Flore: And what if I'm not teasing?

Eugénie: Then ... I don't understand what you mean ...

Flore: You'll understand soon enough, I hope. Has Mr Brown seen you?

Eugénie: Yes, he spoke with me. He seems like a very nice man. But what are you getting at, Flore? Oh, if only I could see Guillaume! Just talk to him for a moment ...

Flore: Easiest thing in the world. Wait for him, right here.

Eugénie: I'm going to run home for a moment, and be right back! (*She leaves.*)

SCENE II
Flore, *alone*

Poor Eugénie – I really feel sorry for her. Ah! – men, men!

SCENE III
Brown, Flore

Brown: Ah! – womens, womens! Hurray for womens, forever! Right, Miss Flore? My dear Miss Flore, I should maybe might say, no? (*He puts his arm around her shoulder.*)

Flore: (*pushing his arm away*) Come! Please, Mr Brown ...

Brown: Oh, don't be a fear of nothing – me not want to make you hurt. Oh no, my dear heartsweet!

Flore: Careful! If Baptiste catches you with me, I wouldn't want to predict what he might do!

Brown: Baptiste? Oh, he big friend of me! He just ask me to do at you a little flavour for him.

Flore: He asked you to do something for him? Well, *what* then?

Brown: He ask me to give you for him one little smooch. (*He attempts to kiss her.*)

Flore: (*pushing him away*) Mr Brown!

Brown: Okay then, it is not being my fault if I no can do what he want – you must be my witness!

Flore: Quite so, sir: it's not your fault, and I shall be happy to tell him so!

Brown: (*looking about him*) But I am hoping to find the other miss here – the pretty one is name ... How she name?

Flore: Eugénie.

Brown: Yes – that is, exactly! Miss Yewjenny. Me much like to see this young person.

Flore: She left here just a moment ago, sir, but should be back soon.

Brown: She your friend, no? She seem as nice as she seem pretty.

Flore: On that subject, sir, I don't know a finer person than she is. She is an angel brought to earth!

Brown: With no joke, I think me love this girl. Like you says in French, me ah-moo-roo!

Flore: Amoureux.

Brown: Ah-moo-roo: I say it right, no?

Flore: Not exactly: A-mou-*reux* ... *eux* ... *reux* ...

Brown: Ah-moo-roo ... roo ... roo! (Flore *laughs.*) Is no matter. This damn language! I no can pronounce other way. He has boyfriend, this young miss?

Flore: I don't think so.

Brown: Oh, now I much happy! I want to see also your cousin. I want him to take to fishing. He is much bore here. (*He leaves.*)

SCENE IV
Flore, *alone*

Have I guessed right? Has he fallen, as the expression goes, for Eugénie? If the poor girl could only manage to forget that dumb cousin of mine, this could be quite a windfall for her! My uncle says the most flattering things about this man ...

SCENE V
Flore, Baptiste

Baptiste: (*enters, laughing loudly*) Ha, ha, ha! Oh, I wouldn't of missed that fer half a dozen prize ewes, an' me own fine little filly in the bargain! Did he ever take a dive! Ha, ha, ho, ho!

Flore: Well, you're certainly in a good mood now!

Baptiste: (*still laughing*) Ha, ho, ho! Hoo, hee, ha!

Flore: Well, what do you have to laugh so heartily about?

Baptiste: Yer cousin! Oh, ha, ha, ho!

Flore: Well?

Baptiste: Ho, ha, ha! ... First, let me tell you that yer cousin Guillotte (oh, ha, ha, hoo!) ...

Flore: (*slapping him on the back*) He's going to die laughing! Come on, speak!

Baptiste: Okay ... We was hidin' behind the little alder bushes on the shore, watchin' him get in the boat, an' when he gets a ways out from shore, I pulls on the cord, an' ...

Flore: What cord?

Baptiste: Oh, the cord I tied to the big bung-stopper I made for the bottom of the boat. I give it one good yank, all of a sudden, an' it unplugs the hole, an a couple a minutes later, the boat starts goin' down, sinkin', sinkin' – an' under she goes! An' there goes yer cousin, into the water, swimmin' fer it! Oh, ha, ha, ha! ... Holy mackerel! (*Looking off-stage.*) Ain't that him comin' now? Ha, ha, ho! ... Ain't it a good one, eh? Ain't it a good one?

Flore: No, Baptiste, that wasn't a very good thing to do. You shouldn't have ...

SCENE VI
Actors, *as before*; William

William: (*holding his jacket on his arm, shaking his wet hat and striding from one side of the stage to the other*) (*aside*) That damned boat! Brown saw me there in the water, too, and instead of coming to help me, he starts laughing! If he weren't my future brother-in-law, I'd sure make him pay for that!

Baptiste: (*choking with laughter*) Ha, ha, ha! Oh, ha, ho, ho! ...

William: You too, you worthless wretch, I saw you there on the bank, laughing at my misfortune ... instead of helping me!

Baptiste: Aha – so you reco'nizes me now, huh? Funny, ain't it, how a bit o' water can clear up yer eyesight!

William: (*aside*) Oh, what a mess, what a mess! I'm afraid Malvina may see me like this!

Baptiste: What'd he say? ... Yessir, fer sure I woulda let you drink the whole lake dry, afore I'da been so bold as to raise me finger to help ya out. I wouldn't a wanted to hurt your *diganitty*!

William: (*aside*) I can't stay around here in this condition. (*Aloud.*) Flore, dear sweet little Flore, could you find some dry clothes for me to change into? I don't know where my father's gone, and he has the key to our suitcases with him.

Baptiste: Well now! (*Mocking* William.) 'Flore, dear sweet little Flore ...'! I find you're rather familiar these days, sir!

William: Arrgh! I'm losing my temper ...!

Baptiste: Darn shame, Mr Gwillium, what happened to you, there! Ain't it? Didja see the bottom o' the lake, then? Poor guy – that's twice you's had a narrow 'scape of it. Jest watch out for the third time: water seems to kinda like ya, eh, Mr Gwillium? Borry him the lend o' one o' yer skirts, Flore!

Flore: (*rummaging about in a trunk*) Goodness! I don't know what to give him ...

William: Just give me something – anything at all!

Flore: (*handing him some clothing*) Here are some old clothes belonging to my father.

William: (*grabs the clothes and starts to leave*) Good! I'm going to lock myself in my room. I'm not in for anyone – you hear me, Flore? Anyone! (*He leaves.*)

SCENE VII
Baptiste, Flore

Flore: (*laughing*) Ha, ha, ha! ...

Baptiste: Oh yeah, *now* you're laughin', when I ain't laughin' no more! Hey, what you laughin' at?

Flore: You didn't notice what clothes I gave him?

Baptiste: No, I didn't take no notice, but ...

Flore: Real farmer's clothes – homespun, big enough for someone twice his size. What a face he's going to make over that!

Baptiste: That's a heck of a lot better'n he deserves, an' I think it was darn good of ya to give 'im anythin' at all!

Flore: I was only doing my Christian duty, Baptiste. Aren't we supposed to return good for evil?

Baptiste: Yer darn tootin', by cracky! – The schoolmarster was sayin' that jest the other day, in his speechifyin' about ... pullet ticks!

Flore: Pullet ticks?

Baptiste: Yeah – pullet chicks, poultry ticks ... whatever. An' then the notary told 'im he shouldn't be gettin' into ... you know, pullet chicks, an' that the school-marster didn't have no elegance.

Flore: Eloquence, you mean.

Baptiste: Ello ... Ellie ... Ellyquence – same difference!

Flore: Yes, yes – clever chap, that notary. *He* never gets involved in politicking, and in fact he calls the whole science of politics a joke. (*Aside.*) Maybe he's right!

Baptiste: That's fer sure! An' he even reads stories by Gene Stew and Victor Gigot![20] – Quite the books, what *they* write!

Flore: A man who goes to see plays!

Baptiste: An' he even acts in them plays!

Flore: Yes, an amateur performer![21]

Baptiste: Yeah, a hamster reformer. My, you talk nice! I kinda wish I had went to convent school like you an' Eugénie ... But to come back to Guillotte (or Gwillium, as they calls 'im), at least I had me a real good laugh, on him. I was so proud o' meself, that I done that, that here I finds meself on me way over here, without even thinkin'. An' me that wanted to stay away from you for a while yet! Anyways, by cracky, here I be. Hey, let's you an' me be good friends agin!

Flore: (*flirting*) I'm not too sure about that ...

Baptiste: What? Someone been makin' eyes at you, while I been away?

Flore: (*flirting*) Well, I'm not going to deny it ...

Baptiste: (*angry*) So who then? Who done it? By tarnation! ...

Flore: Oh, one of your friends.

Baptiste: Who? Jean-Gnace, Marie Gadoury's son?

Flore: No, that's not the one.

Baptiste: Oh – Guillotte's friend?

Flore: That's right, but it was with your permission. Didn't you ask him to ...

Baptiste: ... to give you a little smooch?

Flore: Well ...?

Baptiste: Yes, that's true.

Flore: Well in any case, I'm sorry, but he wasn't allowed to carry out the errand. So let's not say any more about it.

Baptiste: Okay then, let's make up. (*He tries to kiss her; she fends him off.*)

Flore: That's already been done for you ...

Baptiste: (*making a fist*) But Guillotte better not come back here, by tarnation! (*Confusedly.*) Them foolosophers can preach all they want about doin' bad deeds fer good – I ain't gonna listen!

SCENE VIII
Actors, *as before*; Brown *enters, laughing*

Brown: (*jovially*) Where is he? Where is he?

Flore: You mean Mr William?

Brown: Yes, right exactly. I wish to un-bore him. Oh, Baptiste! (*He shakes* Baptiste's *hand*) – your girlfriend she is sharp one! ... He is gone?

Flore: No, sir, he's in his room.

Baptiste: That is, he ain't really in his room.

Flore: Pardon me?

Baptiste: You know he said he ain't in fer nobody ...

Flore: Actually, sir, my poor cousin isn't feeling too well.

Brown: Oh yes, and me knowing why him not feeling well. He very much wet, when he is come here?

Baptiste: Holy cow! You bet he was – wringin' wet like a mop! But wasn't you there when ...

Brown: For sure I were! He go in water, head first! His fault, too – he not wanting to wait for me. Too much hurry, hurry!

Flore: He seems annoyed with you, that you didn't help him.

Brown: Not my fault. I not can help, because I laughing too much. (*He laughs.*) Oh goodness, so funny, so funny!

Baptiste: By gum, I was laughin' too, seein' him flounderin' around!

Brown: Him mad, what? I go un-mad him pretty quick. I go quick to his room. (*He leaves.*)

SCENE IX
Baptiste, Flore

Baptiste: Well, I reckon I better not hang round here much longer ... gotta get back to me hayin'. Like the fella says, ya can't let the hay grow under yer feet! (*He starts to leave.*)

Flore: (*calling him back*) Baptiste!

Baptiste: (*turning back*) Yeah?

Flore: Do you know what I want to say to you?

Baptiste: Yeah.

Flore: What is it, then?

Baptiste: Go ahead an' say it ...

Flore: I know *one* thing ...

Baptiste: ... an' I know a thousand. But never mind, tell me yer one thing.

Flore: My uncle Joe [*sic*]²² wants cousin William to get married right here in the village.

Baptiste: Aha! – to Miss Malvina, that pretty gal who ain't stuck up at all!

Flore: Yes.

Baptiste: He done proposed to her yet?

Flore: No, nor even hinted at it, I suspect, but the whole thing's supposed to take place pretty soon.

Baptiste: (*starting to leave*) Is that all?

Flore: No. Well, you see, my father would really like to see the two weddings take place at the same time.

Baptiste: Oh, now I gets ya. No problem, Flore, I'll marry ya at the same sarmony. Ain't it gonna be great, eh? Two cousins married at the same weddin' mass! ...

Flore: And maybe there'll even be a third wedding. Who knows? – a sort of matrimony in treble!

Baptiste: Aw, I don't understand what you mean by 'mutter-money an' troubles' ... Anyways, I gotta go! (*He leaves.*)

SCENE X
Flore, *alone, staring off-stage*

Well! Here comes poor Eugénie ... With her head down. You'd almost think she was looking for something she's lost ...

SCENE XI
Flore, Eugénie

Eugénie: My bad luck's still with me, Flore. I've lost the only thing of his I had left – the letter he wrote me a few days after he left here, and that I had treasured so carefully, along with the daguerreotype portrait he had sent me at the same time. Oh, Flore, did you see them, perhaps?

Flore: No – wherever might I have seen them?

Eugénie: I usually carried them here in my bosom, next to my heart, and when I wanted to look at the portrait and read the letter for the last time, before giving them back to him, I noticed I had lost them. Since I had come this way, I thought I might have dropped them on the ground ...

Flore: No, Eugénie, I haven't seen them, in any case. So you're finally going to make an effort to forget him?

Eugénie: Yes, dear friend, I've decided to chase him from my mind, no matter how hard that may be.

Flore: Well, that's a good start. I predict you'll be a lot happier if you can do that!

Eugénie: As far as happiness goes, I hardly have the courage to expect that. Perhaps Providence will help me ... but I really must find those things! I'll keep on looking. (*She exits on one side of the stage, as* Louis, Joseph, *and* Malvina *enter from stage rear.*)

SCENE XII
Flore; Louis, *carrying a bouquet of roses*; Joseph; Malvina, *also carrying a bouquet*

Malvina: Who *is* that young woman who just left here – she looks so sad!

Joseph: Oh, that's Flore's friend. Quite a girl, isn't she, Flore? By gosh, brother Louie here knows her quite well, too. His son – William, as he now calls himself ... (Flore *gestures to him not to continue.*) What? But there's no harm saying she and your son were pretty close. Right, Louie?

Malvina: I beg your pardon? I don't understand.

Flore: My father means to say that Mr William ... when he was quite young ... still just a child, you know ... (*aside*) I really don't know what to say.

Joseph: Well listen, now, Flore – he wasn't that much of a child just a year ago, when we all thought he was going to marry her!

Malvina: Oh, I think I understand now. Mr William mentioned her yesterday, when we were out for a stroll together. And yet when we did meet her, it seemed to me that Mr William didn't think too much of her. (*To* Louis.) Your son courted this young woman, didn't he?

Louis: It's true that ... I mean ... I heard that William had seemed to pay her special attention, but ...

Joseph: All right, all right – 'special attention,' call it whatever you want. I know what the situation was ... but it's none of my business. (*To* Malvina.) Well now, Miss Malvina, what do you think of my garden?

Malvina: Oh, it's wonderful, sir, and I must thank you for the pleasure it gave me!

Joseph: That's what all the big city-folk tell me when they come here with their friends. And I can tell you that gives me a lot of pleasure.

Malvina: How lucky you are, to be living in the country! I hope I won't be unhappy on that score myself for very long, since my brother and I are thinking of becoming neighbours of yours in the near future.

Joseph: I should be only too honoured ...

Malvina: My brother really loves the country. He's terribly fond of hunting, fishing, and other country pastimes. That's why we're going to buy the stone house near here, the one we're told is up for sale.

Joseph: The one belonging to Michel-José-Jean-Gnace? Well, well, what do you know – that's Eugénie's father! You know, the girl who seemed so sad ... (*As* Joseph *mentions* Eugénie's *name,* Malvina *takes a letter from her bosom, checks the address, and puts it back.*)

Malvina: Did some misfortune happen to the family, that they're letting their property go like this?

Joseph: By gosh, Miss, that's easy enough to answer: It's the result of a lawsuit, which always spells ruin for a farmer. The lawyers pumped him dry, and I don't know what will become of the poor man and his wife and daughter. Poor girl – so well educated, and all. I really do feel sorry for her. (*He wipes away a tear.*) She's such a *good* girl, miss. Never complains, and yet she has so many problems ...

Malvina: Sir, I admire your good-heartedness, and I'm really touched by this girl's unfortunate situation. In fact, I hope to be able to be of some help to her, one of these days.

Joseph: On her behalf, Miss, I thank you. (*He stares off-stage.*) But who's the chap on his way here now with your brother?

SCENE XIII
Actors, *as before*; Brown; William, *dressed outlandishly, with huge homespun trousers, jacket much too large, red homespun tuque, etc.*

Brown: (*holding* William *by the arm*) Come with, come with ... Now you be dry, like so!

William: (*struggling to free himself*) Let me alone, I tell you!

Joseph: For gosh sakes! (*To* Louis.) It's your son! I bet it's another joke his friend's pulling ... (*Laughing.*) Ha, ha, ha! – that lad's quite the prankster!

William: (*aside*) Curse the luck! – Malvina seeing me in this damned get-up!

Brown: I wanting to take tour of village with him, but him not like one damn bit!

William: (*still trying to free himself*) [*in English*] Brown, my friend, if you please ...

Joseph: And just look at the kind of clothes he's wearing! He doesn't look any better than us, dressed like that!

William: (*trying to escape*) Please, Brown!

Brown: (*holding him back*) Whoah back! What the heck – you looking good like so! You looking like nice big farmer!

William: Please excuse the way I'm attired, Miss Malvina ...

Malvina: Whatever for? It suits you splendidly!

Brown: This is true – 'slenderly.' (*To* William.) Come with, we make one little tour.

William: (*angrily*) Brown ! (*He breaks away suddenly.*) Let me go!

Brown: (*surprised*) Oh! – you still anger? (*Clapping him on the back.*) There, there now ... You always say you be bore. Okay, me try to un-bore you, and now you not want!

William: (*aside*) I'm so angry!

Brown: Oh – me forget to tell you: I invite much of your friends. She all come quick soon. We wait here for them.

William: Who do you mean?

Brown: One little hunchback guy ... and a fiddle-man. Oh, you will see. We dance like hell, no?

William: (*exasperated*) Ahh!

Brown: Here they be – right now!

SCENE XIV
Actors, *as before*; Baptiste; *Men and women from the village, including a* Hunchback *and a* Musician

Brown: (*greeting the newcomers*) Good, good! My friend and me much happy to see you. Come here, my good friends, come! (*To* William.) Shake the hand on your friends.

William: Brown, you're going to pay for this!

Brown: (*to the villagers*) My good friend William she very much satisfy to see you.

William: (*aside*) You English scum!

Brown: He now dressed proper for occasion.

William: (*aside*) Bloody prankster!

Brown: He in such big hurry to see you, he want to go meet you!

William: (*aside*) Oh, the swine!

Hunchback: (*shaking* William's *hand*) G'day, Guillotte! Everyone okay at your place? Y'know, it's a funny thing – they all said you was so stuck-up an' all, an' here you be togged out jest like us, after all! (*The other villagers shake hands with* William.)

Brown: (*to the villagers*) Genitalmens, I am having the honours to present my sister, who is speak Franch almost so good like me. (Malvina *greets the villagers.*) Oh – shake her hands, shake her hands. Not to be shame! She my sister. She soon have big pleasure to be farmer like you. She good for milking cows; me too. And now my great friend he will come too, I think. See – already he is put on farmer clothings!

Hunchback: (*to* William) What! You gonna come help drive the oxen agin? (*Shouts.*) Gee! Ha! Go, Big Red! Go, Buttermilk!

William: (*aside*) Now I'm really livid!

Hunchback: You was pretty good, but I beat you at it, just the same. 'Member when you used to cut across me furrows, after I had made 'em straight? (*To* Baptiste:) But hold on now – you told me he treated you awful. You musta been imaginin' things, eh?

Baptiste: Yeah? You jest don't notice what's goin' on. Anyways, I knows what I knows, by tarnation! (*He offers his handkerchief to* William.) Don't worry – it's clean!

Joseph: (*to* Baptiste) Why the handkerchief?

Baptiste: (*to* William) So's you can wipe your hands, Mr Gwillium, eh? (*He bows mockingly.*)

William: (*aside*) Bloody idiot!

Brown: (*to* Malvina) Come, shake hands! (Malvina *shakes hands with all the villagers.*)

Hunchback: Ain't she the game one, this here Miss Malvanilla! She ain't no more stuck-up that we is!

Baptiste: Her brother neither!

Hunchback: Yer darn right! Nice, fine people they is, no matter whatcha say!

Baptiste: Ain't it a shame they's Protestants! ...

Hunchback: Hush! That don't make no difference! That there's just fanuticalism, as them upper-class folks says ...

Baptiste: Yeah, but you know what the catty-kissem book says –

Hunchback: Aw, forget yer catty-kissem – You wouldn't understand a real mystery, nohow! An' anyways, that ain't none o' our business.

Joseph: (*to* Malvina) Your brother is someone who really likes to have a good time.

Brown: Well, we come special for that, you know!

Joseph: Oh, I don't doubt that! You go ahead and have as much fun as you want – I like to see that. Have you got a musician?

Malvina: Yes indeed. Oh, Miss Flore, we're going to dance! I simply *adore* music and dancing!

Flore: So do I, I swear!

Malvina: Mr Musician, a waltz please. Come on, Mr William, be a proper gentleman now ...

William: I beg you to excuse me, Miss. I couldn't dance dressed like this.

Malvina: You look just fine! Come on. (*She takes his hand. To the* Musician.) You know how to play a waltz?

Musician: A Welsh? No, Miss.

Malvina: Well then, could you please play a polka?

Musician: I don't know none, Miss.

Brown: Play us a *galope*! (*He dances and hums.*) Tum, tiddy tum, tiddy tum, tiddy tum ... okay? You play it?

Musician: No, sir. (William *takes his hand from* Malvina's.)

Malvina: No matter – play whatever you can, then.

Musician: I know the *jack-de-gris*, the *mistigris*, and the *ostination*.[23]

Malvina: You don't know any quadrilles?

Musician: Well ... maybe that's what I calls 'casse-reels'?

Malvina: No, no!

Brown: Me, I'm for a strathspey.

Musician: I don't know no straw spades.

Brown: All right then: a reel!

Musician: Reels? Them's me best, reels an' jigs. (*He tunes his fiddle and bows a bit of country music.*) A reel?

Brown: Please. (*The* Musician *plays some country-style music, but nobody dances.*) Oh, she is good, this fine reel! Now, a jig.

Musician: A jig. Here ya go, sir! (*He plays the same tune.*)

Brown: She darn good, this jig, but me find she much like your reel!

Musician: Yessir, they's like brother an' sister. Oh, I forgot to tell ya, I can play the cotillion too, as good as any city-type musickers!

Brown: Let's hear. (*The* Musician *plays the same tune.*) Funny thing, this one she very much like other two you playing!

Musician: Yes, by gum, sir – it's jest the title that makes the difference.

Brown: I thinking so. Okay, play again the first.

Musician: Right. A reel, right? (*He plays, and the dancing begins.* Baptiste *dances with* Flore. Brown *tries to get* William *to dance, but he refuses. Finally,* Brown *dances with* Malvina. *The* Hunchback *and the others dance.*)

William: (*aside*) Bunch of hayseeds! (*He leaves, as the others go on dancing.*)

SCENE XV
Actors, *as before, except* William

Brown: (*aside, when the dance has stopped*) Hey, my friend William she run away, I see!

Hunchback: (*out of breath*) Whew! That gets yer circulation goin', like the schoolmarster says! But where's Guillotte gone to?

Baptiste: Dumb question – he weren't very comfortable here!

Hunchback: How so? He sick or somethin'?

Baptiste: Yeah – sick o' seein' us!

Malvina: (*to* Louis) Your son *has* left! I guess he doesn't like people.

Louis: I suspect he's just gone to change his clothes.

Malvina: (*to* Brown) By the way, why was he dressed like that?

Brown: Oh, him all soaky wet. Must change. He go for swim, all dressed! I tell you quick later.

Malvina: (*to* Brown) Just the same, it's not very polite of him to run out on his friends like this.

Brown: Oh, I apologizing for him. (*To the villagers.*) My friend, I am you much oblige, and I beg you scuse my friend, Mr William. He not feel so good.

Baptiste: Yeah – his eyes an' ears is sore from what he seen an' heard here!

Hunchback: Darn shame, jest the same. (*The villagers bow, and are about to leave.*)

Brown: (*stopping them*) But ... you please wait ... just one teeny bit. One song, one little song! (*To the* Hunchback.) You will please be obliging us, sir?

Hunchback: (*mocking* Brown's *speech*) Ah, my sir, me not know how to singing!

Brown: Oh you know, you know good – I see from your face!

Hunchback: (*aside*) Thing is, I don't remember any songs ... (*To* Brown.) [*in English*] Elle [*sic*] don't remember any song, sir.

Brown: (*surprised*) [*in French*] Hey ... you can speaking English? Bravo! (*He claps him on the back.*)

Hunchback: (*coughing*) Oh ... hey! ... When you hit me in the back, you 'minded me of me song.

Brown: What?

Hunchback: Me grandma used to sing me a little song, and when she sung it, she used to rap me with a broom-handle, jest to keep time. Anyways, she sung it to me so often she give me a camel's bump that I can't get rid of, no-how! (Brown *and the others laugh. The* Hunchback *coughs.*) Anyways, I know that one, an' you jest reminded me of it. It ain't no great shakes of a song, but I'm gonna sing it to you, anyways. Here she goes! (*He sings, 'Roule ta bosse ...' The others repeat in chorus, 'Roule ta bosse,' etc.*)[24]

Brown: This is singed very good, for surely! And much thank-yous to you! And now, laddies and gentlemans, if you be so good to go in that door (*pointing*) I come join you soon, for some refreshingmints.

Hunchback: (*does a little jig*) Whoopee! Me hump is dancin' fer joy ... anyways! (*The villagers bow and leave in the direction indicated by* Brown. Baptiste *leaves with* Flore, *conversing as they go.* Brown *leaves, in the same direction as the villagers.*)

SCENE XVI
Louis *and* Joseph, *conversing at stage rear;* Malvina, *stage front*

Malvina: I must have a look at these papers I found. (*She pulls a letter from her* *bosom and reads the address.*) Eugénie! – It's that lovely girl Flore spoke to me about. (*She opens the letter.*) Let's see what it says. (*She finds a miniature portrait which she holds up, surprised.*) Oh, Mr William! Yes, it's certainly he. So what his uncle wanted to say, in spite of all the signals his daughter was giving him, is only too true! Let's read the letter. 'Dear Eugénie ... hmm, hmm, hmm ...' Well, it's all very tender and full of passion ... (*She reads again.*) 'Hmm, hmm, hmm ... No, Eugénie, I shall never stop loving you, with the purest and most sincere love ... hmm, hmm, hmm ... I'm just waiting for the time when I'll finally be admitted to the profession I've chosen, when I can fly to your arms and ask you to marry me. Yours devotedly, etc., Guillaume Durand.' *Guillaume?* ... Let's check the date. Aha! – exactly a year ago. All right, I must go see William! (*She puts the letter back in her bosom.*) And here he comes right now.

SCENE XVII
Actors, *as before*; William, *dressed as at beginning of play*

William: [*in English*] Oh, Miss Malvina, are we free at last from the importunities of those fellows?

Malvina: [*in French*] I beg your pardon?

William: [*in French*] Oh, sorry – I always forget, when I'm with you. Yet as you're well aware, there is nothing in the world I wouldn't do to please you. Question of habit, you see! All right – it's settled. Not another word of English.

Malvina: Very good. And now I have a few words to say to you on the subject of a certain young woman from this village, a girl you knew quite well, it seems, and whom you should certainly still be able to recognize.

William: A girl?

Malvina: A girl whom you love tenderly, and to whom you write charming love-letters.

William: (*surprised*) You must be jesting. There's only one person in the world whom I love, and most deeply!

Malvina: Well then, why shouldn't this young woman be the one you're speaking of?

William: Oh, Miss – why are you trying not to understand me? All right, since you're talking like this about some girl, I would certainly like to know what her name is.

Malvina: You remember the girl we met this morning, and whom you refused to recognize?

William: (*blundering*) Oh – Eugénie! (*Aside.*) Numbskull! What have I said?

Malvina: Precisely. But how is it you didn't know her name this morning, when I asked you, and when in fact I criticized you for the rude way you behaved towards her?

William: (*stammering*) I ... uh ... don't know ... I think ... I think someone told me her name, since then ...

Malvina: Is it really true you didn't recognize her? Come, be honest about it!

William: Well, perhaps I did ... But I must say, you surprise me, Miss. What are you getting at with all these questions, if you don't mind?

Malvina: Actually, I'm quite interested in this girl – who is in love with you, or at least who *was* ...

William: Would it be too much to ask you to tell me why it is you're so interested in a mere peasant like her?

Malvina: I've several reasons. (*Pulling the letter from her bosom.*) But here's the one which will perhaps best explain, far better than I could with my own words, why this mere peasant, as you call her, has all my sympathy. (*She hands the letter to* William, *who reads the address and remains dumbfounded.*) You recognize *that*, I'm sure! There's a certain portrait which goes with this letter, too. (*She hands him the portrait.*)

William: (*aside*) Damned rotten luck! (*He tears up the letter and destroys the portrait. Aloud.*) I suppose this little fool's actions – it was probably jealousy that drove her to hand these things over to you – have won you over too, and now your sympathy ...

Malvina: (*interrupting*) Please, sir! Don't add to your discredit with accusations against an innocent person! I found these things while I was out for a stroll near here. No doubt the poor girl lost them. Here's how things appear to me at the moment: either you *were* really in love with this girl and are now treating her shabbily because she still loves you (which amounts, at the very least, to ingratitude and cruelty); or else you've simply acted like a lot of heartless men of your age: you simply took advantage of her vulnerable state and her gullibility – and that's not the way a decent man behaves. I'm sorry to be lecturing you like this. I wouldn't be doing so, if I didn't know you're too intelligent and mature to be offended by it ...

William: All right, Miss, if I must ...

Malvina: Yes?

William: I do admit that ... I was once in love with that girl.

Malvina: Well, why hide it from me, then? And why treat her so harshly?

William: (*hesitantly*) Oh, Malvina! ... It's because I ... I was afraid ... you wouldn't like that ...

Malvina: You can't be serious!

William: Malvina, since I first met you, I call heaven to witness, you are the only person on earth that has all my love and affection. I couldn't tell you ...

Malvina: (*surprised*) Pardon? I don't understand. This is the first time I've ever heard you speak to me like this, Mr William. It's true I was brought up in France, where that sort of thing is taken lightly; but for heaven's sake, never speak to me like that again!

William: (*aside, surprised*) Whatever can she mean? (*Aloud.*) But Miss ...

Malvina: Drop this subject entirely, sir, or I shall lose all the respect I've always felt for you since I had the honour of making your acquaintance!

William: Oh, Malvina! Is respect the only sentiment I have been able to arouse in you up to now? I can't believe I could be this unfortunate! I came here right now to offer you, not only the tribute of a heart that burns for you alone, but also my hand in marriage and the offer of everything I own! (*He throws himself at* Malvina's *knees.*) Oh, Malvina, *please* have pity on me! ...

Malvina: (*bursting into laughter*) Ha, ha, ha! (William *rises to his feet.*)

SCENE XVIII
Actors, *as before*; Brown, *with* Eugénie's *arm in his*; Baptiste; *and* Flore

Brown: Allo! I see you have big fun by here? (*To* Eugénie.) Miss Yewjenny, I have the honour of introduce you my sister Malvina (Eugénie *bows*.) Malvina, this is Miss Eugénie, who is agree to marry with me! (*To* William.) My dear friend, I inviting you at my wedding ... and Baptiste, she invite you to his also. We have two wedding on same time!

Baptiste: Hey, I hope they's gonna be three! You ain't countin' out Guillotte's weddin'? Maybe his missin'-trophy will get cured by then, jest like his sore eyes an' stuff, etcetera, amen ...

Malvina: (*still laughing*) Ha, ha, ha! ...

William: (*to* Malvina) How cruel you are!

Malvina: Ha, ha, ha! ...

Brown: Why in devil she laugh so much? (Louis *and* Joseph *arrive, looking surprised.*)

Malvina: Mr William absolutely insists he wants to marry me!

Brown: (*laughing*) Oh, ha, ha, ha! – Me forget to tell ...

William: I really don't understand what's so laughable about this ...

Brown: Oh, she is be already marry!

William: What!

Malvina: Don't be angry, Mr William – or if you really want to hold anyone responsible, it should be your good friend, my brother here. I strongly suspect he's the cause of this whole misunderstanding ...

Brown: (*to* Malvina) I was always tell him and everyones that you still not marry. And I tell especially Mr William that you be very found of him.

William: (*aside, clenching his fist in exasperation*) Oh, the wretch!

Malvina: (*to* William) Did you hear that? Since you never asked me I always assumed, up till now, that you were aware my husband is in France, and will in fact soon be coming to this country to join me ...

Brown: And anyways 'Miss' and 'Mrs,' they be nearly sinny-names, no? (*He laughs.*) Ho, ho, ho!

Malvina: So! – There's another of his tricks, I suspect. (*To* Flore.) Miss Flore, are the words 'mademoiselle' and 'madame' really synonyms in this country, as my brother informed me?

Flore: We say 'Mademoiselle' or 'Miss' to ... to an unmarried woman ...

Malvina: Enough! – Oh, that terrible brother of mine! I'll never trust him again.

Brown: Oh, Malvina, that is not much easy to believe. You not so dumb like that. You know well a 'Miss' is not a 'Mrs,' but you be half French, and so you like all other womens, you liking your role in this affair. So I not the only one who be guilty!

Malvina: (*laughing*) Ha, ha, ha! ... You're always such a hoaxer! ...

Brown: (*to* William) My friend, I beg many pardonings from you. This be all only for fun, you know. I hope you not being angry?

William: (*aside*) Oh, you despicable huckster! ... (*Aloud.*) I have no more need to be nice to you – and you'll pay for this! (*He leaves.*)

Brown: (*aside*) Oh! he be damn anger now!

SCENE XIX
Actors, *as before; except* William

Malvina: (*taking* Eugénie's *hand*) Miss, I was already informed of your virtues and your admirable qualities, and I am delighted with this marriage, which will bring honour to my brother and to my whole family, and which will no doubt lead to life-long and intimate friendship between the two of us!

Eugénie: (*to* Malvina) Miss – or rather, Madame – I don't know how to show my gratitude ...

Baptiste: (*To* Flore) My! Them townsfolk, they's funny people! Say, you sure *you* ain't already married, huh?

Flore: (*laughing*) I'm not really sure ...

Joseph: (*to* Louis) I'll be hanged if I understand the least bit of all this.

Louis: (*to* Joseph) Well, I can tell you I'm astounded by the whole thing, too ... But after all, thinking it over ...

Joseph: (*to* Louis) It was a misunderstanding, as far as I can see, and ...

Brown: Yes, genitalmans – and I think me act also much rashly, and now my friend William terrible angry to me. But I soon chase angriness away from him, I swear at you! (*To* Louis.) I am hope, sir, this little surprising happening not will change friendness who exist between us – or I be plenty sad!

Louis: On the contrary, sir, I am more your friend than ever, and I hope the silly little things that happened today – I hope William will learn from them – will not in any way disturb our enjoyment here. I hope we can stay at my brother's, at least until the two weddings take place, if he doesn't object ...

Joseph: (*to* Louis) Come, come – how can you talk like that? (*To the others.*) First, I'm going to go see Guillotte; and then ...

Brown: (*interrupting*) I will un-bore William plenty quick ... but not now. Oh, he terrible mad now!

Joseph: And later – tomorrow, that is – there'll be marriage contracts, the wedding ceremony, good food and drink, singing and dancing, fun, and pleasure for all, by cracky! Oh – while I think of it, and before I go to see Guillotte, it'd be a good idea for us all to take a little stroll by the lakeshore. You don't get to see this spot too often, and you'll enjoy it. Come along, friends!

He exits, singing 'À la Claire Fontaine.' Brown and the others follow, singing as well. When the villagers have disappeared in the wings, there is a rapid scene change showing a wood, with Lac Calvaire in the background. The villagers cross over again, further backstage, still singing, and disappear at rear. The curtain falls, and the orchestra continues to play 'À la Claire Fontaine.'

V

Félix Poutré

INTRODUCTION

1. History of the Play

Félix Poutré was by far the most popular play by a Canadian author to come out of nineteenth-century Quebec. Its première took place on the evening of 22 November 1862 at Quebec City's Salle de Musique, where Petitclair's *A Country Outing* had also been first staged five years earlier. The performance had been preceded by an extensive advertising campaign in the capital's newspapers, for the occasion was to be a special one: the cream of Quebec society was to be in attendance, there would be a full orchestra, and it would play a selection of patriotic songs to enliven the intermissions. And the author – the authors, more precisely – would be in attendance.

This was astute advertising, for the name of the titular hero-'author' had come to special prominence by the late autumn of 1862. The best-seller of the year had been the memoirs of forty-eight-year-old Félix Poutré, published in the spring with the title, *Échappé de la potence: souvenirs d'un prisonnier d'état canadien en 1838*, republished in French and in English translation (*Escaped from the Gallows: Souvenirs of a Canadian State Prisoner in 1838*)[1] before the end of the same year, which is in itself proof of the thin book's astonishing popularity. Now, a dramatized version, the work of a young poet and occasional essayist, Louis-Honoré Fréchette, currently articling for the legal profession, would be presented.

The première was, by all accounts, a brilliant success. Fréchette gave a short, stirring speech before the curtain rose, the twenty-three year old dramatist and the author of the memoirs were both warmly applauded by the large audience, and afterwards newspaper accounts were glowing.[2] Two months later the play was revived. Within two years it had become a classic of the amateur stage; within two decades it would become the play most often staged throughout French Canada and the Franco-American communities of New England, and it would remain so until the advent of *Aurore l'enfant martyre* in the 1920s. Jean Béraud, one of the first historians of Quebec theatre, recounts that a journalistic colleague, Aimé Blanchard, managed to carve out a second, lifelong career in the title role of *Félix Poutré*, one of the most sought-after roles until well into the twentieth century.[3] Its most recent revival was as a one-hour radio adaptation by Radio-Canada in 1953.[4]

How does one explain the astounding success of this play, in the light of its serious imperfections when viewed by any critical eye? A good part of the answer undoubtedly lies in the timing of its première; the rest must come from an analysis of Fréchette's text itself, in its virtues as well as its defects.

2. The Historical Context

The timing was impeccable: twenty-five years less a day after the battle of Saint-Denis – the first serious confrontation in the uprisings of 1837–8 in French Canada, and the only military victory achieved by the Patriote side – a new, corrective perspective on the rebellion was now offered, purportedly through the eyes of a major participant in the conflicts of 1838. In the interval most of the surviving leaders, along with virtually all the exiles, had returned, and many were now active in politics (the best example being George-Étienne Cartier, a Patriote veteran of the battle of Saint-Denis and currently co-premier, with John A. Macdonald, of the united Province of Canada). The hardships, the injustice, and all the unresolved issues stemming from the two uprisings, as perceived by the generation that had lived through them, were depicted for his own generation by Louis Fréchette, born the year after the conflict had ended. This was the first treatment on the public stage of the rebellions, and it came at a time when Lower Canada (Canada East), ever mindful of its past, was seriously re-examining its current role and its prospective future within the united province.

In a North American context, moreover, with the Civil War worsening to the south and threatening to engulf Canada, many French Canadians saw the whole status of their nationhood again open to question. The defeat of the Cartier ministry in May 1862 on the question of a standing militia to defend Canada's southern border had aroused bitter memories, old fears, and old options, particular for those who, like the still influential Louis-Joseph Papineau, overtly favoured union with the United States. (His ardent admirer, Fréchette, would later adopt this stance as well.) The remarkable success of Poutré's poorly written, mendacious memoirs shows how deep the currents ran that he had managed to tap.

3. The Relationship between Fréchette's Play and Poutré's Memoirs

Then there is the play itself. Critics have concentrated almost exclusively on its textual proximity to Poutré's memoirs, thereby tying the play's fate to that of its spurious source.[5] Nowadays it seems more appropriate, and more illustrative of Fréchette's skill as an adaptor, to concentrate on the major differences between the two texts, for it would have been utterly impossible to transpose the memoirs to the stage without serious modifications.

The most striking of these differences is what comprises the first act in published editions of the play (some or all of it had apparently been a Prologue in the first stage version),[6] in which the villain Camel's treachery is revealed, then countered, and the newly recruited hero's solemn swearing-in by the other conspirators – he has come to Montreal for the occasion – is impressively depicted. The *Souvenirs* had presented, with typical blandness, a very different version of how Félix had been recruited on his father's farm near Saint-Jean-sur-Richelieu, and of his motive for joining the rebellion. For the sake of contrast, this is how the episode reads in the curious, often gallicized English of the 1862 edition:

On the third of September, 1838, whilst working with some dozen men on my father's farm, I saw two men coming towards me through the fields. One of them was Dr. Côté,[7] of Napierville. I was slightly acquainted with him, he shook hands with me and introduced me to his friend, Dr. Robert Nelson.[8] After a few words of conversation, I gradually retired until out of hearing of the men who surrounded me. Dr. Côté then suddenly addressing me, said: 'Poutré, we are on our march to overthrow the government, will you join us?' I had then just 21 years; I was strongly affected by anglophobia; boiling with rage since a long time, not only on account of the useless outrages committed that year, but I had moreover at heart to humble our St. John's loyalists,[9] and repay with bitterness their shabby tyranny, the stupid vexations to which we had continually been subject to [*sic*]. I fancied that I saw them pass before me with their haughty air, their disdainful look, with an expression of satisfaction at our humiliation, and I could not help saying unto myself: 'Ah! That I could for once have my turn.' Besides I found that labour was rather hard; a revolution promised me an excellent means of advancement and an only chance of appearing with haughty mien before our enraged loyalists. I therefore replied to Côté:
– That will do for me. It will exactly suit my plans; the heat is powerful in the fields, and I would to a certainty prefer to be governor of the country.
– Not so fast, not so fast, replied he; you are not the only one to be provided for.[10]

Fréchette, to his great credit, must have seen how ineffective this original text would be on-stage, and how ambiguous the rationale for his protagonist's commitment to the Patriote cause might appear. In its place he created a compelling scene, with its atmosphere of highly organized conspiracy, charged with tangible, personal danger. The most striking and original element of the first act is the portrayal of the arch-villain Camel's scheme, its subsequent discovery, and his apparent punishment. Camel's role, although lacking in certain vital dimensions, is central to the play. It must also be stressed that he is almost entirely Fréchette's creation (there is only a brief reference to a traitor, identified as 'D ...,' in Poutré's memoirs). Whereas the memoirs had pitted Poutré diffusely against ineffective, dishonest Patriote leaders (Côté and Robert Nelson) and various representatives of governmental authority, the principal, visible conflict in the play is between Félix and his nemesis, Camel. The result is an economy of structure and heightened, personalized intensity of dramatic emotion. The combined dynamics are far more effective theatrically, albeit far closer to those of a 'recipe' melodrama of the type then immensely popular in European and American theatre.

Another difference between the play and the memoirs is the introduction by Fréchette of frequent visual and verbal humour, especially the unconscious and unsophisticated verbal humour of Toinon, the stereotypical country bumpkin who is the main victim of Félix's mad pranks and a character totally absent from Poutré's text. This combines with yet another important factor in the contemporary success of Fréchette's adaptation: the injection of popular speech and of popular and patriotic songs into the text itself (we have noted that songs and musical accompaniment were also provided for the intermissions). Thus, after the strong impact of act 1, the second act opens with a troop of Patriote recruits singing, at first in the distance, then nearer, until they cross the stage and exit. Their song echoes the vocabulary of the 'Marseillaise' and the French Revolution, with lines borrowed from Casimir Delavigne's *La Parisienne*,[11] and would no doubt have been accompanied by the orchestra that we know was present. Act 3, set in prison, lets us hear the final words, off-stage, of the Patriote leaders Cardinal and Duquette before the gallows-trap is sprung beneath them. Duquette's last gesture is, again, to intone the first words of the 'Marseillaise' while the prisoners kneel and sing a patriotic response, as they will do again later in the act to affirm their solidarity. As to their speech, only the caricatural Toinon uses what Fréchette intends as popular *québécois* idiom. As with Petitclair's servants in *The Donation*, however, his diction is not really convincing, owing far more to the worn traditions of Molière's rural domestics than to the linguistic reality of contemporary working-class Quebec. Moreover, and again in line with other models in nineteenth-century Quebec literature, non-standard speech is here equated with low intelligence – an attitude only too characteristic of the educated, professional class to which the young dramatist aspired to belong.

The first act is the only completely original one, but Fréchette must also be given credit for the dramatization of Poutré's lifeless text in the rest of the play as well. The following examples illustrate this. Act 1 ends with the young hero at the summit of his fortune, proclaiming that 'in six months Félix Poutré will be dead, or be a great man!' Act 2, only slightly longer than the very brief act 1, presents the rapid evolution of his fate and that of his co-conspirators: misled by Côté and Nelson and betrayed by the escapee Camel, he surprises the audience by surrendering, in the last scene, in order to save his father's life and property. The gloomy prophecy of act 1 is about to be fulfilled, it appears. In the memoirs the events of act 2 take twenty-two dense pages to recount – half the length of Poutré's entire text, because the text is interlarded with digressive tirades against British authorities, failed Patriote leaders, and unjust governmental policies towards the rebels. In the memoirs Félix hides out in the woods for a fortnight and only surrenders to the authorities *after* he has hatched his plan to save his skin by feigning madness. In the play his surrender takes place on the same day he returns to his father's house from the disastrous battle at Odelltown. Even minor touches are revelatory of Fréchette's dramatic sense: in the memoirs Félix has just arrived at his father's house when he is told that the British troops are only half a league or twenty minutes' march away and are on their way to seize him, but in the play this becomes a quarter of a league and he has only ten minutes to decide whether to flee to the woods or stay and surrender.

These changes mainly heighten dramatic suspense but there are more important dimensions to some of them as well. Félix's feigned madness, effective but hardly heroic, is a carefully planned strategy in the memoirs, developed while the narrator is in hiding. Fréchette, conscious of the ambivalence of this central action in the memoirs, has Félix decide to play the madman only after his imprisonment and the execution of Cardinal and Duquette, when he realizes he also will soon be tried summarily for treason. In a conversation with his friend Béchard, Félix asks the latter's advice, explaining to him that the idea of feigning insanity first came to him in a dream the night before his arrest. Béchard doubts the ploy will succeed, but agrees that it is the *only* chance he has. Obviously all this preparation serves to attenuate the effect on the spectator and reader of this 'unheroic' device to save his own skin. It also underlines one of the most fascinating aspects of the play's structure for modern readers, its dependence on refractive role-playing within the larger 'play,' and in turn the play's refraction of Poutré's memoirs, which themselves play outrageously with what we now know as historical truth (they were, it appears, in large part ghost-written – or at least rewritten – by the journalist Médéric Lanctôt).

Other touches that are added by Fréchette, such as the visit by Félix's father to his 'mad' son in prison, inject pathos into the dry text and increase our sympathy for both men. Cardinal and Duquette, whom patriotic historians had by 1862 made into martyrs for the Patriote cause, are mentioned only in passing in the memoirs but are given important roles in the play, especially in act 1 where they entrap Camel, and act 3 where, after eloquent (and unhistorical)[12] final exhortations to their comrades, they die heroically – off-stage but within our hearing. Finally there is the expansion – often amounting to 'milking'– of some incidents barely mentioned in the memoirs, for well-documented stage effect. The most notable of these are Félix's verbal and physical assaults on judge, sheriff, and lawyers in act 4, scene 2, and his physical revenge on the francophobic prison doctor, Arnoldi (based on a historical character)[13] in act 4, scene 7, scenes that were apparently expanded *ad lib* by amateur actors to thunderous local acclaim.[14]

In short, the play's demonstrable on-stage success owes more to what Fréchette added than to what he borrowed from Poutré's *Souvenirs*, and the young author's willingness to share the spotlight with Poutré at the première in 1862 was rather generous for the time. If Fréchette had been as forthright with regard to his later dramatic works, the sad reputation they bear would have been avoided. The sorry tale of his plagiarisms from other authors (*Le Retour de l'exilé* of 1880 'borrowed' without credit from the novel *La Bastide* by French author Élie Berthet; *Véronica* in 1903, written in large part by his acquaintance Maurice de Pradel, for financial considerations) has been fully documented elsewhere.[15] It is certainly legitimate to suspect that the almost universal dismissal by later critics of *Félix Poutré* is to some degree due to their awareness of these subsequent plagiarisms. Putting aside such considerations, the reader is invited to approach the text as a unique example of what really 'turned on' popular theatre audiences and as an extensive illustration of the *mise en abyme*, or play-within-a-play phenomenon, which is very rare in nineteenth-century French Canada.

4. Language

The language used in this play is generally standard, 'international' French, and it is sometimes disconcertingly literary when Fréchette stays too close to his source, reproducing for example, the verbal tenses (*passé simple* and *imparfait du subjonctif*) that have long disappeared from the spoken language (direct quotations from the stilted English of Poutré's memoirs are introduced in act 2, scene 6 to demonstrate their parallel effect on the reader). There are two exceptions: the language of Toinon, a caricature of non-standard, rural speech, and the fractured, heavily anglicized French of Dr Arnoldi, which I have chosen to render into fractured English, as I did for the character Brown in Petitclair's *A Country Outing*.

[LOUIS-HONORÉ FRECHETTE] [16]

Félix Poutré

A HISTORICAL DRAMA IN FOUR ACTS

CHARACTERS

Félix Poutré, twenty-one years old
Poutré Senior, Félix's father, sixty years old[17]
Béchard, forty years old
Cardinal, member of Parliament, thirty-five years old
Duquette, a law student, twenty-one years old
Toinon, a peasant,[18] twenty-one years old
Camel, a traitor, thirty years old
Dr. Arnoldi, sixty years old
Sheriff
Jailer
A Judge
First Conspirator
Second Conspirator
Third Conspirator
A Policeman
Hangman; English Soldiers; Policemen; Patriotes;
Prisoners; Officers of the Law

ACT ONE

Setting: *Rue Saint-Jean-Baptiste in Montreal, at night*

SCENE I
Camel, a Policeman

Camel: (*wrapped in a heavy overcoat*) You see that door, don't you?

Policeman: Yes.

Camel: Well, that's the one. You're to arrive at midnight, understand? That's when all the Patriotes will be meeting.

Policeman: Are there many of them?

Camel: That depends. In any case, come well prepared, because those outlaws are armed and may offer stiff resistance. And be sure you protect me, in case they turn on me ...

Policeman: Don't worry! What part of the building are they meeting in?

Camel: You'll be led to it. Since it's strictly forbidden to use any sort of light in the hallway, they won't see your uniforms until you've been let into the meeting room itself. The password is 'Vengeance and Liberty!' And when they ask, 'Who goes there?,' you're to answer, 'Brutus!'

Policeman: Very good.

Camel: Understood, then? See you at midnight.

Policeman: At midnight. (*He leaves.*)

SCENE II
Camel, *alone*

Aha! I've got them now – they won't get away this time! Caught in the same net, almost the whole lot of them! The government will certainly be beholden to me. There'll be a nice reward, too! Oh, but what a lot of patience, tact, and courage I've needed to get to this point! Passing myself off as a Patriote, getting accepted by the conspirators themselves, convincing them all with my loud declarations of devotion to their cause ... I've done all that with skill, with talent, with genius! Camel, Camel, you're a great man indeed! Destined to become prime minister, at very least! ... Well, it must be ten o'clock by now, and they should all be there together. Let's go in. (*He knocks three times on a door at stage rear, pausing between knocks.*)

Voice: (*off-stage*) The password?

Camel: Vengeance and Liberty! (*The door opens and* Camel *enters. The setting changes to represent a basement room. Several conspirators are gathered around a table. Weapons of all sorts hang from the walls.*)

SCENE III
Cardinal, Camel, Conspirators

Cardinal: Is there any news from the United States?

First Conspirator: Yes, two of our people are in New York City organizing support committees. Number 36 left for Washington, to meet with the authorities there. Number 17 writes from Burlington that a large quantity of arms is to be shipped from Albany and that he's making preparations to get them to us at the first sign that our insurrection is to begin. On the whole, the Americans are entirely sympathetic to our cause, and will no doubt supply all the arms and ammunition we shall need.

Conspirators: Bravo!

Cardinal: (*consulting his notes*) Has number 20 returned from Quebec City?

Second Conspirator: Here I am. I attended the Brothers'[19] meeting on Saturday. For the moment, I don't think we can try anything in Quebec City. Apart from a few enthusiastic and committed young men, the whole population is wallowing in terrible apathy. The general feeling is, if there isn't a serious uprising everywhere in the country, there's no use counting on Quebec.

Cardinal: That's about what I've been told as well. And Trois-Rivières?

Second Conspirator: I stopped off there. The local people are even more negative than in Quebec. Impossible to budge. But there is a rather active organization made up of a small number of committed Patriotes who are in close contact with our comrades in Nicolet. They found out from their affiliate in Quebec City that the government intended to send a considerable shipment of arms and ammunition to Montreal, and so they came up with a plan to seize the shipment with one bold stroke. But they don't want to act rashly, and especially not prematurely, so they're awaiting our instructions.

First Conspirator: Why, that's a splendid idea! We need those arms, whatever the risk!

Camel: Arms and ammunition: that's all we need! (*Aside.*) Another bit of useful information. You'd be tempted to think Providence itself is on my side!

Cardinal: And number 27 – is he back in Montreal?

First Conspirator: Yes, we're expecting him right here at any moment. They say he's accomplished wonders south of here. When he gives a speech, the whole countryside rises, to a man! If we succeed, we'll owe a large share of our success to him.

Cardinal: Stout fellow! If everyone had the same courage and the same sort of dedication ... (*A knock is heard at the door.*) Hush! – perhaps that's him now!

Third Conspirator: Who goes there?

Duquette: (*off-stage*) Brutus!

Cardinal: That's his voice. It's him!

Third Conspirator: The password?

Duquette: (*off-stage*) Vengeance and Liberty!

Third Conspirator: (*opening the door*) Come in! (Duquette *enters.*)

SCENE IV
Actors, *as before*; Duquette

Duquette: Brothers, peace be with you, and God save Canada!

Conspirators: God save Canada!

Cardinal: (*leading* Duquette *to stage front*) My dear Duquette! (*He takes his hand.*)

Duquette: My dear Cardinal!

Cardinal: Be very careful – something tells me there's a traitor in our midst.

Duquette: A traitor!

Cardinal: Yes, I've had my eye on him for quite some time, and right now I'm trying to trick him into betraying himself. I hope it works!

Duquette: And then what do we do with him?

Cardinal: We'll see. For the moment, the most important thing is to smoke him out.

Camel: (*aside*) I'd give a lot to know what they're talking about so secretly. If they're hatching some plot, they're certainly not expecting what's going to happen to them tonight!

Cardinal: (*to* Duquette) What about your trip? They say you accomplished wonders.

Duquette: I did succeed, in fact better than I had even hoped. The whole population is very well disposed towards us. Four thousand men are already enlisted and ready to move as soon as we can provide them with weapons. But let's talk about that when we have more time. I did see that young man from Napierville you told me about.

Cardinal: Poutré?

Duquette: Yes.

Cardinal: Well, then?

Duquette: Twenty-one years old, with an athlete's build. A wrist of steel and a heart of oak. What's more, he's really popular with the country folk. He's certainly just the man we need for that region. Dr Côté spoke with him, and asked me to bring him to Montreal for your instructions.

Cardinal: He's here?

Duquette: Yes, in the next room. Shall I bring him in?

Cardinal: Right away! (Duquette *leaves.*) Brothers, the news from the countryside to the south of us is extremely encouraging. Within the next three weeks, the banner of independence will be unfurled in several places at once; and within a month, I hope, the whole country will rise as one to put down its oppressors!

Conspirators: Hurrah!!

Cardinal: But let's not be overhasty – that was our undoing last year. Our campaign was heroic, but untimely and poorly planned, and that imperilled our cause. Too much heart and not enough head! Let's have no wild enthusiasm, but rather cool-headedness in our planning and lots of energy in its execution. And dedication, above all! This year we shall succeed where last year we failed. But make no bones about it: we need courage and caution, for we are risking the fate of an entire nation on one roll of the dice! (*Knocking is heard at the door.*)

Third Conspirator: Who goes there?

Duquette: (*off-stage*) Brutus!

Third Conspirator: The password?

Duquette: (*off-stage*) Vengeance and Liberty!

Third Conspirator: (*opening the door*) Enter! (Duquette *and* Félix *enter.*)

SCENE V
Actors, *as before*; Félix

Duquette: (*to* Cardinal) Here he is.

Camel: (*aside*) Félix Poutré! That wretched creature hell keeps casting in my way! He, above all, is the one I must get!

Cardinal: (*to* Félix, *shaking his hand*) Well, well, young man! You know what the situation is: are you with us?

Félix: Gentlemen, if your aim is to overturn the government and give the English a good strong enema, you can count on me. I've been itching to do that for a long time, and by damn I can hardly wait to rough up a few redcoats!

Cardinal: All in good time – you'll have your wish before long! Since you're an intelligent lad, full of goodwill, and a good Patriote to boot, you can play an important role if you want to. But you have to be ready for anything.

Félix: Don't worry – I am!

Cardinal: Think about this carefully. It's a very serious business we're getting into. The lives of all of us are at stake, and once we start, there's no pulling back. We have to see it through to the end, come what may!

Félix: I'm not the type to worry about pulling back. And I've done all the careful thinking I need to. I want to free my country and I'm behind you all the way, whatever may happen. But all the same, we would do well to be careful this time, because sometimes things can go against us ...

Duquette: It's precisely because we *didn't* succeed last year that we shall have experience on our side this time. You see, we now know where our mistakes were made ...

Félix: I can tell you right off where your main mistake was made: sending the farmers off to fight armed with muskets that didn't even have any locks! How did you expect us to drive off the Englishmen with guns no better than wooden sticks? You want us to fight? Well, we're ready to. And you'll find real men, I can tell you! But give us arms, at least: muskets, cannons, gunpowder, and ammunition. With those, I promise you, the English will get a real drubbing.

Cardinal: You'll get your guns and bullets. We've taken all the necessary steps. Right now, we have agents in the United States who are busy obtaining all those things for us. At the moment, the most important thing is to secure financial support. There are two urgent considerations: first of all, the organization of committees that will become military companies later on; and secondly, to raise as much money as possible to purchase the armaments we need. You're well known in the region of Napierville. Will you take on both those tasks for us?

Félix: You know my answer.

Cardinal: Good! I expected no less, knowing your patriotism, Félix Poutré. I am going to swear you in, and you can set to work immediately. (*He hands him a Bible, and all the conspirators surround* Félix, *raising their right hands.*) Do you swear to God and to your country to devote all your energies and all your courage to drive the English from Canada's soil, and do you swear never to cease in your efforts while a single one remains within its borders? (*He kisses the Bible and steps back.*)[20]

Conspirators: Amen!

Cardinal: The country is counting on you now, Félix Poutré. Keep this Bible and canvas the countryside, administering the same oath to all who wish to join us. At the same time, we shall be soliciting contributions to be used to buy the weapons we need for our success. Will you do that, conscientiously and at the same time discreetly?

Félix: I so promise, on my own head, and on my honour![21] (*A knock is heard.*)

Third Conspirator: Who goes there?

Voice: (*off-stage*) Brutus!

Third Conspirator: The password?

Voice: Vengeance and Liberty!

Third Conspirator: (*opening the door*) Enter! (*Ten policemen enter.*)

SCENE VI
Actors, *as before*; Policemen

Conspirators: We've been betrayed!!

Camel: (*aside*) So soon! They weren't supposed to be here until midnight!

Duquette: Come on, let's defend ourselves! Death to the traitor!

Cardinal: Calm down, Duquette – let me handle this.

Camel: (*going to the policemen*) These men are all conspirators. They have sworn to overthrow Her Majesty's government. I denounce them! (*Pointing to* Cardinal.)

There's their leader! (*Pointing to* Félix.) And here's their latest recruit, who's perhaps the most dangerous of all!

Conspirators: The traitor!

Cardinal: The scoundrel!

Camel: (*showing the policemen a paper*) Here are my orders, signed by the sheriff. Officers, arrest them all! (*No one moves.*) Arrest them all, I say – don't let a single one escape!

Cardinal: (*to the policemen, pointing to* Camel) Brothers, seize this traitor. (*To* Camel.) Oh, you coward! – I've suspected for some time that you were betraying us, and I've been watching you. You've been setting traps for us, but like a fool you've fallen into one yourself! You thought these men were mercenaries of that government to whose vile interests you yourself toady, but in fact they're our own people, as you can see. I had them put on these uniforms just to get you to drop your mask. And now that we've seen what you really are, we know what we have to do with you ...

Conspirators: Put him to death!

Camel: Mercy! For the love of God!

Cardinal: Mercy? You filthy spy! If you were worth the trouble, I'd blow your brains out like an old, rotten pumpkin, and throw your foul carcass to the dogs! But the arms we have taken up for our country's liberation must not be soiled by the blood of a traitor. Into our jail, you swine! There you will await the punishment your treachery deserves! (*They throw* Camel *into the cellar.*)

Conspirators: Well done! Bravo!

Cardinal: Brothers, we've just escaped great danger. Let us thank Providence, which is so obviously protecting the cause for which we are fighting! And now let's get to work. Here are your sealed orders, in which each of you will find the password and our leaders' orders. Take them. Be *very* careful – and God save Canada!

Conspirators: God save Canada!

Cardinal: (*to* Duquette) Come with me. (*To* Félix.) It's settled, young man? Farewell, then: in life or in death! (*He shakes* Félix's *hand.*) Let's go. (*All exit.*)

Félix: (*remaining behind, alone*) In six months Canada will be free. And what about me? In six months Félix Poutré will be dead, or be a great man! (*He exits.*)

ACT TWO

SCENE I
A highway. Singing is heard in the distance. The sound draws nearer, and a band of Patriotes *enters stage right, singing.*

One of the Patriotes:
Onward! March on! (*etc.*)
O Canadians, brave race,
Liberty opens her arms to you again!
They told us: Slaves you will remain!
And we answered: We'll be soldiers instead!
So, to arms! Proud Patriotes!
Let us revive the sansculottes![22]

Onward! March on
Against the cannons,
Through fire, sword, and the enemy's ranks!
March on! And down with all tyrants! (*bis*).

Chorus: Onward! March on! (*etc.*) (*All exit left, still singing.*)

Toinon, *alone on-stage, with a huge, rusty sabre on his shoulder*

By Saint Anne's boots, if I could just clobber me one Englishman! Even just a teeny-weeny one, wit' me dead grampa's sabre here! Poor ol' guy sure woulda liked that! (*Starts to exit, singing off-key.*) 'Onward! March up! ...'

[Toinon, Cardinal, *and* Duquette]

Cardinal: (*to* Toinon) Boy! Wait! I want to talk to you. (*To* Duquette.) You say he's escaped?

Duquette: Yes, here's the letter I've just received. (*Reads.*) 'Camel escaped yester-day from the cell where we had imprisoned him. Even as I write, we have no doubt that all of us have been identified and betrayed. I am told the traitor left for Napierville this morning. So be on the alert! Signed, number 12.' As you can see, there's no time to lose.

Cardinal: Then he's probably in Napierville right now.

Duquette: Very possibly.

Cardinal: (*to* Toinon) Do you know Captain Félix Poutré, boy?

Toinon: Well, I sure guess I do!

Cardinal: Good. Run along to Napierville, then, and tell him that Camel has escaped from prison, that he must be in that area right now, and that he must be intercepted at all costs. Go on – you'll be rewarded for this.

Toinon: Right you is! (*Exits left, singing.*) 'When the fire hit the fir-trees, it sure made flames, sure made flames ...' (Cardinal *and* Duquette *follow him. The stage opens to represent the inside of* Poutré's *house.*)

SCENE II
Poutré Senior, *and* Camel, *seated*

Camel: I tell you he *was* there, and that damned mob had the gall to attack Odell-town,[23] where the loyalists were making a stand. The rebels fought for two whole days, like the crazy criminals they are. Luckily they were only armed with a few inferior muskets and the government troops had no trouble repelling their attacks.

Poutré: Poor lads!

Camel: Oh yes, 'poor lads' indeed! – Rebels who, if the government gets its hands on them, will surely get what they deserve! You understand, I hope, Monsieur Poutré, that your son may soon be trying on a bit of neckwear that's a lot less comfortable than a groom's necktie!

Poutré: But who told you Félix has joined the rebels? He left for Lacolle a week ago, to take care of some business for me.

Camel: Come, come! – I know what I know! What if I were to tell you that for the past month he's been prowling the countryside, swearing in rebels and raising funds to buy weapons in the States? That he's persuaded more than three thousand misfits to join, has organized committees, held meetings, and collected that whole mob which, I'm very glad to say, has now been made to scatter!

Poutré: (*aside*) The traitor knows everything! (*Aloud.*) What you say is impossible, Camel. My son has never been involved in this country's problems. But I must say, you're certainly plying a despicable trade, slandering your fellow-citizens and making insinuations like that about people's actions ...

Camel: Blah, blah, blah! Listen, old man, if I followed my conscience, I'd report them all, and the government would be most grateful to me! (*The sound of singing is heard in the distance: 'Onward! March on!' etc.*) Listen! Here they come now. (*Gunshots are heard.*) Do you hear that shooting? Probably a skirmish on the other side of the river. It's 7 p.m. right now, and before 11 o'clock tonight the troops will have seized the village. Goodbye, Mr Poutré. (*He leaves.*)

SCENE III
Poutré Senior, *alone*

Goodbye indeed, you damned gallows-feeder! If anyone's to be chased out of this country, they should start with swine like you! ... But Félix still hasn't returned! I do hope nothing has happened to him. Who knows what his headstrong temperament might make him do! O Lord, he's the only hope for my old age! (*A group of Patriotes enters, singing. They are armed with pitchforks, scythes, and crude firearms.*)

SCENE IV
Poutré Senior, Béchard, Toinon, Patriotes

Poutré: Well, Béchard? (*He shakes his hand.*)

Béchard: What about Félix?

Poutré: He's not with you? Good heavens, what's become of him!

Béchard: Last night he left for Lacolle, to look for guns. We're looking for him. And time is running out – he should have been back a long time ago! (*Félix enters.*)

SCENE V
Actors, *as before*; Félix

Béchard: Here he is! Oh, Félix – we've been looking for you for four hours!

Félix: (*discouraged*) No arms, my friends, no arms! Not a single musket, not a single bullet! Friends, we've been cheated, betrayed, sacrificed. Where is he, so I can tell him to his face what sort of man he really is?

Poutré: Who do you mean?

Félix: Dr Côté.

Béchard: They say he's left.

Félix: Damnation! I'm too late! How could I have been so unsuspecting? Oh, the coward! – he's saved his own skin. Ah, if I had only been here he wouldn't have gotten away like that ...!

Béchard: No one saw him leave. We suspect he stole away before daybreak.

Félix: The traitor! Listen, friends, I'll tell you just how treacherous a man can be. You know all the fine promises he made us? Well, after the disastrous attacks on Odelltown, I went to Napierville, to *Dr Côté, and asked of him whether we would be supplied with muskets and guns or not. 'What can we do without cannon,' said I, 'to drive out these rascals from the church? If we have no arms, better to give up at once! Where are the arms promised? Without arms, you know full well that you are leading us to nothing but useless slaughter.' Although he tried to put on a good countenance, I saw by his embarrassment that he had no good news to impart. He appeared to me to be keeping back a secret which tormented him, and I thought he did not look as usual. He recommended me to visit him at Napierville.* I left him, in a bad mood. *I therefore said in my mind: 'We shall see tonight what they will say. It is time that all that nonsense should be put a stop to! To fight against walls with musket balls, would require two months more! If we only had two small guns, how quickly we would dislodge those rascally volunteers! And to think that since upwards of two months they promise to supply us with arms, and not a single musket has arrived yet! And all these confiding and honest men who are all here, are compromised by madmen or traitors! For after all there is no middle course, if they have arms and do not bring them on at once, it is an imbecility without a name; if they have none, these men have been betraying us since two months!*[24] If they had told us right off, 'we can't get any guns for you,' would you even have thought of leaving home?

Patriotes: No! No!

Toinon: No way, I reckon!

Félix: Are we supposed to get ourselves massacred by English soldiers, or swing from the gallows' tree, just for their benefit?

Patriotes: No! No!

Toinon: No way, I reckon!

Félix: But here's the end of my story: that evening I went back to Dr Côté's house. They wouldn't let me in. Around nine o'clock I showed up again: same result. It made no sense to me. Finally I went back at 11 o'clock, determined to get through to him, over ten dead bodies if need be. To my great surprise I entered without difficulty, and Côté said: 'My dear Poutré, we have just heard that troops are marching in the direction of Napierville. They are still five leagues from here, so they should arrive here tomorrow between four or five in the morning. It is reported that they form a column of 5,000 men. Start at daybreak, and proceed to Lacolle where our armaments must have arrived by now. You should find 5,000 muskets there, along with ammunition.' I didn't bother waiting for daylight, but set out for Lacolle, determined to carry out my mission honourably. On the way, I stopped at every house where I expected to find a horse and wagon, and ordered rather than asked people to follow me and pick up the weapons we had been awaiting for so long. When I got to Lacolle, I asked about them. Nothing there! And then the truth hit me like a bolt of lightning: we had been sold out, and Côté had wanted me out of the way so that he could slip away more easily. One less witness against him!

Béchard: Oh, the scoundrel!

Poutré: So what are you going to do now, Félix? The English troops are only a few miles from the village!

Félix: What do you expect us to do against 5,000 regular soldiers, with our 400 shoddy muskets? Oh, if only we had guns, *real* soldiers' guns! But what's the use – it's all over now, that's quite obvious. Let's split up, my poor dear friends, and let's each of us go his separate way. I pity anyone they get their hands on!

Béchard: You're right, Félix, it's all over – for now. The hour of freedom has not yet struck. Let's separate. Farewell, farewell brave friends! (*The Patriotes shake* Félix's *hand, and all leave.*)

Félix: Farewell, brave comrades! May this treachery have no more serious consequences for us!

Toinon: (*aside*) An' t'think I didn't even get to clobber even half o' one of 'em!

SCENE VI
Poutré Senior, Félix, Toinon

Félix: Yes, it's all over. Oh, the traitors! (*He gazes at his musket, then kisses it.*) Farewell, faithful musket! This is the second time you've fought for your country; and in better days ahead, may you again defend the right cause! (*He hangs his musket on the wall, and sits down sadly.*)

Toinon: Cap'n? (*Silence.*) Meanin' no disrespects, Cap'n, sir ...

Félix: What do you want?

Toinon: Well the thing of it is, Cap'n ...

Félix: Enough of this damn 'Captain' stuff – what do you want?

Toinon: (*aside*) By Saint Anne's boots! – he sure is jittery! (*Aloud.*) Like, I been given a sort o' message to give you ...

Félix: Well, what is it?

Toinon: Well, there was this important-like fella ... some sort o'general, I guess, an' he says to me, 'Do you know Félix Poutré?' he says. 'Young Felisk, ol' Poutré's son?' says I. 'Well I sure reckon so!' I says. 'You're to go and find him,' he says to me. 'Well okay,' says I – oh, did I mention they was two o' them there generals?

Félix: Are you going to tell me or not? What's the message?

Toinon: Well, here she be: 'Tell Mr Felisk,' he says to me, 'that Camel ...'

Félix: What!

Toinon: ... 'that Camel is around here somewheres, an' you gotta git holt o' him, 'cause ...'

Félix: Camel, out of prison! That's impossible!

Poutré: Impossible? He was here less than an hour ago.

Félix: I'm doomed! That man has sworn to destroy me. He's already reported me, I'm sure!

Toinon: So there you be. Me message is made, so I'm gonna put away me grampa's sabre now. See you later! An' hey – that Camel guy, he ain't no big problem ... (*He leaves.*)

SCENE VII
Poutré Senior, Félix

Poutré: Well, my dear Félix, now what are you going to do?

Félix: I wouldn't mind having an answer to that, myself!

Poutré: They're going to come and arrest you.

Félix: Quite likely, but what can I do about it? Perhaps they'll let me go: I haven't done all that much, after all ...

Poutré: Not *much*? Think for a minute, Félix! You organized units; for more than a month you went from village to village, swearing in Patriotes; you spoke against the government; you were captain of a company and you fought at Odelltown. And you say you haven't done much? Well, I say you've done more than enough for them to ... poor lad! (*He wipes away a tear.*) Come, no weakness now! The greater the danger, the greater the need for a show of courage. Listen, Félix, the only thing you can do ...

SCENE VII
Félix, Poutré Senior, Béchard

Béchard: Félix had better not stay here a moment longer – they're looking for him! (*Seeing* Félix.) Get away from here; clear out right away! Colonel X just gave orders for your arrest!

Poutré: O God! What can we do?

Félix: How in hell did he found out I was here?

Béchard: Even if he didn't see you, he suspects you're here. And as I was going by that old scoundrel of a colonel's quarters, I noticed Camel coming out ...

Poutré: Oh, the wretch!

Béchard: And the old colonel said as he shut the door (I saw him just as I see you, with his red woollen tuque, and his eyes big as a screech owl's): 'Listen! Get Félix first – if he's with his father, the old man has a sharp nose and won't keep him long. Go to his place at once! I wouldn't want to miss that fellow – I've been watching him for a year.' I understood right away that he meant you and I cut across the fields to tell you. If the roads had been good, I might not have been here in time. But with the condition of the roads right now, they must still be nearly a mile from here. So you have only about ten minutes left. Use your time well: it's urgent, as you can see!

Félix: Thank you, my dear Béchard! (*He shakes his hand.*)

Béchard: All right – and goodnight to all! I'm in a hurry, since I'm not sure about my own situation, either. But listen, Monsieur Poutré, I've done so much running that a wee drop wouldn't do me any harm ...

Poutré: (*bringing a bottle and glasses*) Oh, poor lad! I didn't even think of it, fool that I am! You know, sometimes a person just doesn't have one's wits about him. Please excuse me – it's not my custom to treat my best friends so badly!

Béchard: Think nothing of it, Monsieur Poutré – I know your heart is certainly in the right place! (*They clink their glasses.*)

Poutré: To better days ahead!

Félix: To a free Canada!

Béchard: To a free Canada! And with that, farewell, brave friends – and good luck! (*He leaves.*)

Félix: Farewell!

SCENE IX
Poutré Senior, Félix

Poutré: You can see there's not a minute to waste, Félix! Run! Run and hide in the Thirty-Acre Woods back there! I'll bring you food, tomorrow. (*A knock is heard.*) Go this second, for the love of God! (Félix *exits stage left.*) Who's there?

SCENE X
Poutré Senior, Camel

Camel: (*off-stage*) Open up, Monsieur Poutré! Surely you're not afraid of your friends?

Poutré: Here he is, the scoundrel! (*He opens the door.*)

Camel: (*entering*) Good evening to you, Monsieur Poutré.

Poutré: Good evening.

Camel: Times are hard, Monsieur Poutré.

Poutré: Yes, the poor Canadians have some difficult times ahead of them.

Camel: It's their own fault. Why did they have to rebel against the government? Is there a single country in the whole world as fortunate as this one?

Poutré: Hmm.

Camel: What? You don't think Canadians are lucky to be living under our good government?

Poutré: Look here, Camel, don't try to trap me into anything. I haven't done anything – I thought it was madness, and in fact that's what I told those young men. Unfortunately, once the whole thing started, nothing could hold those poor youngsters back. I would say what they did was foolish, but that's a long way from saying that our government is good. Mind you, I'm not saying it's bad: I'm just not saying anything. Before I would say it was good ... well, you know what I mean, chum. But in any case, that's not why you're here. What do you want?

Camel: So, Monsieur Poutré! You think our government isn't a good one!

Poutré: I'm not saying anything, Camel, as you can see. But let's drop that subject. Tell me why you're here.

Camel: Oh, I just dropped in for a chat, on my way by. But you're up rather late, aren't you, Monsieur Poutré? Waiting for someone?

Poutré: And you're rather inquisitive! I think I have every right to stay up as late as I want.

Camel: Come now – no need to lose your temper, Monsieur Poutré! Have you heard the latest? They say there's been a lot of unfortunate incidents – a lot of people arrested, in particular.

Poutré: That's too bad.

Camel: Why too bad? Don't those scoundrels deserve to be punished for their actions?

Poutré: They're not the ones who would be suffering, if the real guilty ones were to be punished.

Camel: And who are the ones really guilty, then?

Poutré: Listen, Camel, the real guilty ones are those who betray their countrymen for money, honours, or titles!

Camel: Come, come, Monsieur Poutré! You're losing your temper again. Certainly I don't intend to report anything bad about a man like you. But if you're talking about the sort of scum that went and fought at Odelltown, then I think a person can say what he thinks about them.

Poutré: Is it fair to call them 'scum' – decent people who simply made a mistake? As far as I'm concerned, the people who are a hundred times more despicable are ...

Camel: The ones who are punishing them?

Poutré: No, those who are out hunting them down. Look here, Camel, when we see a bird like you hovering around, we know something unpleasant is in store for us. And if you think you can fool me with your show of innocence, then you're the one who's mistaken. I know all about your cowardice and your treachery. Look – I even know you infiltrated the ranks of the Patriotes so that you could betray them to the government. I also know that, once you were found out, you owe the fact you're still alive to the humanity of the very people you sought to destroy. I know you escaped, somehow or other, from the cell they had locked you in. In short, I know as well as you do why you're here. And what's the worst thing about you is, you're trying to get me to say the wrong thing – to turn stool pigeon, as the saying goes, against myself, so that you can drag away two people instead of one. Oh, I've long known what sort of person you are, Camel!

Camel: Alright, let's do what must be done, then. I wish someone else had to do it, Monsieur Poutré, but since I've been given the task, I have to see it through.

Poutré: Let's drop the hypocrisy, Camel. You've come for Félix, but you'll return empty-handed: he's not here. And if you get scared on your way back – that often happens! – just sing, 'I've found the rabbit's den';[25] maybe that will keep you from shivering every time you hear the leaves rustle. Félix is not here, so clear out of here right now, because I'm not going to put up with your servile, mercenary mug in this house any longer!

Camel: Monsieur Poutré, I have a warrant here that I must serve. Since the Colonel is aware that Félix is here, there's no use denying he is. I must search for him, Monsieur Poutré, and I must find him.

Poutré: Go ahead, then – search!

Camel: You might as well spare yourself some trouble, Monsieur Poutré. What's the use of denying it – Félix came back here today! Come on, we know what's going on! Why force me to ransack this house and look in every corner?

Poutré: (*seizing* Camel's *arm*) Not another word, understand? If I say Félix is not here, that's the truth! If you don't believe me, go ahead and search. Do your dirty job, then clear out of here – fast! You'll wind up right where you're sending these other people, you snake! So go ahead and do your searching.

Camel: Look, Monsieur Poutré, I know you couldn't lie to me ...

Poutré: None of your base flattery! You've got a duty to fulfil, you say? Well, do it fast and spare me your presence!

Camel: If you'll just give me your word of honour that Félix isn't here, Monsieur Poutré, I'll be satisfied with that.

Poutré: Search, you coward! Don't pester me with your propositions. I don't want to seem even remotely beholden to you for any special treatment.

Camel: I can see that a search would be useless – the rascal is well hidden. And in that case, Monsieur Poutré, I've only one thing to say. Your son is a traitor to the government. He's in hiding, but you must know where he is. And since you won't tell where he is, I have the right to arrest you as a suspect, as someone concealing a fugitive. (*He takes a whistle from his pocket and blows it. Several soldiers enter.*) Soldiers, arrest this man! (*The soldiers obey.*) Now, Monsieur Poutré, you're going to prison, and you won't be released until you reveal where your son is. And if you don't, your property will be burned, and you will continue to be detained.

Poutré: You scoundrel!

Camel: Quiet! One last time, Monsieur Poutré, I order you, in the name of the law, to tell me where your son, Félix Poutré, is.

SCENE XI
Actors, *as before*; Félix

Félix: (*entering*) He's right here!

Poutré: Oh my God!

Camel: Soldiers, release that man and arrest this one. Félix Poutré, I arrest you, in the name of the English Crown. You'll be joining your friend Béchard, whom I've just had arrested as well!

Félix: Poor Béchard, victim of his own devotion!

Poutré: Poor Félix! What have you done!

Félix: Poor father! Well, I'm the one who's poured this cup and now I must drink it. I would never let you suffer for something I alone am guilty of. Forgive me for all the sorrow I've brought you, and let's leave the future in the hands of Providence, which will now watch over your son's life. (*He kisses him.*) Farewell! (*Curtain.*)

ACT THREE

The setting is the inside of the prison in Montreal

SCENE I
Several prisoners, amongst whom Cardinal, Duquette, Béchard, *and* Toinon, *sit in sadness.* Félix *sits alone, at stage front.*

Félix: Well, Félix, what's left now of your fine dreams of greatness and glory? How ironic fate is! A few weeks ago, I imagined that I would soon be a handsome officer, armed from head to toe, with pistols in my belt, a sword at my side, and a good rifle in my hands, marching triumphantly at the head of a regiment of victorious Patriotes. I could almost hear the cheers of the crowd as I marched by! There they were, calling me one of my country's liberators! ... And now, poor fool, my whole universe is nothing but the walls of this dungeon, where I'm crowded in with my companions in misfortune. And the time may not be far distant when I shall have as my only pedestal ... the scaffolding of a gallows! Condemned to death! Hanged! – now there's a word I don't like at all! In fact, I would almost rather look like an Englishman all my life, than the way I will that day! Hanged! And to think that today it's poor Cardinal's turn, and poor Duquette's! Poor lads! Yes, today, Wednesday the 21st of December. The government has chosen its first victims ... and my turn can't be too far off. How awful it was to see poor Cardinal kissing his wife and four children yesterday, and Duquette kissing his poor old mother good-bye. That was heart-breaking! Barely twenty-one years old,[26] his mother's sole support, and he's to die ... on the gallows! Oh! (*He buries his face in his hands.*) They're opening the door. And here's the sheriff. Yes, it's about that time. O God – the hangman! The sentence ... (*The* Sheriff *enters, followed by several soldiers, the* Jailer, *and the* Hangman. *The* Sheriff *wears a sword at his side; the* Hangman *is dressed in black, and wears a mask.*)

SCENE II
Actors, *as before*; Sheriff; Jailer; Hangman; Soldiers

Sheriff: Joseph-Narcisse Cardinal, come here and raise your right hand. (*He reads.*) 'Having been properly and legally convicted of the crime of high treason, with the avowed intention of overturning the government of our sovereign in Canada, the Queen; you, Joseph-Narcisse Cardinal, have been condemned by a court martial legally established in this province, to be brought forth on Friday, the twenty-first day of December in this year of Our Lord one thousand eight hundred and thirty-eight, to the usual place of execution, and there to be hanged by the neck until death ensues. And may God have mercy upon your soul!'

Cardinal: Long live liberty!

Sheriff: Joseph Duquette, it is your turn to approach and raise your right hand. (*He reads.*) 'Having been properly and legally convicted of the crime of high treason, with the avowed intention of overturning the government of our sovereign in Canada, the Queen, you, Joseph Duquette, have been condemned by a court martial legally established in this province, to be brought forth on Friday, the twenty-first day of December in this year of Our Lord one thousand eight hundred and thirty-eight, to the usual place of execution, and there to be hanged by the neck until death ensues. And may God have mercy upon your soul!'

Duquette: Long live liberty!

Sheriff: Joseph-Narcisse Cardinal and Joseph Duquette, prepare to follow me. (Cardinal *and* Duquette *shake hands with the other prisoners, some of whom are in tears.*)

Cardinal: Weep not, my friends, we shall meet again in a better world! In the meantime, we shall show our enemies that Christians and French Canadians know how to die. Farewell! Pray for us – and long live Canada! (Cardinal *and* Duquette *embrace, then kneel down.*)

Duquette: I offer my soul to God, and my life for my country.

Cardinal: Amen!

Sheriff: Are you ready?

Cardinal and Duquette: (*together*) Yes. (*They leave, escorted by soldiers and followed by the* Hangman, *the* Jailer, *and the* Sheriff. *The prisoners remain silent, but the noise of the crowd outside can be heard.*)

Cardinal: (*off-stage*) Canadians! We are going to die for our native land. May our blood provide fertile soil for the future of Canada!

Duquette: (*off-stage, sings*) 'Allons, enfants de la patrie/Le jour de gloire est arrivé ...' (*A loud noise is heard, followed by the cries of the crowd. The prisoners kneel and sing softly.*)

Prisoners:
   To die for one's country
   Is a fate most noble
   A fate most enviable! (*bis*)
(*The prisoners rise.*)

SCENE III
Félix, Prisoners

Félix: Friends, listen to me. Two men, irreproachable in their conduct, two men universally esteemed and respected, two noble hearts, two devoted citizens, have just met the fate reserved for criminals, thieves, and murderers. The awful truth is there before our eyes. Two of our friends have just been torn away and sacrificed for partisan revenge; for, indeed, there is so little that is at all criminal in this attempted insurrection that sooner or later the English government will be forced, by the evolution of events and by public opinion, to rehabilitate these victims of an atrocity almost unparalleled in human history. From every conceivable point of view, an execution for purely political reasons is really murder and an inexcusable cruelty. The government that orders this is thereby more dishonoured than those who suffer it. But take heart, my friends: Cardinal and Duquette and all those who will have the honour of following them to the gallows will forever be considered martyrs for liberty since they've sacrificed their own lives for their convictions! Moreover, Attorney-General Ogden,[27] the real perpetrator of these murders, will forever be pilloried by history and held up for public execration, while public sympathy and national mourning will raise monuments to his victims. Friends, let us admire the stoic courage with which our comrades have just made the supreme sacrifice. If we too are to suffer the same fate, let us all swear to die as they did, with heads held high and the word 'Liberty' on our lips!

Prisoners: *(raising their hands)* We so swear! (*The* Sheriff *and the* Jailer *enter.*)

SCENE IV
Actors, *as before*; Sheriff; Jailer

Sheriff: *(entering)* Charles Hindelang,[28] you are summoned for interrogation. Follow me. (*The* Sheriff *and* Jailer *leave with one of the prisoners.*)

SCENE V
Actors, *as before, except the* Sheriff *and* Jailer

Félix: *(leading Béchard to stage front)* I believe, my dear Béchard, that there's a strong chance we shall soon be following in the footsteps of poor Cardinal and Duquette.

Béchard: I must say, I don't feel at all safe. The government is seeking revenge, and now that it's decided to do so, it will avenge itself as thoroughly as it can. I don't really understand what sort of madness has seized the people governing this country!

Félix: Just the same, you have a better chance of surviving than I do: you didn't recruit 3,000 men, and what's more important, you didn't let everyone know what you were up to!

Béchard: True enough, but it's possible to have a poorer chance than you do, and yet have *some* chance of surviving!

Félix: But in fact, you think my situation is hopeless?

Béchard: To be perfectly frank, my friend – we are men, and we can face the truth – I'm rather surprised they didn't start with you.

Félix: Hell! You're not much comfort!

Béchard: What do you expect? There's no sense deluding ourselves! Better be prepared for anything.

Félix: That's true; and after what's just happened, I can't help telling myself I'm a goner. But that reminds me ... You know, there might be a way, just the same ...

Béchard: A way to do what?

Félix: A way to save my own skin.

Béchard: Huh! I really doubt that!

Félix: Tell me, Béchard – you're older than I am – have you ever heard of them hanging an insane person?

Béchard: No, but I don't think *we're* insane!

Félix: We certainly aren't – but it's possible to *pretend* to be.

Béchard: Are you really out of your mind? I assure you, it's a lot harder to feign insanity than you think, my friend! For half an hour, all right! But for weeks, or perhaps months? It's impossible – there's not a man alive who could play that role successfully. How could you ever keep yourself from laughing? Because that's the

214 The Drama of Our Past

real sign of insanity, and the most difficult one! You're finished, if you fail to keep a straight face even once! No, may as well forget it – your idea itself is insane!

Félix: Listen, Béchard, you are the only man in the world I would ever dare to tell something like this. I'll tell you what gave me the idea. The night before they arrested me, I dreamed they had captured me and I was on trial. I was about to be condemned to death, when one of the judges, more humane than the others, declared that I was insane and should be set free. Since then, the idea keeps running around in my head. Yes, my friend, I shall indeed play the fool and do all the craziest things you can imagine, and I *won't* laugh! No, as far as keeping a serious face is concerned, I'm quite sure I can do that. Have a good look at me, Béchard: here I am, completely 'off my nut,' as we say here in Canada. If they find me out, they can't hang me *twice* for it! So I'm going to take the risk. I've been thinking about it for a long time, and it seems to me that any way of saving your own life is worth trying.

Béchard: Well, I'm certainly not going to stand in your way; but I haven't much faith in your plan. If you succeed – fine! – you'll save your own head. But the idea of going all that time without laughing – that's impossible! But I suppose, when you do feel the urge to laugh, all you have to do is think about the noose – maybe that will keep you in a serious frame of mind ...!

Félix: Exactly! So then, I shall be a madman, a real one – and before very long, I can assure you! But listen – be careful not to give me away. You have to pretend to believe that I'm indeed quite mad.

Béchard: Oh, don't worry about that. Once you've decided, I'll do everything I can to help. And frankly, I don't think you've any way out except that one!

SCENE VI
Actors, *as before*; Sheriff; Jailer; Two Soldiers

Sheriff: Félix Poutré, you're next! Follow these men to the interrogation room. (Félix, *soldiers, and* Jailer *exit.*)

SCENE VII
Actors, *as before, except* Félix, Soldiers, *and* Jailer

Sheriff: Prisoners, I have something to say to you. From the terrible punishment that has just befallen two of your companions, you can see that Her Majesty's Government is determined to proceed with the utmost severity against those who took part in the recent uprising. However, in my position as clerk of the court martial, I am authorized to inform you that the law is prepared to act with some leniency with regard to those who are willing to provide any information that might help us discover those primarily responsible for this rebellion.

Béchard: Sheriff, that's a very cowardly statement you've just made. Do you really think you have the right to insult us, just because we're in chains? You've renounced your proud identity as a French Canadian in exchange for your wretched job; for vile lucre you've made yourself the servant of those who execute your fellow citizens, but don't try to dirty us with the mire you've besmirched yourself with! Have a good look at these honest men here: tomorrow they may die, but posterity will avenge them, and you shall get what you deserve, sooner or later! In the meantime, even if you haven't the courage to follow them in their commitment, at least show respect for their misfortunes! Shackle us with chains, pour insults upon us, treat us as badly as you wish, take our lives on the scaffold – yes, take our lives even: we shan't resist! But if you try to impugn our honour, you may as well stop right there! So go back and tell the people who sent you that the only traitors are in their own ranks and not among those who are offering their lives for their country. As far as I'm concerned, as long as the hangman's noose hasn't choked off my last breath I shall still have the courage to shout 'Down with tyrants, and long live Liberty!'

Prisoners: Long live Liberty!

Béchard: Traitors among us! Traitors among us, indeed! Traitors among the Patriotes – never!!

Prisoners: Never!!

Toinon: No way, I reckon!

Prisoners: (*singing enthusiastically*)
   To die for one's country
   Is a fate most noble,
   A fate most enviable! (*bis*)

SCENE VIII
Actors, *as before*; Félix; Soldiers; Jailer

(*Cries and loud footsteps are heard in the corridor, and the soldiers enter, carrying* Félix *in their arms. The prisoners all rush forward.*)

Prisoners: What's happened? What's going on?

Sheriff: Has he had a stroke? (*They place* Félix *on a chair; he is convulsing violently.*)

Jailer: He just fell down flat, crying out frightfully! I've never been so scared in my life! Did you hear him?

Béchard: The poor lad! I didn't realize he was epileptic. It's a real shame, because he's an extraordinary man!

Toinon: Yer dang right! There's a guy with a head on 'is shoulders, even if he's sorta fast to take offence ...

Sheriff: We've got to help him. Send for the prison doctor right away! Jailer, go and fetch Dr Arnoldi. (*The* Jailer *leaves.*)

Toinon: Whaddaya want the doctor fer? We're all gonna be hung, anyways!

Béchard: First things first – give me some water! (*He throws water on* Félix*'s face.*) Move back, the rest of you – give him some air! (*He splashes water on his face, and* Félix *slowly regains consciousness. Suddenly* Félix *stands up, and begins to stride solemnly back and forth.*)

Félix: (*in a terrifying voice*) On your knees! Here's the governor! (*No one moves.*)

Toinon: Well! Is he gonna make us parade now?

Félix: On your knees, I say! (*Seeing no one move, he rushes at all those he can reach and pounds them with his fists. The* Sheriff, Jailer, *and soldiers manage to evade him and exit.*)

Béchard: Good God! He's gone mad – he's delirious! He's going to kill someone, for sure!

Félix: You scoundrels! *I'll* teach you how to follow orders properly! (*He starts punching again, seizes* Toinon, *floors him, and tries to strangle him.*)

Toinon: Ow! ow! By Saint Anne's boots! Ouch! Don't hurt me, cap'n – I'm a good guy, really! I'll pray to God for ya! ... Ow! Ouch! ... Help! Murder! (*All rush to help.* Félix *allows them to intervene, then suddenly knocks down two or three of them, struggling frenziedly.*)

Félix: Aha! you smarties! Aha! you scamps! (*All shrink back from him.*) All right, try to resist now! You'll soon find out just who you're dealing with. I'm warning you, I took lessons from Her Majesty the Queen herself, who has no peer when it comes to boxing! Things have got to change around here – I'm not governor for nothing, and I'll soon show you how an officer of the government commands respect. First, you're going to do your drills. Take your guns! Hey! – are you going to obey or not? By the Lord livin' ...

Prisoners: (*to each other*) Has he really taken leave of this senses?

Félix: So! You won't obey, eh?

Toinon: Oh yeah! Yeah, I wanna obey! (*Aside.*) By Saint Anne's boots, what's to become of us? (*The* Jailer *enters.*)

SCENE IX
Actors, *as before*; Jailer

Félix: Stop, thief! Stop! (*He lunges at the* Jailer, *knocking him down.*)

Jailer: Oh! Ow!

Toinon: Aha – thing's ain't goin' none too good fer him, neither! (*Some of the prisoners go to help the* Jailer.)

Béchard: He nearly killed him!

Jailer: The man is mad! He's got to be tied up!

Toinon: Yeah, tie 'im up! Just you go ahead an' try! He's as strong as two teams o' oxes! Too bad he didn't go off his nut earlier – he woulda made short work o' them Englishmen!

Jailer: Is he suffering from delirium tremens?

Toinon: We'se the ones gettin' the leeriest trimmin's from him!

Béchard: It's the after-effect of his epileptic fit. Better to be gentle with him, to calm him down.

Jailer: The damned fool! I thought my last moment had come. We can't keep a wild animal like that in here. They'll have to get rid of him, or else I won't be a jailer here any more!

Toinon: Yeah? Then I don't wanna be a prisoner no more, neither!

Félix: Enough idle chatter, all of you! Throw that thief out the door! Do you hear me, by thunder? Do I have to wring his neck for you?

Toinon: By good Saint Anne's boots! There he goes again!

Béchard: For heaven's sake, jailer, leave right now, because if his crazy spell returns, he'll wind up killing someone! (*The* Jailer *leaves.*)

SCENE X
Actors, *as before, except* Jailer

Félix: Now that's the way to do it! That's the way to treat thieves! The Queen is going to give all of you a medal, when I tell her about this. Now let's all shout together: 'Long live the Queen of England!' (*All remain silent.*) That's the way – bravo! bravissimo! But hold on a minute – what's become of the government's hay? By thunder, I've got to have my share of it. I'm not governor for nothing! Meanwhile, I'm going to auction it off. Come here, all of you! (*He climbs on a chair.*) We're going to sell, to the highest bidder, the 500,000 ricks of hay that are to arrive in port this morning. Now there's *real* hay for you, I say – hay, not straw! *Real* hay. The very picture of hay! (*These ravings and those that follow are constantly interrupted by peals of laughter from the prisoners,* Toinon's *being especially loud.*)

Béchard: Has he really gone mad, then?

Toinon: Some question! An' me with a busted rib somewheres, too!

Félix: Silence, all of you! If you don't keep quiet, I'll throw all of you out of here and conduct my auction by myself! (*To* Béchard.) Beadle, while I think of it, heat me up a mugful of water on the stove – I've got to say my Mass before long. (*To two of the other prisoners.*) You two will be my acolytes, I'll give you a hundred bucks a day. Hey! – this is no skinflint you're dealing with! It's government money; no need to hold back. And since I like to show my staff a good time, after Mass I'll take all of you out fishing for bears and hunting whales.

Toinon: Fishin' fer bears! ... an' he calls that a good time!

Félix: But before saying Mass I have to announce the marriage banns. Your attention, please! There is a promise of marriage between Félix Poutré, adult son of Ignace Poutré and Charlotte Descarreau, both of this parish, on the one side; and on the other – the Queen of England. Anyone knowing of any impediment to this marriage is asked to come forward – and be thrashed to death! We recommend to your prayers Louis-Joseph Papineau, Dr Chénier, Dr Côté, Dr Nelson, Dr Arnoldi, and all doctors ... and all the scum of this parish. Brethren, I bring you great good tidings: I have been chosen by the Almighty to accomplish great things. He has sent me here to wage war on the devil. And I have fought with him, and slain him ... and I'll kill all of you, too, if you don't watch out! Such is the joy I bring you, and with all my heart, amen! (*To* Béchard.) Beadle! Have you heated the water for my Mass?

Béchard: Yes.

Félix: Right, then – on to the *Asperges, me, Domine!*[29] (*He dips his handkerchief in the boiling water and splashes it on the prisoners, who shrink back, shouting.*)

Prisoners: Oh! Ow! Damned fool! He's scalding us!

Toinon: (*seated in a corner opposite* Félix) Ha, ha, ha! Look at 'em run! So where you all gonna hide? Feels good, eh? Everyone gets his turn! Everyone's gotta take what he's got comin'!

SCENE XI
Actors, *as before*; Jailer

Jailer: (*entering*) How is he now?

Béchard: Still mad, raving mad! He's scalding us, and threatening to kill us. Is the doctor coming?

Jailer: We've contacted him. He should be here pretty soon.

Félix: (*to the* Jailer) Well! How are you, illustrious champion of immortal legions, sublime dweller in the celestial townships? You've come, no doubt, on behalf of the Almighty to congratulate me on the brilliant victory I've just achieved over His Omnipotency's enemy? Come near – come and gaze upon me! (*He points to* Toinon *sitting in a corner.*) There sits that dethroned monster, that fallen archangel – Satan, in a word!

Toinon: Yikes! – here he comes with another one!

Félix: I floored him! I blasted him! I pulverized him! And there he is now, like a defeated gladiator, biting the dust of the arena, stained with his own blood!

Toinon: He's right on with that one – I can't take no more!

Jailer: There's no way we can keep this poor lad here if his madness persists. I'll talk to the sheriff. Meanwhile, try not to excite him. With his strength, he could really be dangerous – I can testify to that! Anyway, the doctor should be here in a moment. We'll see what he has to say. (*The door opens.*) Ah, here he is.

SCENE XII
Actors, *as before*; Doctor, Sheriff

Félix: (*aside*) Good Lord! The doctor! The jig's up. But I'd better take heart – I've nothing to lose and everything to gain.

Doctor: [*in English*] What is it? [*In French.*] What's going on? (*Aside.*) [*In English.*] I'll be glad when I get rid of all those damned Canadians! (*Aloud.*) [*In French.*] What's going on?

Sheriff: (*pointing to* Félix) This is the one. He collapsed into what I think was an epileptic fit just a little while ago.

Doctor: Bienne, bienne, tray bienne. Very well! ... So?

Béchard: And then, while we were washing his face with cold water, he jumped up in a rage, and ever since then he's been behaving like a madman.

Toinon: Yeah, an' clobberin' everybody!

Doctor: Bienne, tray bienne, very well!

Toinon: (*mocking*) Bienne, tray bienne, very well! An' the same to you, you goddam lunkhead!

Doctor: (*taking* Félix's *pulse*) Bienne, bienne, very well! He is eat good?

Toinon: Yeah, sure! – dry bread, like the rest of us!

Doctor: Bienne, bienne, very well!

Toinon: (*aside*) Bienne, bienne, very well! I wonder if he'd find it 'very well' too, if he didn't have nothin' but that to eat!

Doctor: [*in English*] What do you say? [*In French.*] What you is say?

Toinon: (*mocking*) Me is say ... me is say ... he'd rather eat roast chicken, if there was any – an' the same goes fer us!

Doctor: [*in English*] Oh, don't bother me, you damned rascal! [*In French.*] Jailer, you be go find bucket of cold water. We be give him cold showers. (*To the* Sheriff.) We be give him cold showers, you know, and we'll see. (*The* Jailer *leaves.*)

Sheriff: Do you think his type of insanity is dangerous?

Doctor: Oh, non ... no, no, not dangerous, pas dangerouse.

Toinon: (*mocking*) No, no, pas dangerouse! ... By cracky, when we're all dead, 'twon't be dangerous at all! Doctor – hmm! You is maybe know some good cure for punches? (*The* Doctor *grimaces scornfully, and everyone laughs.*)

Jailer: (*entering*) There's an old man asking to see the prisoner Félix Poutré. His papers are in order.

Sheriff: Would it be all right to let him in, Doctor?

Doctor: [*in English*] Oh! yes, yes!

Sheriff: Have him come in. (*The* Jailer *brings in* Poutré Senior, *who rushes to embrace his son.*)

SCENE XIII
Actors, *as before*; Poutré Senior

Poutré: Félix! My son!

Félix: (*stands, staring wild-eyed at his father*) Why yes, I do think we've met ... haven't we, old-timer?

Poutré: My poor Félix!

Félix: (*bursts out laughing*) Ha, ha, ha! What have we here? This is dreadful – it's terrible! You! You're the one who assassinated Henri IV![30] You're the one who had Mary Stuart beheaded! You smiled as you gazed on her lovely, bleeding head ...

Poutré: Félix!

Félix: Gentlemen, the man who stands there before you, that wild-looking man there ... he's a coward! An assassin! A hangman!

Poutré: Stop, Félix!

Félix: I shall have that man crucified! (*He falls back on his chair.*)

Poutré: That's the last thing I needed for my old age: Good Lord, my son is mad! (*The curtain falls.*)

ACT FOUR

A courtroom. Lawyers are seated around a table with the Sheriff. *A* Judge *is presiding.*

SCENE I
Sheriff, Judge, Lawyers

Judge: Has the man named Félix Poutré been summoned?

Sheriff: He'll be here in a moment

Judge: Good. We'll attempt some sort of interrogation. Perhaps in his madness he'll make statements that could be very useful to us. They tell me he's still quite insane. He's lucky: you might say his sentence has already been pronounced!

Sheriff: Allow me to point out, Your Honour, that the poor young man has been out of his mind for more than two months now. The prison doctor's treatment has had no effect. His condition continues to deteriorate, and is in fact threatening to become dangerous both for himself and for the other prisoners. They're continually exposed to all sorts of assaults from him. Twice a day he suffers epileptic fits and is taken with dreadful convulsions. And when the crisis passes he attacks his companions, beating up everyone he can get his hands on. Six men at a time are nothing to him. He breaks the prison windows, spills the prisoners' water, throws their clothing in the fire, assaults the guards, to the extent that the chief jailer is the only one who can set foot in there. Just a few days ago he nearly set fire to the whole prison. He had gotten it into his head that the stove wasn't level, and had to be plumbed up. So he put five or six pieces of wood under the stove legs and plumbed and replumbed the whole thing so well that stove and stove-pipe got knocked over, and the flooring had caught fire by the time we managed to intervene. It's not hard to see that that sort of madness can have very dangerous consequences, and it's my opinion that we should send the poor young wretch home. Returning under his father's roof may help him recover his sanity, which his fear of the gallows has probably made him lose.

Judge: Very well. I'll discuss it with the authorities, and we shall see.

Sheriff: I've sent for him, along with another prisoner, a certain Béchard, who's the only one who seems to still have any influence on his state of mind. He's the only one who's been able to get him out of his cell.

Jailer: (*entering*) The prisoners are here.

Judge: Bring them in. (Félix *and* Béchard *are brought in.*)

SCENE II
Actors, *as before*; Félix; Béchard; Jailer

Judge: Félix Poutré, come forward and answer the questions we shall ask you.

Félix: All right. But first of all I must tell you, you'll have to begin by clearing out of all those seats you're in. You have no business here. I've got an army of ten thousand men due to arrive here soon, and there won't be any seats to spare!

Sheriff: (*to* Judge) My Lord, as you can see, there's no way we can get a sensible word out of a person in his state of mind.

Judge: Félix Poutré, you stand before a court. You should be aware that we have the power to deal with you as we wish. The best thing for you would be to answer promptly the questions we shall ask you. First of all, tell us ...

Félix: First of all, I'm going to tell *you* that you're a bunch of loafers, in your big black robes and starched white fronts! Judges? You're a lot of thieves! You've been stealing government money for a long time, and just lazing about. And now that I'm Governor, that sort of nonsense has got to stop, understand? I don't know why I don't run you all out of here, right now. I've been made head of this country for good reason, and you're going to have to watch yourselves – there's fair warning! And that's all I've got to say to you.

Judge: Look here, Félix Poutré, if you continue to insult the court, I shall be forced ...

Félix: Here now! I can see you don't understand something that's as obvious as the nose on your face! I'm telling you once and for all that I'm the governor, and if you don't know how to govern yourselves, then I'll govern you properly!

Judge: Silence! Once again I call upon you, Félix Poutré ...

Félix: Aha! You want to argue, do you? Just hold on – this'll only take a minute. First I'll pay you, and then put the run to you. Loafers, good-for-nothing scoundrels, rogues, thieves, blackguards that you all are, I've had enough of you! You're going to pack your bags and clear out without any fuss or ceremony! You want to resist, eh? Well, I'll settle your accounts right now! (*He grabs a book and starts to write in it.*)

Sheriff: Hey – he's going to ruin that book! (*He takes it away from him.*)

Félix: Oh, you really do want to resist, do you? All right, let's have some fun! (*He strikes the* Sheriff.) Here, take this for a start! (*He knocks the lawyers about.*) Now your turn, you lot! (*To the* Judge.) And as for you, you big gawk, just you wait! (*He* *knocks the* Judge *down, overturns tables, chairs, etc., throwing everything into the wings. All run off stage, except* Béchard.) Hurray for me! Long live the governor! Bring on more of your black robes and white dickeys! Welcome, all you gentlemen with your big books, and my compliments to your families! (*He looks around, then turns to* Béchard.) My dear Béchard, here we are alone, finally! (*Takes his hand.*) Tell me now, do you think I know how to play the fool?

Béchard: What? You mean you *aren't* insane?

Félix: No more than when I went to prison. But don't talk so loudly – you'll give me away.

Béchard: Well, I never! Really, is it possible you're in your right mind?

Félix: Did you really think I was mad, then?

Béchard: Good heavens, yes! Stark raving mad – crazier than all the madmen in the world put together! I've never seen anything like it!

Félix: So what do you think of the way I'm putting them through their paces?

Béchard: He *is* sane! ... Well, I can tell you, you don't just pretend, when you decide to do it – there are several prisoners here who've wished you were in hell! The jailer told me they can't keep you here much longer. But listen – I still can't believe this! I can't believe you're not mad!

Félix: But I told you I would do it ... (Camel *appears at stage rear.*)

SCENE III
Félix, Béchard, Camel

Béchard: I know you did. But good Lord! how could I imagine that a man in his right mind could do such crazy things? When I saw you behaving so insanely I believed, as sure as my name is Béchard, that God had punished you for that thought and had really driven you mad. I would have taken an oath that you were insane. Are you sure you're *not*, really?

Félix: Not at all. Everything I do is pretended: the things I say are just made up in my head.

Camel: (*aside*) Now there's a useful bit of information!

Félix: So I guess I'm not pulling my punches, eh?

Béchard: Holy cripes, you've been slaughtering them! That's what really made me believe you *were* insane – thrashing everyone the way you did. And you treat your friends the same as the rest!

Félix: Except you, Béchard. (*He takes his hand.*)

Béchard: You know, that hadn't even occurred to me!

Camel: (*aside*) Bloody fool!

Béchard: I just thought that, since we were such close friends, you recognized me better than the others, that's all. But tell me, how do you manage not to laugh? As far as I'm concerned, I didn't laugh because I was so distressed by the whole thing. But how do you manage, when you see them all frightened stiff, staring at you and then running away like sheep with a wolf at their heels ...?

Félix: That *is* the most difficult part! But whenever I'm tempted to laugh I follow your advice and ask myself how much I would be laughing if I saw myself with the noose around my neck and a white hood over my head. Once I think about that for a bit, my temptation to laugh disappears completely! But I take it you think I'm doing a good job of playing the fool?

Béchard: It's as though you had never done otherwise in your whole life!

Camel: (*aside*) But not quite good enough, even so ...

Béchard: You really are brazen – attacking the sheriff, the judge ...!

Félix: Actually, you know, that's what's saved me.

Béchard: I'd have to agree: that's not going to make them want to keep you around here much longer!

Félix: But there *is* something I'm worried about ...

Camel: (*aside*) Aha! He *does* have some misgivings, it seems!

Félix: It's that damned doctor. The old scoundrel seems to look at me as if he suspects something. He keeps on taking my pulse and staring into my eyes. If he comes back, I'm going to have to cook up something special for him. Do you think the fellow can find me out, just checking my pulse?

Béchard: I don't think so – he seems too dumb for that.

Félix: He just keeps staring at me in the strangest way, the old skinflint.

Béchard: Oh well, if you keep on doing what you've done so far, you're safe.

Camel: (*aside*) We'll see about that!

Félix: I didn't want to do anything to him, since I was always afraid he would notice something. After all, a doctor should know something about madness ... more than other people, anyway! Do you remember the medicine he gave me last night?

Béchard: Yes?

Félix: Guess what I did with it.

Béchard: You didn't take it?

Félix: No, I poured it in my boots.

Béchard: What a thing to do!

Félix: But don't you see, he could have poisoned me! In any case, if he comes back again I'm going to teach that fellow a lesson. He shouldn't get off any easier than my friends did. You just try to be there, and when you come to rescue him I'll stop, but not before. Before you do, I'll shake him like an old sock. Long and skinny as he is, he shouldn't put up much of a fight.

Béchard: Good idea – shake him up a bit, it'll do him some good! He takes on such superior airs, the old Limey. Never misses an opportunity to label us 'damn Canucks.' Choke him a bit – that'll teach him a lesson!

Félix: Well, since you agree, he'll get his comeuppance. I can tell you, Béchard, I'm really happy to chat a bit with you. For nearly two months I've been trying to get you aside. Now that you know the whole score, you must be very careful, because the least little thing could give me away.

Béchard: Don't you worry about that! (Camel *moves between the two of them, smiling*.) Camel!!

Félix: Curses! I've given myself away!

Camel: My warmest greetings, gentlemen. Delighted to see that our friend Félix's – um – *indisposition* is not as – uh – *serious* as was reported ...

Béchard: (*aside*) Poor Félix! Now his goose is really cooked!

Félix: (*exasperated*) Camel! You've followed me everywhere, like some evil spirit! You've had me thrown in prison, along with hundreds of my comrades, two of whom have already died on the gallows. Tomorrow I'll be hanging there too, and the next day my poor old father will die of sorrow! Are you happy, Camel? All right, but in the meantime it's just the two of us, once and for all! (*He rushes at* Camel.)

Camel: Help! Murder! I'm being killed! Oh! Oh!

Béchard: Félix! Félix! For God's sake, don't kill him!
(*The* Sheriff, *the* Jailer, *and soldiers rush in.*)

SCENE IV
Actors, *as before*; Sheriff; Jailer; Soldiers

Sheriff: What's he doing *now*? Good Lord!

Jailer: Come on – he's going to kill him, for sure!

Béchard: Félix, dear Félix, again I beg you, let him go!

Félix: (*releasing* Camel) There you go, you snake! I'd skin you alive, but I just can't overcome my disgust for your foul carcass! Get out of here, you cur!

Sheriff: He's getting more and more dangerous.

Camel: Sheriff, this man is a base impostor. This man, who has succeeded in passing himself off as a madman, is no more insane than you and I. It's all put on. He's pulled the wool over the eyes of all of you!

Jailer: (*laughing*) Ha, ha, ha! Come on now – Look's like we've got another one with a screw loose!

Sheriff: What proof do you have for what you're saying, Camel?

Félix: The best proof that I'm no madman is the very fact that for a moment at least I had the urge to rid the world of a worthless scum like you!

Camel: Proof? He provided it, on his own. I heard him confess to his friend Béchard.

Béchard: Yeah – as if madmen *usually* admit that they're mad ...!

Félix: (*aside, to* Béchard) Thank you, Béchard, you've saved my life!

Jailer: He's never admitted he's insane. Far from it, in fact – he keeps insisting he's the governor of this country!

Félix: Alright, enough idle chatter! Soldiers, seize that man (*pointing to* Camel), and hang him high and dry on the main yard of my frigate, which is docked here. Otherwise the whole lot of you will face the firing squad tomorrow morning!

Sheriff: (*to* Camel) You can see he's out of his mind.

Camel: But I tell you he isn't!

Sheriff: Then you're wrong, Camel.

Camel: I tell you he *isn't* crazy, Sheriff – and I know what I'm saying!

Sheriff: Well, *you* may know what you're saying, but *we* know what we're doing. Let's go. Jailer, take the prisoners back to their cell. (*He leaves with* Camel.)

Camel: (*aside*) How stupid of me! (*Shaking his fist at* Félix *as he leaves.*) Just wait – I'll get my chance again!

Félix: (*to himself*) Take care now – that was a narrow escape!

Jailer: (*to* Félix) Governor, your servants are acting up, and your gracious presence is requested, to help put things back in proper order.

Félix: Right away. Oh, but don't forget to tell my coachman to harness my two white horses to my carriage, and get seventy-five pairs of snowshoes ready for my retinue. I'm off for England tonight: the Queen has sent for me!

They leave. The setting changes to show the inside of the prison. The prisoners are in the background.

SCENE V
Toinon, Prisoners

Toinon: Well, our madman's been gone for quite a while. A bit o' peace for us, anyways! Hell of a thing – goin' off his nut like that, all of a sudden! Right starkers! Tain't funny, neither: he's gonna bust someone's bones one o' these times. I can tell ya, sure makes me lonesome for home! Like the man says, it ain't no fun dyin' for your country! I just as soon never put a hand to me grandpa's sabre. Darn tootin'! An' like as if it wasn't enough to be locked up like criminals, an' fed dry bread, an' hung one after the other – no, we gotta be kicked an' punched around by that there madman! An' me that's got a kinda delicate constitution! I'm so kinda like *sensitive*, that the tiniest kick in the ass really hurts. An' that's what gets you down, after a while. An' you might even say he seems to be doin' it to me on purpose! When he wants to beat up on someone it's always *me* he looks for! Well okay, I'm willin' to die for me country this time, but I ain't never gonna get mixed up in no patriotics no more, I can tell you that, me chum! Tain't no fun at all, that stuff! (*The door opens.*) Hey, here's our madman! Oh, I knew it wouldn't last long! (*The* Jailer *brings in* Félix *and* Béchard, *then leaves.*)

SCENE VI
Actors, *as before*; Félix; Béchard

Félix: So! It seems you've all been up to your usual tricks, while I was gone! Even though you know I'm going to make you pay for it, as usual. (*To* Béchard.) You know, Lieutenant, I've never had this kind of trouble with anyone else. If it keeps up, I'm going to have to throw them all in prison!

Toinon: Ha! Now that's all we needed!

Félix: Come here, you, you rogue. I'll start with you.

Toinon: Me agin! Beggin' your pardon, Mr Madman ...

Félix: Mr *Mad*man?

Toinon: Uh, er – I mean Mr ... Mr ... Mr Governor! That's what I meant to say!

Félix: Turn around, so I can give you a good kick.

Toinon: Oh God! – mercy, Mr Madman – Oh no! – Mr Governor! I won't say it no more, I promise, I won't say it no more!

Félix: Here, this'll teach you to act smart! (*He pulls* Toinon's *hat down over his face.*)

Toinon: Oof! oof! By Saint Anne's boots! how come all this sufferin's happenin' to me? Me new hat! Ain't I gonna look nice now, when I go courtin'!

Félix: That's the way to make you people behave. I can't leave here without all of you acting up. I may have to have the lot of you hanged, in the end!

Toinon: Now there's a great idea, what? – As if they wasn't enough Englishers to do that, already!

Félix: But if you had all behaved I would have taken you to England with me tonight, to see my wife, the Queen. She's trying on a new robe this evening, the little sweetheart! But hey – who's gone and set this stove up all crooked? Now I've got to straighten it again. Where's my plumb-line? (*Checking his pockets.*) Ah! here it is. (*He starts to straighten the stove, humming a popular tune.*)

Béchard: Félix, can't you see it's standing straight as it is?

Félix: Mind your own business, all of you! Who are the idiots responsible for setting up a stove this way? Let's do it right. (*He puts pieces of wood under the stove legs.*)

Béchard: Stop! Stop it! Can't you see it's straight? You're going to tip it over, and we'll be smoked out again!

Félix: (*continuing his adjustments*) To hell with the lot of you! What sort of fools would install a stove this way!

Toinon: By Saint Anne's boots! it's gonna tip over, an' this time we're all gonna fry! Well, I sooner be hung. Good God, ain't we an unlucky bunch! (*The* Doctor *and* Jailer *enter.*)

SCENE VII
Actors, *as before*; Doctor; Jailer

Béchard: Quick, Jailer – he's levelling the stove again!

Jailer: Oh no! ... Here, Mr Governor, let me help you. (*He removes the pieces of wood from under the stove legs.*) How does it look to you now?

Félix: Good! Excellent! You can see it's quite straight now. If they had only set it up like that in the first place, it would've been a lot less work for me!

Doctor: (*to* Béchard) Him is take medicine me is give yesterday night?

Béchard: Yes, I gave it to him myself.

Doctor: Good! good! Tray bienne! It is do something?

Béchard: Nothing at all.

Doctor: Nutting at hall?

Béchard: That's right.

Doctor: Him worser than horse! Okay, okay, tray bienne, we be giving him gooder one toot allure! (*He tries to take* Félix's *pulse.* Félix *seizes his hand, making his knuckles crack.*)

Félix: So, how are we doing now, Mister Englishman?

Doctor: (*trying to free his hand*) Oh! Ow! Ow!

Félix: (*still squashing his hand*) Are your little plum-pudding-grabbers all right?

Doctor: Oh! Oh!

Toinon: All right! At least's it's the Englisher's turn, now!

Félix: Now that I've got hold of you, you must come and have dinner with me.

Doctor: [*in English*] Oh! Oh! By God! Let me go! That hurts – c'est faire mal! Oh! oh! damned fool! – cré fou!

Félix: Me, a fool? You say I'm a fool? Hold on a bit, you old scoundrel. I'll show you what a real fool is like! (*He floors the* Doctor *and begins to choke him.*)

Doctor: [*in English*] Oh! help! help! ... murder! ... for God's sake, take me away! ...

Toinon: Well done! Tray bienne! Very well!

Béchard: Félix! Félix! for the love of God, don't strangle him! (Félix *lets go of the* Doctor.)

Toinon: Let him be, you guys! He's an *Anglais*, after all! They ain't so fast on the jump when I'm the one he's beatin' on! Well anyways, he *did* hand 'im a good thrashin'!

Béchard: (*to the* Doctor) Good heavens, I really thought he was going to choke you to death! Did he hurt you?

Doctor: What, hurt? He is nearly kill me. I never see such a thing before!

Béchard: Well, you can take some consolation in that fact you're not the first to have that happen to him. Why, when the fit hits him, he can manhandle ten men. You're lucky to have gotten off so easily.

Doctor: [*in English*] Why did you not tell me? [*In French.*] Uh – why you is not say me he take fits?

Toinon: [*mocking the* Doctor's *French*] Uh, he is take fits two times in day! Doctor, you is not know some good – uh – remedies for punchings with fist?

Doctor: [*in English*] Oh! the devil! I wish I was rid of those damned Canadians! ... (*He leaves, and the prisoners all laugh and applaud.*)

SCENE VIII
Actors, *as before; except* Doctor

Jailer: (*to* Béchard) What a bloody madman! He's pretty lucky, though – there is serious talk of releasing him. He nearly killed the judge and sheriff, and they'd ask for nothing better than to get him off their hands. Every time I come in here I'm afraid of finding someone dead. That young man really must be removed from here. And the doctor's experience will no doubt set some people talking, so perhaps ... In any case, he's calm right now, so I'll leave you. I have to give the other prisoners their rations. (*He starts to leave, then returns.*) Here comes the sheriff – good news, I think! (*The* Sheriff *enters, accompanied by a few soldiers.*)

SCENE IX
Actors, *as before*; Sheriff; Soldiers

Sheriff: Félix Poutré, we have obtained your pardon from the governor general. Here are your discharge papers, signed by Sir John Colborne.[31] You may now leave this prison and return home. Jailer, free this man.

Toinon: What's all this gibberish mean?

Félix: (*aside*) God help me to handle this carefully! (*Aloud.*) What are you rambling on about, with your 'John Cold Barn'? With your 'Governor'? *I'm* the governor, and you'd better watch what you're saying!

Sheriff: We've brought you this letter of pardon. You may leave now.

Félix: Me, leave? Leave the Queen's service, without notifying her? Who do you think you're dealing with? Listen, you'd better just be on your way, understand?

Sheriff: Oh no – are we going to have to force you to leave?

Félix: Force me? You couldn't force me out, with all the cannons in the Citadel in Quebec! I am here on the Queen's service, and shall remain here. So be on your way, and mind your own business!

Sheriff: There's no use trying to reason with him any further. Come, soldiers, throw this man out.

Félix: (*punching and shoving the soldiers*) Here you go, my hearties – try this on for size! (*The soldiers run off.*) That's the way I have to handle you people! (*Aside.*) There's another little thrashing for the redcoats, at least!

Sheriff: Now that's the last straw! There's no way to get him out of here!

Jailer: Let me try. I think I know how to do it. (*To* Félix.) Would Your Honour care to have a little drink with us, Governor?

Félix: Eh?

Jailer: Come along, we'll drink a little toast to the Queen's health.

Félix: Hmmm ...

Jailer: Just a wee drop, no fuss about it ...

Félix: Hmm ... There's an offer hard to refuse! Lieutenant, you take care of everything here, in my absence. (*He leaves with* Jailer.)

SCENE X
Actors, *as before*, except Félix

Toinon: Sure, that's the way things are these days – crazy people are better off than sensible folk!

Jailer: (*closes the door as soon as* Félix *is safely outside. Peering through the grating of the door.*) Go on, be on your way, you poor fool – we've had enough of you!

Sheriff: We're rid of him, thank heavens! Come along, Jailer, we've got to visit the other prisoners. (Sheriff, Jailer, *and soldiers exit on the other side.*)

SCENE XI
Actors, *as before; except* Sheriff, Jailer, *and* Soldiers

Toinon: (*peering through the grating*) I just gotta see what direction he's gonna be headin' in. Let's see – oh, by Saint Anne's boots! He's beatin' up the sennatree. (*Laughs.*) Ha! Good! Good! There's the senatree now, lyin' on his back. (*Laughs.*)

Looks like it's them redcoats' turn now, eh? Good ... now he's takin' his gun an' marchin' around with it! Oh, by Saint Anne's boots! here comes a whole gang of 'em. They got bayonets – Oh, I can't stand to look no more! ...

Béchard: What? Is this your idea of another joke of some kind? (*He goes to look out the grating.*)

Toinon: (*stopping him*) Oh! don't look, don't look! (*He returns to the door, and immediately bursts out laughing.*)

Béchard: What's happening?

Toinon: (*laughing*) Wow! Is he ever crazy! ... He's a nut!

Béchard: What's he doing?

Toinon: (*laughing*) He's takin' 'em off ... He's takin' 'em off. He's got 'em off! What a nut! What a nut!

Béchard: Tell us what's going on, you idiot!

Toinon: (*holding his sides with laughter*) He took 'em off, an' now he put 'em on his back!

Béchard: *What?*

Toinon: His boots! An' there he goes, barefoot in the snow! By Saint Anne's boots! – his poor toes!

Béchard: But he's gone!

Toinon: Yeah, an' I don't think anyone's too sorry about that!

Béchard: Poor lad! May the good Lord give him guidance.

Toinon: I can sure tell you, I had my fill of him!

The setting changes to represent the inside of Poutré's house.

SCENE XII
Poutré Senior, *alone*

Poutré: *(entering)* No news! Another useless trip! Oh, this will be the death of me! My poor Félix, the last of my children! The only hope for my old age, dragged off to the gallows like a murderer, just because he loved his country too much! Oh Lord, surely you won't permit this! Let me die, but save my son! Poor child, driven insane by his fear of execution! And I didn't even have the consolation of embracing him one last time – he brushed me aside with curses! He didn't even recognize his own father. And there's my reward for seventy years of honesty and hard work! Oh, the traitors! The tyrants! Come, feed on my suffering! Come and enjoy the despair of a poor old man whose last consolation has been snatched from him! You're thirsty for victims' tears – well, there are plenty of tears here, from this white-haired old man! Come and see, all of you: it's a spectacle worthy of your attention!

SCENE XIII
Poutré Senior, Camel

Camel: *(entering)* Well now, Monsieur Poutré, have you heard the news?

Poutré: Out of here, you traitor! No – come here! I suppose you're not satisfied? All right, put the finishing touch on your foul deeds, you coward! You've sent my son to the gallows; he won't be alone: arrest his father, too! Complete your mission! I despise the vile tyrants whom you serve, do you understand me? I despise them, I revile them, and I'd spit in their faces if they were here. As for you, you're nothing but a coward.

Camel: Come, come, Monsieur Poutré. Still holding a grudge against me? I only did my duty, you know. It was never my intention to hurt you. I know you've helped me more than once, so just to prove to you I'm not ungrateful I've come to bring you news from Montreal.

Poutré: What more news could you have for me, traitor? Probably Félix's death sentence?

Camel: No, not quite, but ten of his comrades have just been sentenced to death, including de Lorimier, the notary.[32]

Poutré: No mention of Félix? But they told me ...

Camel: Hold on a bit – they can't hang twenty-five men all at once!

Poutré: The poor lad!

SCENE XIV
Actors, *as before*; Félix

Félix: (*entering*) Father!

Poutré: Félix!

Camel: Him! (Félix *and his father run to embrace each other.*)

Poutré: Free! You're free! Thank you, Lord!

Félix: (*turning to* Camel) What, you again, you scoundrel! No doubt you're here to arrest me again. But I don't care a damn about you now! Here – read this! (*He shows him a document.*)

Camel: A letter of pardon!

Poutré: He's pardoned!

Félix: Yes.

Camel: Well, well – my dear Félix, I'm very happy for you, and hope you won't hold anything against me. It was merely my duty, my duty, you know ...

Félix: What! You have the gall to ... (*Two policemen enter.*)

SCENE XV
Actors, *as before;* two Policemen

Camel: The police! I'm saved! Officers, arrest this man. He's escaped from prison! He has a letter of pardon obtained under false pretences. I'll prove it! Arrest him!

Policeman: Is there someone here by the name of Joseph Camel?

Camel: That's me.

Policeman: Then I hereby arrest you for forgery. Here is my warrant.

Camel: Curses! (*The policemen seize him.*)

Félix: Good for you, you wretch! Now it's your turn!

Poutré: God is just! (Camel *and the policemen exit.*) So it's really you, Félix, finally! But they told me you were sentenced to death!

Félix: Yes, but they couldn't even put me on trial. I pretended to be insane. Not exactly heroic, but it saved my life.

Poutré: You mean you *weren't* insane?

Félix: No more than I am today. And I must beg your pardon for the way I treated you. I did it to save my own life, and to save you further sorrow.

Poutré: My dear Félix, let's not even talk about it! (Béchard *enters.*)

SCENE XVI
Actors, *as before*; Béchard

Béchard: Freed, me too!

Félix, Poutré: (*together*) Béchard! (*They all embrace.*)

Béchard: They had no proof against me – as simple as that!

Poutré: Boys, let us thank Divine Providence, who never forsakes those who have faith in it!

Félix: Indeed, father, let's thank Divine Providence for watching over us and let's pray for those poor victims, less fortunate than us, who have paid on the gallows for the crime of loving their country too much! They died as brave patriots and Christian heroes. May their deaths prove a fertile ground for patriotism, and may the soil that has drunk their blood bear the finest fruit for the future of Canada! (*Curtain.*)

VI

Archibald Cameron of Locheill, or an Episode in the Seven Years' War in Canada (1759)

INTRODUCTION

1. History of the Play

This last text, *Archibald Cameron of Locheill ou un épisode de la Guerre de Sept Ans en Canada (1759)*, was composed for the college stage, a very active and important dimension of indigenous theatre in nineteenth-century Quebec. First performed on 19 January 1865 at the Collège de L'Assomption near Montreal, it is adapted from what is generally considered to be the outstanding French-Canadian novel of the century, Philippe Aubert de Gaspé's *Les Anciens Canadiens*, published two years earlier and translated subsequently as *The Canadians of Old* and as *Cameron of Lochiel*.[1] The adaptation, by a priest-in-training at the Collège de L'Assomption, almost immediately became the most popular play in Quebec's system of *collèges classiques* and, by the last decade of the century, in the youth organizations known as Les Cercles de Jeunes Gens. Its last performance to which reference has been found was on 26 October 1936 at the Collège de L'Assomption.

Two printed editions of the text exist, the first published in 1894 and the second in 1917.[2] In addition, there is a heavily rewritten manuscript draft completed in 1864 (and which is probably closer to the text first performed in 1865), as well as a full manuscript version prepared for a repeat performance at the Collège de L'Assomption in 1868.[3] The original text was essentially the work of twenty-four-year old Camille Caisse, then a subdeacon awaiting ordination to the priesthood, with thirty-two-year old Arcade Laporte, supervisor of studies at the Collège de L'Assomption (and, like Caisse, a graduate of that institution), supplying only the general outline, as affirmed by Laporte in a note that precedes the 1868 manuscript version. Neither of the published editions gives any credit to Caisse or to Laporte, the first, in 1894, purporting, on its title-page, to be by Aubert de Gaspé himself (he had died in 1871), the second saying 'drawn from the popular novel by P. A. de Gaspé.' Because of the impressive number of similar plays that were 'drawn' from other authors and 'arranged' for youth organizations by the prolific J.G.W. McGown (the 'arrangement' usually involving the excision of female roles and of any references remotely offensive to local tastes) and because the two published editions of the play append a list of McGown's adaptations, including, after a misleading division-bar, the title, *Les Anciens Canadiens*, along with others known not to be by him, he is often credited as the adaptor – and indeed, he may have had something to do with the preparation of the printed versions, which are virtually identical. The text I have chosen to translate is the earliest surviving complete version, the manuscript prepared for a special performance in March 1868 and which is retained at the Collège de L'Assomption.

2. Relationship between the Novel and the Play(s)

The play has sometimes been dismissed as quite unoriginal, a mere copy of the dialogue and events in the novel.[4] A comparison of the texts does not justify this judgment, as we shall see, although the 1868 manuscript is closer to the original text than are the published editions of the play.

Aubert de Gaspé's novel opens in New France, some fifteen years before the climactic events of 1759–60. A young Scots nobleman, Archibald Cameron of Locheill, whose mother was French, has had to seek refuge in Canada from unjust persecution of his family in Scotland. He is befriended by the seigneurial d'Haberville family, and especially by its scion, Jules, who is of the same age as Archibald ('Arché' or 'Archie'). The two become inseparable friends – 'brothers' – during their college years in Quebec. Upon graduation they both choose military careers, Archie with the British Army, Jules with the French. They wind up fighting on opposite sides in the battle for New France. Archie, forced to carry out cruel measures against non-combatants that are ordered by his family's nemesis, Major Montgomery, is despised because of this by the Canadians who had loved and befriended him, including Jules.

After participating heroically in the battles of the Plains of Abraham and Sainte-Foy, Archie and Jules eventually become reconciled and resolve to live in amity in the new Canada resulting from the Conquest. Archie's happiness is incomplete, however, for the woman he has long loved, Blanche, Jules's sister, refuses on principle to marry him, despite the love she bears for him. (Jules, on the other hand, marries an English woman, and thus the novel ends with a confused symbolism that has engendered much critical speculation.)

The play, naturally, compresses the action, opening a day or two before the battle of the Plains of Abraham, a little over halfway through the plot of Aubert de Gaspé's novel, but with frequent retrospective references. Act 1 presents the French-Canadian militia in preparation for military engagement, as they learn of

the apparent extent of Archie's ingratitude. Six of its seven scenes take nothing textual from the novel except for one brief remark by Saint-Luc in scene 1, referring to
the arrival of British troops led by Archie at Rivière-Ouelle. Scene 3, the longest in
this act, is the only one borrowed directly from Aubert de Gaspé. In it, José, whose
family has served the d'Habervilles for generations, recounts at great length his
father's encounter with the legendary La Corriveau[5] and the ghosts and demons of
the Île d'Orléans. This folkloric digression (somewhat compressed by comparison
with the novel) obviously represented an attractive hors d'oeuvre for contemporary
readers and audiences, as evidenced by the fact that at least one other play was spun
off from the novel with this episode as its title and central focus.[6] José's tale is arti-
ficially interrupted in the 1868 manuscript, assumedly in order to retain the audience's suspended interest, then resumed and ended in act 2, scene 7. (Perhaps the
episode had lost some of its interest by the 1890s, for the two printed versions
return to the novel's strategy, leaving the tale intact, in act 1, scene 3.)

Most of act 2 is inspired, textually as well as thematically, by the novel. Much of
it is devoted to Archie, the dilemma he faces because of Montgomery's cruel orders
– including the directive to burn the d'Habervilles' seigneurial mansion and other
properties – his capture by Indians loyal to the French cause, and his eventual rescue by a Canadian whose life Archie had once saved. The action then returns to the
Canadian militia as they listen to the end of José's tale. Act 3, on the other hand,
represents a considerable departure from the novel. Textually, there is virtually no
resemblance: a faint echo or two of Aubert de Gaspé's dialogue is all that remains
of the original. Thematically, the two texts have little in common as well. The
novel had painted briefly the outcome of the battle of the Plains of Abraham in
September 1759, followed immediately by a longer description of the battle of
Sainte-Foy in April 1760 (often called, as it is by Aubert de Gaspé, the 'Second
Battle of the Plains of Abraham'), in which French and Canadian troops under
François de Lévis defeated the small army of Wolfe's successor, General Murray. As
the British troops retreat hastily behind the fortifications of Quebec, where they
would successfully withstand the siege undertaken by Lévis, Archie and Jules meet
by chance, long enough for the wounded Jules to taunt his former friend for his
actions. Ten days later Archie seeks Jules out in the makeshift hospital where he lies
inside the city walls and manages to persuade him, without great difficulty, of the
sincerity of his intentions and the guiltlessness of his actions. The two reaffirm
their former bonds and will spend the rest of their unclouded lives as friends and
neighbours in the new Canada.

The play, on the other hand, in the 1868 manuscript version, presents only the
first battle, through descriptive off-stage commentary by Indian allies of the French
(act 3, scene 1). Scenes 2 and 3 present Montgomery's traitorous scheme (which
has no basis in the novel) to have Archie murdered during the battle. In scenes 4

and 5 the beaten Canadians regroup and resolve to face their future with courage. Jules joins them in scene 6, exhorting them not to lose hope. They march off, leaving Jules alone (scene 7) to soliloquize on his nation's military disaster and the personal disappointment he feels at Archie's betrayal. Thus scene 8, the longest and the climactic scene of the play, has been well prepared, for Archie happens to appear at this point, having escaped the machinations of the evil Montgomery. After much explanation and anguished pleading by Archie and much anguished soul-searching by Jules, they are about to agree, in a scene far more emotionally effective than in the novel, to forget the past and to re-establish their friendship. Montgomery happens upon their reconciliation (scene 9) and threatens to denounce Archie as a traitor. But Montgomery's plot to kill him has been discovered by General Murray, who has dispatched a letter to Archie appointing him to Montgomery's post. Archie explains to Jules that he has refused the promotion and resigned from the British Army, a decision that makes his complete reconciliation with him (scene 10) all the more convincing. The play ends with the two friends, the Indians, and José all returning to share their joy. Again, in all this there is little or no resemblance to the novel. (There is simply no reference in the play to Archie's ill-fated love for Blanche, and in any case one would expect no such reference in college theatre at that time.)

As this brief comparison shows, Caisse did not slavishly follow the plot or reproduce the dialogue of the novel: nearly two-thirds of his text is different, sometimes in major ways, from the original. It is also obvious that the young author had a certain sense of dramatic structure, influenced by classic French tastes. Whereas the novel depicts the tension between Archie and Jules as a secondary theme, allowing it to subside fairly easily once Archie has a chance to explain his actions, Caisse has made of their conflict the very substance of his play: apart from the digression represented by José's tale, every scene prepares for the culminating emotional confrontation between the two heroes in act 3, scene 8.

3. The 1868 Manuscript

The full title and description given the 1868 manuscript by its authors is 'Archibald Cameron of Locheill, or an Episode in the Seven Years War (1759) in Canada. A full-scale drama in three acts drawn from Les Anciens Canadiens by Monsieur Philippe Aubert de Gaspé. Play performed at the Collège de L'Assomption on 19 March 1868, for the benefit of the Canadian Zouaves.' About 85 per cent of the manuscript is identical to what is reproduced in the two printed editions of 1894 and 1917. There are structural differences between the manuscript and published versions of the play, however, the most important being the consolidation of José's long tale, as we have seen, into one connected whole in the printed versions (act 1, scene 3), whereas the manuscript interrupts the story begun in act 1, scene 3, then resumes and finishes it in act 2, scene 7. And there is a major thematic transposition of considerable interest to historians: whereas the manuscript version deals only the battle of the Plains of Abraham in 1759, the printed versions depict the battle of Sainte-Foy. Thus in the published texts the reconciliation of Jules and Archie takes place in the heady atmosphere of a French victory rather than after a crushing defeat. These differences and other textual variants of any significance are indicated in my notes.

It is not difficult to understand the drama's appeal in all of its versions to contemporary audiences, particularly the educated, idealistic segment of society present for end of term exercises at a *collège classique*. Both Archibald and Jules exemplify the loftiest of ideals and the noblest of sentiments. Both are passionately committed to French Canada, although Archie's oath to the British Crown as a commissioned officer leads to the despicable actions he is forced by his superior, Montgomery,[7] to implement. Readers of the novel had all seen its symbolic dimensions on the national level in the atmosphere immediately preceding Confederation, and the play magnifies through concision the force of part of that symbolism. As we have seen, however, Blanche d'Haberville's adamant refusal to wed Archie, despite their strong mutual attraction, is, in the novel, a symbolic but clear affirmation of her and her country's intention to remain culturally distinct in their coexistence with English-speaking Canada. By its omission of this theme – in which an adaptor for the college stage had no choice, let us recall – the play's message is noticeably impoverished.

The thematic weight of the play falls elsewhere, in the psychological conflict pitting Archie against Jules, glorifying the nobility of the French cause, and affirming faith in the future. It is not coincidental that Aubert de Gaspé's novel appeared in 1863, exactly a hundred years after the Treaty of Paris which sealed the fate of New France (and let us recall, Caisse's original adaptation was completed the following year). The glorification of the *ancien régime* was already well under way in French Canada, and Aubert de Gaspé (whose family had fought for the French Crown but had stayed on after the Conquest to fight for the British) presented a glowing, nostalgic portrayal of the society in which his family had enjoyed so many privileges. Through these rosy lenses all the French-Canadian characters are honest, loyal, happy, and amusing, and utterly dedicated to their seigneur and captain, Jules d'Haberville. Traditional songs and music, colourful native Indian costumes and speech, melodramatic coincidences and miraculous escapes, visually compelling tableaux depicting marching scenes and skirmishes, plus a strong seasoning of local folklore – all conspire to fix a patriotic audience's attention, in the familiar setting of an amateur entertainment attended only by parents of students enrolled in the college, plus a few invited dignitaries.

4. College Theatre in French Canada before Confederation

College theatre in Quebec was rather different from what we are familiar with today in Canada's schools, universities, and colleges. It was very strictly limited in scope, choice of texts, time of performance, and audience. The tradition was almost as old as the history of education in New France, for the Jesuits, following the pedagogic principles of their order, had introduced it into their first school in Quebec soon after its inception in 1635 as a means of instilling confidence into their students and giving them edifying models to emulate, with most of the texts written by members of the Jesuit Order. There are frequent references to this type of dramatic activity for the rest of the seventeenth century. But college theatre virtually disappeared for a time after the memorable confrontation between the bishop of Quebec and Governor Frontenac in 1694, and then resurfaced vigorously immediately after the Conquest. It had been carefully inserted into the curriculum of the extensive network of *collèges classiques* that was developed during the first half of the nineteenth century, and that offered virtually the only advanced humanistic education in Quebec for male francophones.[8] Indeed, it is one of the curious contradictions that public theatre long remained suspect – and often explicitly condemned – in French Canada, while at the same time a strong interest in stage arts was inculcated into all educated Québécois – all the males, at least – through their upper schools.

Before *Archibald Cameron of Locheill*, the best known college play written in Quebec had come from the pen of twenty-year-old Antoine Gérin-Lajoie in 1844 while he was still a student at the Collège de Nicolet.[9] But his case is exceptional, and most of the repertoire came from other sources: plays by Jesuit authors published specifically for schools; adaptations of well-known French classical plays, especially by Molière, Corneille, and Racine (with all female characters and love themes removed, of course); and texts composed by priests or other religious teaching in the *collège classique* system, a notable example being Father Hospice-Anselme Verreau's *Stanislas de Kostka*, performed at the Collège-Séminaire de Sainte-Thérèse in 1855.[10]

The play's première took place, as we have mentioned, on 19 January 1865, at L'Assomption, and it was enthusiastically received according to contemporary reports. In the absence of the bishop of Montreal, in Rome at the time, Monsignor Farrell, bishop of Hamilton, Upper Canada, had made the journey in the dead of winter, to consecrate a new altar and attend the concert and dramatic performance scheduled to celebrate the occasion. He was lavish in his praise of the play, as were others who were present.[11] A former student at the college, one Major Charles Guilbeau, had returned to play the role of Archibald and had apparently acquitted himself exceptionally well. But a far more impressive performance took place at the college that summer on 11 July. The elderly novelist, now approaching his eighti-eth year, was present, arriving with great pomp in a steamboat from Montreal to a rousing welcome from staff, students, and parents. There were stirring speeches before and after the three-hour performance, with Aubert de Gaspé expressing his delight at the unique honour accorded his work and himself. A medal was even struck to commemorate the occasion, a minor theatrical summit but certainly one of the cultural highlights of the decade in Quebec.[12]

5. Language

Compared with the other texts in this volume, the French used by most of the characters is straightforward, 'correct,' or 'international,' as would befit perfor-mance in an educational institution. The speech of José and Fontaine is unlettered, rustic, and colourful, but without the often exaggerated deformations found in *Félix Poutré* or in *A Country Outing*. A different nuance is heard in the speech of the native Indian characters, however, who express themselves in solemn, formal French flavoured with similes and metaphors drawn – at least that is the apparent intention – from their natural surroundings. Not all of these ring true: the frequent references to lions and tigers in the mouth of Great Otter, for example, may seem difficult to accommodate to the realities of North American zoology. Nonetheless, the adaptation is certainly kinder to Amerindian values, speech, and mores than was the original.

Archibald Cameron of Locheill, or an Episode in the Seven Years' War in Canada (1759)

Drawn from *Les Anciens Canadiens* by
Monsieur Philippe Aubert de Gaspé[13]

This play was performed at the Collège de L'Assomption on
19 March 1868 for the benefit of the Papal Zouaves.[14]

CHARACTERS

Archibald Cameron of Locheill (Archie), a Scottish officer serving in
the English army
Jules d'Haberville, a Captain in the Canadian Militia
Dumais, a soldier in the Militia
José, Dubé, Fontaine,[15] Pierrot, Canadians
Saint-Luc, Platoon commander in the Militia
Montgomery, a Major in the English army
Another English officer
Great Otter, Chief of the Indian allies
Talamousse and Ouabi,[16] Abenaki Indians
Six other Indians
Seven other Canadian Militiamen

ACT ONE

Setting: *A Canadian military encampment*

SCENE I
Jules d'Haberville, Saint-Luc, *both seated*

Saint-Luc: From the rumours I've heard it will be a terrible fight, Captain d'Haberville. They say England has made impressive preparations and that she's decided to do her utmost to seize the colony.

Jules: All the better for us! It'll be a chance to add new lustre to our arms!

Saint-Luc: I haven't the slightest doubt as to our soldiers' courage, Captain. But let's not deceive ourselves: virtually abandoned by the mother country, Canada is in a rather precarious situation.

Jules: Indeed. The situation is growing darker for New France, day by day. But what of it? (*He stands.*) I have faith in the future of my country! I have faith in Providence, which never abandons those who rely on it to defend their rights. Don't we have God, and our own stout swords, on our side, Monsieur de Saint-Luc? For a brave man, for a real *Canadian*, that should be enough! By the way, do we know who's commanding the English troops?

Saint-Luc: They say it's Wolfe,[17] one of the most distinguished generals in the whole British Army.

Jules: Wolfe? That's a name long familiar to me. He's a worthy adversary for our brave Montcalm!

Saint-Luc: Among his leading officers they say there's one you used to know quite well.

Jules: (*surprised*) That *I* used to know quite well?

Saint-Luc: Yes, Captain – and I might add, whom you honoured with your respect and friendship as well.

Jules: I don't understand.

Saint-Luc: A few people from Rivière-Ouelle,[18] on their way through here this morning, informed us that two English regiments had landed on their shores, and that their leader was a young Scottish officer ... to whom your father, Captain d'Haberville, once offered hospitality as ...

Jules: (*interrupting*) Stop right there, Saint-Luc! You're talking about Archie, but don't you realize Archie is my friend, and that the suspicions you're raising about that noble officer amount to an insult, as far as I'm concerned?

Saint-Luc: Yes, I know that. Realizing that it's only a vague rumour at this point, I had decided not to mention it to you. But since it's Jules d'Haberville himself who asked me, I though I should be perfectly frank and open with him.

Jules: Yes, my noble friend, you judged me by your own standards, and I thank you for it! But what do you think of this rumour? Is there any foundation to it?

Saint-Luc: (*hesitating*) Captain ... without giving it much weight ... I can't help ...

Jules: (*forcefully*) What! The very idea that Archie would bear arms against Canada, which sheltered him in his misfortune! That Archie would betray my father! Betray *me*, his friend and brother! If that were the case, I would detest him as much as I used to love him, the wretch! (*Striding back and forth.*) But I know Archie, and there's no way this can be true. You're mistaken, Saint-Luc! (*The militiamen are heard, singing as they arrive.*) I can hear our soldiers coming, so I'll leave you with them for a while. Just as well they don't find out what we've been talking about, for the moment.

Saint-Luc: You may count on my discretion, Captain. (*Jules exits.*)

SCENE II
Saint-Luc, Militiamen

(*The soldiers perform a military salute for the audience: 'Platoon – halt! About – turn! Present – arms! Open order – march!'*)[19]

Saint-Luc: Brave members of the militia, we have quite a task before us today! But first of all, let's sing us a nice military song, as we Canadians like them. You there, my good fellow, give us the key for the 'Soldier's Refrain'!

A Soldier: (*sings*)

> O Sons of France, O soldiers brave
> Liberty beckons us with open arms.
> They said to us, 'You shall be slaves!'
> And we replied, 'We shall be soldiers!'
> Come brave men all to the field of honour;
> Come! You shall not be slaves!
>
> Chorus
> Forward! March on
> Between the cannons
> Through smoke and fire and enemy troops
> Speed on to victory! (*bis*)[20]

Saint-Luc: Well sung, friends! Your war song fills our hearts with courage and joy. And that's the true Canadian soldier: ever merry and carefree in camp, but fierce as a lion on the battlefield!

Fontaine: So's to speak ...

Dubé: What d'you mean, 'so to speak'?

Fontaine: Well, so's to speak, 'merry 'n carefree in camp' is fine for me, as long as the enemy ain't too near. But as far as the battlefield – no siree! I ain't cut out for to be no soldier! I'm too fond of my fellow-man.

Saint-Luc: How so?

Dubé: (*laughing*) He's right, sir! – to the point that big Fontaine here, bravest of the brave, went and hid in old man Michon's cellar, as soon as our marching orders came!

Fontaine: That's right, an' you're the one who went and squealed on me to the recruitin' officer! You'll pay for that, you big tattle-tale!

A Soldier: Come on, Fontaine – I can't believe my ears! And you a direct descendant of the heroes who founded this colony!

Fontaine: Let me tell you, the only thing I ever descended was the path between us an' our neighbour Gendreau's that leads to the parish church! An' if they told you anythin' else about me, they was lyin'! (*All laugh.*) Ain't nothin' to laugh at! If I'm here wagin' war today, it's because of people like you that talk too much! You've went and give me a real reppytation, now! Okay – you're the ones that's gonna be responsible for any blood I spill!

Dubé: Don't worry about that: I'll take responsibility for everything, as long as it's not your own blood you shed, because that's too precious.

Fontaine: Well, that's exactly why I don't wanna take any risks. God, just think! I was so happy back home, doin' my chores an' chattin' up my dear Josette in the evening! (*He starts to sob.*)

Saint-Luc: It's a good thing Canadians like you are a rarity, poor lad (Fontaine *bows to him*), because otherwise the English flag would soon fly victorious over our great river!

Dubé: At least be good enough to treat us to a drink, Fontaine, so we can toast your health!

Fontaine: Gladly! I prefer to spend my money with good Christians like you, rather than see it stole from me by them English hairyticks! Here you go, Pierrot – go on over to old Missuz Dupré's an' bring back some of her good stuff. Tell her it's for Édouard Fontaine, son of André Fontaine his father, beadle of the parish of Saint-Jean-Port-Joli. You got that?

The Others: Now you're talking!

SCENE III
Actors, *as before*; José

(*All rush to surround* José.)

Saint-Luc: Well hello, Papa José! We've been hoping for the pleasure of your company for quite a while. What do you think – are the soup and black bread here in camp as good as Captain d'Haberville's fritters or Uncle Raoul's flatcakes?

José: Sir, with all due respect an' all, I can tell you that whatever duty commands is okay with me, an' I'd consider meself unworthy of sharin' the fate of Captain d'Haberville if I didn't get to share his toils an' depreevations, too!

All: Well said! Three cheers for Papa José!

Dubé: Now there's a son worthy of his father, the great, immortal François the Boozer, who fought one whole night against witches, werewolves, hobgoblins, and all the assembled devils of the Île d'Orléans that wanted to drag him along to their sabbath!

Fontaine: What kinda flapdoodle you talkin' now, Dubé?

José: It ain't no flapdoodle, you big know-nothin'! It's an adventure that happened to my dear departed father – he's dead an' gone, now – an' it's the absolute truth, as sure as you're the biggest blockhead in this whole county!

Saint-Luc: Come now, José, don't be angry at Fontaine. Instead, sing us that nice song that your dear departed father – who's *dead and gone now* (*he stresses these words*) – stole from the evil spirits of the Île d'Orléans. What's more, this generous son of Bellona here (*he points to* Fontaine) is going to whet our whistles with a draught as sweet as the nectar served by Ganymede to the dwellers of Olympus ...[21]

José: Sir, I don't know those countries you're talkin' about, an' as far as booze goes, I ain't finicky. I was always happy enough with the brandy my captain gets sent from Quebec, an' never asked for no granny's mead from a Limpus. Meantimes, I'll be happy to sing you my late father's song. But I'll be beggin' your pardon 'cause I don't have the voice, the fine larry-nix organ my dear dead departed father had.

Dubé: No matter, you'll do just fine! Here, sit down, Papa José. (*José sits, and all surround him.*)

José: But first I'll have to explain the why an' the wherefore of this song. So listen up – I'll make it short, an' it won't take long!

Fontaine: Good! Give us the why, the wherefore, the who, and the how an' the how come, anythin' you want, we're all listenin'!

José: One day my dear departed father, who's dead an' gone now, had left town pretty late an' set out for home, after tossin' off a few pints with his friends from Pointe-Lévis. He liked to take a drop, y' know, fine, good man that he was. Fact, he even went so far as to carry with him a flask o' brandy in his sailor's sack, whenever he travelled. Used to say that for old-timers, it was like milk!

Saint-Luc: (*sententiously*) *Lac dulce* ...[22]

José: (*peevishly*) With all due respect an' all, Monsieur de Saint-Luc, it weren't no lackadaisy, nor lake water or whatever, it was some of that good, honest brandy that my dear dead departed father carried around in his pack!

Saint-Luc: I'm sorry, José, I didn't intend to slight your dear dead departed father's memory ...

José: No slight taken, sir. Anyways, when my dear dead departed father set out, it was comin' on dark already. His friends did everythin' they could to get him to sleep over, pointin' out that he would have to pass by the iron cage where that Corriveau woman paid the penalty for killin' her husband ...[23]

Fontaine: (*interrupting*) A Corriveau who kilt her husband? I never heard nothin' about that!

Dubé: Hush! Don't keep interrupting the man when he's talking, you big nincompoop!

José: So anyways my dear dead departed father, who was hard as nails, says to them that he didn't owe nothin' to the Corriveau woman, addin' a whole lot of other things that I forget now. An' he gives his mare a crack o'the whip, and they're off! But when he's passin' in front of her skellyton he's pretty sure he hears some sort o' noise, some sort o' groanin' like, but since the wind was gustin' up pretty good from the sou'west, he thinks maybe it's the wind blowin' through the bones of her skellyton. But that worries him quite a bit, just the same, so he takes a good pull on the bottle to steady his nerves. Like my dear dead departed father used to say, good Christians gotta stick together, when all's said an' done, an' maybe that poor thing was askin' for prayers. So he takes off his cap an' recites a *Diaper Fundy*[24] for her, as devoutly as he can, figurin' if that didn't do her no good, it couldn't do her no harm neither; an' either way he couldn't help but be better off for it ...

Dubé: Darn good thinking on Grampa François' part! I'm not surprised he's got a son like you, the pride of his family, the glory of the county, a son favoured by fortune ...

José: (*continues without paying attention to* Dubé) So he just keeps goin', fast as he can. But once he gets up on the heights near Saint-Michel, all of a sudden he starts to feel drowsy, like. A man ain't a dog after all, as my dear dead departed father used to say!

Saint-Luc: And yet, my friend José, I could quote you a whole raft of philosophers, armed to the teeth with their learning, who would argue against your honourable, respectable – and dearly departed – father, that the only difference between a man and a dog is that one of them has a tail ...

José: Them foolofficers o' yours are idjits, savin' your respect an' all, sir, an' they don't deserve to share in the Good Lord's Eucharist!

Fontaine: You know, I can't thank my mum enough – Lisette was her name – that she didn't send me to school! The way I am, I mighta wound up being a big foolofficer too, learnin' nonsense o' that sort! I'm better off just knowin' me kattykissem –

Dubé: Will you belt up, loud-mouth? Go on, José.

José: 'A man ain't a dog,' my dear dead departed father says to hisself. 'Let's have a bit of a nap. Both the mare an' I'll be better off for it.' So he unharnesses his mare, hobbles her with the reins, an' says to her: 'Here's some good grass, an' you can hear the brook runnin' over yonder. So there you go, an' good night to you!' But just when my dear dead departed father was about to crawl under his wagon to keep the night dew off o' him, he decided to check out the time o' night. Seein' the Three Kings in the south an' the Chariot in the north, he figured it must be midnight. 'Time for all good men to be in bed,' he says to hisself. But then all of a sudden it seems to him the whole Île d'Orléans is on fire! So he jumps up, climbs over a ditch, leans on a fence, opens his eyes good an' wide, an' he stares an' stares ... He stares so hard his eyes – they was a bit fogged up, y'see – they cleared up all of a sudden, an' there he sees a weird sight, I can tell you!

All: What kind of sight? What was it?

José: Just you listen! It was kinda like ... *men*, but strange critters, just the same! They had heads big as half-bushel baskets, with pointy hats on top, a good yard long! An' they had arms, an' legs, an' feet, an' hands with claws on 'em, but no *bodies*, or at least not enough to mention! They had, savin' your presence, their crotches startin' right under their ears! (*All chuckle here.*) Hardly any meat on 'em, they was nearly all bones, like skellytons. An' all them pretty folk had their upper lips split, like harelips, with one big tooth, stickin' out a good foot long, like a rhinoceferous, the kind you see in the book o' supernatural history Uncle Raoul has. As for noses, they was hardly worth mentionin' – nothin' more than pigs' snouts, beggin' your pardon, that they swivelled left 'n' right o' that big rhinoceferous tooth – to sharpen it up, I reckon! Oh, an' I nearly forgot: they each had a long tail too, twice as long as a cow's ...

Fontaine: Hey! Mighta been that comet, that came down from the sky with its little ones!

José: No, you big ninny – they used it to keep the flies off!

Fontaine: (*frightened*) Holy Mother, that musta been scary! Like that long, tall son of a gun I saw once in Master Beaumont's garden, a big ugly thing, sittin' on the end of a stick, as long as the length of a ...

A Soldier: (*interrupting*) Will you shut up, blabbermouth! Don't you realize you're breaking one of the first laws of courtesy, interrupting Papa José in his fascinating story?

José: Aw, I don't hold it against him – he ain't had no eddy-cayshun, y'know ...

Fontaine: *Me*, no eddycayshun? After I spent two an' a half years workin' for Monsieur Bégin the notary, who had a whole closet full o' big books!

José: (*continuing*) My dear dead departed father, well his eyes were just buggin' right out o' his head! But things got worse when they all started to prance an' dance around, without movin' at all. They was singin' too, and the voices on 'em sounded awful, like bulls when they're gettin' strangled! An' here is what they were singin':
  Come along spooks, friends of mine!
  Come along spirits, neighbours of mine!
  Come along gravediggers all,
  Frogs an' toads all to the ball:
  Let's make a feast, a spooky feast,
  Of Christians, of Christians!
'Oh, you bloody carniballs!' says my dear dead departed father. 'You scoundrels want to feast on Christians instead of wine!' But the witches went on with their hellish singin', starin' at my late father an' aimin' their big rhinoceferous teeth at 'im:

> Come along, good friend François!
> Come along now, juicy piglet!
> Hurry up, friend sausage-head,
> Puddin'-head, punkin' head:
> Let's make a dinner, a salt-pork dinner
> Of François, of François the Frenchman!

'All I got to say right now,' says my late father, 'is, if you ain't gonna eat any more fat than you'll get off me, you won't have to de-grease your stew!'

Saint-Luc: Now that's the way to talk to His Satanic Majesty! Dear departed François must have been quite a brave man!

José: All this time the witches seemed to be waitin' for somethin', 'cause they kept turnin' their heads an' lookin' back. So my late father, he does the same thing. An' what do you think he sees, right there on the hillside? A huge devil built just like the others, but as tall as the bell-tower on the church at Saint-Michel! Except instead of a pointy cap, he was wearin' a three-cornered hat with a big spruce tree on top for a plume. He only had one eye, the scoundrel, but it was worth a dozen! He was probably their regimental drum major, 'cause he was holdin' in one hand a big pot, twice as big as our sugarin'-off pots, the ones that hold twenty gallons, an' in his other hand he was holdin' the clapper from a big bell that I s'pose the bloody hairytick had robbed from some church before it was blessed!

Fontaine: (*startled*) What! What's that you say! (*The others stare at him and motion to him to be silent.*)

José: So all of a sudden this giant of a devil starts singin' some devilish song, accompanyin' hisself on his pot, drummin' louder an' louder! An' all them spooks took off like lightnin' – took 'em less than a minute to zip round the whole island! That's when they started to sing that fine song that my late father could only 'member three verses of. I'm gonna sing 'em for you:

> This is our Île d'Orléans
> The land of pretty folk like us,
>   Toura loura!
> Let's dance all around it,
>   Toura loura!
> Let's dance all around it!
>
> Come along now, all you ghosts,
> Wizards, lizards, toads, an' serpents,
>   Toura loura!

    Let's dance all around it,
       Toura loura!
    Let's dance all around it!

      Come along now, all you spooks,
      Pagans, atheists, unbelievers,
      Toura loura!
    Let's dance all around it,
      Toura loura!
    Let's dance all around it![25]

My dear dead departed father was sweatin' blood, but he wasn't through the worst of his troubles yet, the poor man!

Dubé: Now there's a rough situation to be in!

Fontaine: This one's just as scary as the stories my late grampa used to tell me, that used to make me shiver from stem to stern!

José: But right now I'm just dyin' for a smoke, an' if you don't mind, I'm gonna stoke up my pipe ...

Saint-Luc: Good idea, my dear José. I'm dying for something else: according to my stomach it's seven o'clock, time for supper for any good soldier. Let's have a bite to eat, to restore our strength.

Dubé: I second that motion!

All: Me too! me too!

Fontaine: An' I third it, an fourth it! Ain't it nice, though, to be settled down in your camp, knowin' the enemy is a long ways off!

Dubé: And I see Pierrot coming too, in the distance, with a jug under his arm!

Saint-Luc: Splendid! The sweet potion he's carrying will serve as a nice sauce for our bread. (*With feeling.*) My, how wonderful the soldier's life is! I'd bet you all the money in the world that Croesus with all his wealth wasn't as happy as a stout-hearted soldier, fearless and uncomplaining, eating his soup and black bread with an appetite like Lucifer's!

José: (*fervently*) You're absolutely right, sir, especially when the soldier you're talkin' about is a Canadian!

All: (*enthusiastically*) Hurrah for the Canadian soldier!

SCENE IV
Actors, *as before*; Pierrot

Dubé: Come along, Pierrot – we've been waiting for you for ages!

Fontaine: (*mocking*) It's the jug he's been anxious for, not the jug-head who's carryin' it!

Pierrot: There goes Fontaine the joker again. Will you never stop playing the clown?

Saint-Luc: All right now, lads, enough of that kind of banter, if you don't mind.

Dubé: You're right, sir. Right now our task is to eat, drink, and be merry until we get our chance to make the Englishmen dance a jig for us, in time with our cannons! Let's all sit down now, and let every man do his duty. You agree with that, Fontaine?

Fontaine: His duty? Durn right I'll do my duty that way! I just hope my duty never gets no harder than this! (*They all sit, and begin to eat and drink.*)

José: (*sings*)
Can you tell me why, good friends (*bis*)
We all now feel so merry? (*bis*)
It's 'cause the only good meal
Is eaten very simply
Out of your mess-tin!
    Hurrah for the sound (*bis*)
Out of your mess-tin!
    Hurrah for the sound of the soup pot!

A Soldier: (*raising his glass*) To the health of Papa José and his dear departed father, the immortal François the Boozer!

José: Thanks, an' the same to you!

Fontaine: To the health of my mum, Lisette, an' her son Édouard Fontaine, who's gone off to war!

José: (*sings*)
    Do you know why the Romans (*bis*)
    Conquered the whole world?
    Because those doughty soldiers
    – No doubt of it, my lads! –
    Ate from their mess-tins!
      Hurrah for the sound (*bis*)
    Ate from their mess-tins!
      Hurrah for the sound of the soup-pot!

    Friends, let's finish this song (*bis*)
    With the oath of all good Frenchmen (*bis*)
    Swear, let's all swear, friends
    To stick together forever!
    Long live the King of France!
      Hurrah for the sound (*bis*)
    Long live the King of France!
      Hurrah for the sound of the cannon!

Dubé: Well sir, when shall we have the pleasure of testing our mettle against the English gentlemen? I'm starting to get a bit bored with this quiet, humdrum life!

Pierrot: No doubt about it, sir, the Canadian soldier is not made to sit idle. He needs the smell of gunpowder, the roar of the cannon, the challenge of a long, hard battle.

A Soldier: You bet! We'll show 'em that when it comes to our country, all of us Canadians, young and old, are real soldiers!

José: You better believe we're soldiers, an' darn tough ones, too! If them Englishmen show up, we'll lick 'em, same as we did before, no matter how many of 'em there is: five to one, ten to one, twenty to one – we'll still lick 'em!

Saint-Luc: Well said, friends! You demonstrate that you're worthy descendants of the Canadian pioneers, and will defeat your enemies everywhere, bringing glory and prosperity to Canada. For the moment, as we wait for our leaders to guide us to the field of honour, let's all drink to the success of our forces. May the fleur-de-lys wave forever over the frontiers of New France!

All: Long live New France!

Fontaine: Now ain't it nice to fight like this, with cheers an' pretty speechifyin'! That's the sort of stuff that don't do nobody no harm. That's the kinda war I like, with lots o' drinkin' an' eatin', an' where you can beat up on the enemy without havin' to meet 'im! If they was some way of arrangin' it like that with our English friends ...

Saint-Luc: (*interrupting*) Are you a Canadian or not, Fontaine? What sort of blood runs in your veins?

Fontaine: Aw, sir – I can't bear to think about blood at all. Makes me too skeerd! Listen, the kinda guy I am, I'm too kind-hearted to ever be a real soldier. I can't even stand to see a sheep slaughtered without ...

Saint-Luc: (*interrupting*) All right, all right, Fontaine. Let's drop the subject for the moment ...

Dubé: It's no wonder he talks so darn much – he ain't even had a smatterin' of eddy-cashun.

Fontaine: That ain't true! I had a lot o' smatterin', Dubé!

Dubé: Here comes our commanding officer, sir.

Saint-Luc: Take post, everyone!

SCENE V
Actors, *as before*; Jules

(*As* Jules *arrives,* Saint-Luc *has the soldiers present arms: 'Atten-tion! Slope – arms! Present – arms!'*)

Jules: Well done, brave soldiers of our militia. Continue to act as stout defenders of our country, and you'll soon see that if a soldier's life has its trials, it also has its blessings. From what I've seen of you, you certainly won't fall prey to melancholy!

Saint-Luc: If there's one thing that characterizes the soldier of New France, sir, it's his good humour. We're perfectly happy where we are – the only thing missing, as far as we're concerned, is the enemy!

José: Yes, my dear Jules – I mean, sir! – would you please arrange to lead us to battle as soon as you can, so's we can teach them Britishers a good lesson?

Dubé: Oh, I can't wait for a chance to try my luck against those stuck-up islanders!

Fontaine: But what about poor me? ... Durn it!

Jules: From your lofty sentiments I recognize the noble blood that flows in your veins! Friends, this is a very serious situation, for the enemy appears stronger than ever. But what of it! Let's confront the challenge, as Canadians and true Christians!

All: Hurrah for Monsieur Jules d'Haberville!

Jules: Our good friend Dumais should be arriving soon. I sent him on a mission to the Indians to find out where they stand and to encourage them to take to the warpath on our side. On his way back he was to stop off at my father's place to seek information for me on the enemy's strength. As soon as he returns we'll leave here and set up camp north-east of Quebec City. While we're waiting, let's practice our drill.

(*The soldiers carry out bayonet drill: 'Fix bayonets! Charge! Unfix bayonets! Slope arms! Order arms! Stand at ease!' After they receive the order 'Stand easy!' Dumais enters, with a letter for Jules in his hand.*)

SCENE VI
Actors, *as before*; Dumais

Jules: Dumais! Mission accomplished?

Dumais: In full, sir! Chief Great Otter, who has such influence with the Indians, announced that he was joining us, and all the others immediately sided with him, singing their war songs. Great Otter has sent messengers to the chiefs of the other bands. He himself was to set out for here the same day I left their territory. In fact, I'm a bit surprised he hasn't arrived here yet with all his warriors. He should surely be here before long.

Jules: Well done, Dumais.

Dumais: So much for the first part of my mission. As for the second part, which was to go to Captain d'Haberville's place and obtain information for you, I've succeeded in that as well. Here's a letter he asked me to give you.

Jules: Thank you. (*He reads aloud; all listen attentively.*) 'Son, the enemy disembarked here yesterday, and the tents of this impudent foreigner now cover our fields. He brings fire and devastation with him, and we are now in a very grave situation. That ingrate Archibald of Locheill, your childhood friend, is at the head of the enemy's forces here, displaying his bravery by burning down the homes of those who offered him hospitality when he was in need. Adieu, my dear Jules, conduct yourself always as a worthy descendant of the d'Habervilles, and remember that you are fighting for God and for your country. (*Signed.*) Captain d'Haberville.'

Did I really read that correctly? Archie, whom we sheltered in his misfortune; Archie for whom I would have shed the last drop of my blood! And now he's become our enemy, and our country's? Then yesterday's sinister rumour is now cruel reality! Traitor! Is that how you repay a family that was so good to you! – You vile outcast – this land nourished you, along with the noblest of her own children, and it was a serpent that she cradled to her breast! (*Striding back and forth.*) Friends, I'm going to my tent. I must answer my father and then, in just a few hours, we must leave for the position assigned to us. Have no fear, but be prepared for any eventuality!

Saint-Luc: Don't worry about us, Captain! (*Jules leaves.*)

SCENE VII
Actors, *as before, minus* Jules

Fontaine: He's quite a guy, our commandin' officer, when he gets mad! Enough foolin' around, I says!

Dubé: Oh, belt up would you, you windbag!

José: I'm crushed at that stuff about Archie! I raised him, along with Monsieur Jules, an' he always seemed to me like such a nice lad! Ah, it can't be true. But it *is* true, if it's written down on that paper! An' Jules liked his Archie so much, too! O Lord, I beg you, give him the strength to get through this trial!

Dumais: It can't be true. I know Archie too well to believe he could ever be guilty of such treachery. Anyone who risks almost certain death to save a stranger, as Archie did for me when I was almost carried off by the ice break-up at Saint-Thomas Falls,[26] anyone who does that is incapable of such a foul deed. He must have been forced into doing it, for some very good reason! (*The Indians' war cry is heard.*)

Dubé: What are those cries?

Dumais: I recognize them – it's Great Otter and his warriors, calling out to us.

Saint-Luc: Come, friends – let's hurry to meet our allies. Forward – march! Left! Right! Left! (*The soldiers exit, singing.*)

ACT TWO

Setting: *A forest*

SCENE I

Archie, *alone.* (*He seems pensive and sad.*)

After fifteen years' absence, here I am, Canada, back on your soil. But oh! how times have changed, although the countryside looks the same. Yes, this is the forest where I went hunting so often with my good friend, my brother Jules d'Haberville, both of us carefree as mountain deer! Off in the distance, I think I can make out the hospitable manor of my benefactor, my father, Captain d'Haberville. That's where, as a poor orphan in exile, I found another family for myself. Oh, my friends! – now your parlours are silent and bare! No human sound reaches this hill, whose echo, back then, used to repeat your happy voices! Oh my generous friends, you opened your arms and your hearts to the young outcast, but what will you say when you find out that the boy you loved so much has now returned, fifteen years later, to bring death and destruction to your peaceful land? Archie, you are nothing but a coward and an ungrateful wretch! Heaven, intent on punishing you, will pursue you everywhere, for it is written: 'Cursed be he who makes room in his heart for ingratitude!' (*Voices are heard off-stage; a shot rings out, and four Indians rush upon* Archie. *They struggle to tie him up, and shout to their comrades for help. Finally they manage to subdue him, in spite of his desperate efforts to escape. Then Archie, seeing that further resistance is useless, appears to resign himself to his fate.*)

SCENE II
Archie, Great Otter, Talamousse, *and several other* Indians

(*The Indians are seated in silence.*)

Archie: (*bound securely, at stage front*) Is this just a bad dream? Is it all over for me? Must I die, die in the depths of the forest, after the most dreadful tortures! Die without managing to explain myself to my friends! Oh, you've won all right, Montgomery, ambitious schemer that you are! You've been persecuting me long enough with your infernal hatred! No doubt you'll say I deserted to the enemy. Then your joy will be complete, for I'll have lost everything, including my honour! I curse the day I was born! ... Good heavens, what have I just said! Lord, I offer up to you the sacrifice of my life; please accept it, in expiation of my sins. After all, what does men's judgement matter to me, now that my life is over? (*There is a long silence at this point.*)

Great Otter: (*solemnly*) Our friend the paleface warrior is late. He should have met us two suns ago. Perhaps the Great Spirit has brought sickness upon him. Shall we keep our tomahawks idle while we await our brother, or shall we take this English dog to our friends from La Marigotte,[27] to be burned alive? Great Otter has spoken.

Talamousse: The Great Spirit has granted my brother great wisdom in council. The serpent in our forests is less wise than he. Let my brother decide what he wishes, and we shall obey him. Perhaps it would be better to wait a while longer for the paleface warrior? Then our people from La Marigotte will come and we can hand our prisoner over to them.

Great Otter: My brother has spoken well: the Lady of Wise Counsel has enlightened his mind. Yes, let us wait for the paleface warrior and our people from La Marigotte. For now, let us smoke our war-pipe. (*The Indians light and smoke a pipe.*) Let us sing our war song, and death to the English!

All: (*with feeling*) Death to the English!

(*They sing a war song and perform a war dance, after which they sit and smoke the war pipe again.*)

Great Otter: Talamousse?

Talamousse: Brother?

Great Otter: While our brothers were smoking in silence, the ears of Great Otter heard a strange sound. Go see what it may be.

Talamousse: (*exits, and returns shortly*) Talamousse announces to his brothers that the paleface warrior has come.

SCENE III
Actors, *as before*; Dumais

Great Otter: Our brother the paleface warrior is very late. Perhaps he was sick?

Dumais: No, brothers, but I had to spend two whole suns at the wigwam of the Seigneur d'Haberville, to gather information on the enemy's numbers, and so to inform our brothers, the red-skinned warriors. But who is this prisoner?

Talamousse: An English swine whom we shall hand over to our brothers from La Marigotte to be burned alive.

Great Otter: (*after a pause*) Will my brother wait long for the warriors from the portage?

Dumais: (*raising three fingers*) Three suns. Great Otter and Talamousse may leave tomorrow with the prisoner. The French will join them at Captain Launière's camp.

Archie: If there is a Christian among you, for the love of God give me some water!

Great Otter: (*to* Dumais) What does the cur want?

Dumais: The prisoner is asking for something to drink.

Talamousse: Tell the English dog that he will be burned alive tomorrow, and that if he's really thirsty we'll give him boiling water as refreshment!

Dumais: I shall tell him, but in the meantime will my brothers allow me to take some water to their prisoner?

Talamousse: Our brother may do as he pleases. The palefaces have hearts as tender as a woman's!

Dumais: (*giving* Archie *something to drink*) Who are you, in heaven's name? Your voice is very like that of a man who was very dear to me!

Archie: Archibald Cameron of Locheill, once the friend of your countrymen, today their enemy, and who richly deserves the fate which awaits him now!

Dumais: Mr Archie, even if you had killed my own brother, and if I have to split the skulls of these redskins, you will be free within the hour. First I'll try to persuade them before resorting to force. Say nothing for now. (*He returns to his place among the Indians. After a long silence, he addresses them.*) The prisoner thanks the Indians for allowing him to die a man's death. He says the paleface's death-song will be that of a true warrior.

Great Otter: Pouah! The Englishman will be like the owl that cries out when he sees the fire of our wigwams at night! (*He continues to smoke, staring scornfully at* Archie.)

Talamousse: This Englishman speaks like a man, as long as he's far away from the stake. The Englishman is a coward, who cannot even bear his thirst! Weeping, he begs his enemies for a drink, like a little child begging his mother! (*He spits in* Archie's *direction.*)

Dumais: (*lifts his pack-sack and takes from it a few provisions and some brandy*) Would my brothers like to share my meal with me? They know that everything the paleface possesses is theirs as well.

Great Otter: The people of the red skins know the generosity of your heart, brother. Many times they have stayed in your wigwam, and you have always smoked the pipe of hospitality with them. But now they declare, in the presence of the Great Spirit, that they have need of nothing.

Talamousse: (*staring at the brandy*) Talamousse is not hungry, brother, but he is thirsty. He has walked much today. Firewater relaxes the legs. (Dumais *passes him the flask. The Indian seizes it, his hands shaking with anticipation. He gulps a good* *half-pint, and soon begins to show visible signs of intoxication. He hands back the flask.*) That is good!

Dumais: Dumais does not offer any to his friend, Great Otter. He knows he does not drink firewater.

Great Otter: The Great Spirit loves Great Otter. He made him vomit out the only mouthful of firewater he ever swallowed. The firewater made him so sick he thought he would visit the land of dead spirits. Great Otter thanks the Great Spirit for it: Firewater robs a man of his mind!

Talamousse: (*after a moment's silence he reaches for the flask, but Dumais pulls it back*) Firewater good! More drink, brother, I beg you!

Dumais: No, not right now. Later. (*He puts the flask back in his pack.*) The Great Spirit loves the Canadian also: last night the Great Spirit visited him in his sleep.

Great Otter and Talamousse: And what did he say to our brother?

Dumais: The Great Spirit told him to ransom the prisoner.

Great Otter: My brother lies like a Frenchman. He lies like all palefaces. Only the people of the red skins never lie.

Dumais: Frenchmen never lie when they speak in the presence of the Great Spirit! (*He takes the flask from his sack and swallows a small mouthful.*)

Talamousse: (*reaching again for the flask*) Give it to me, I beg you, brother!

Dumais: If Talamousse wishes to sell him his share of the prisoner, the Frenchman will give him another drink.

Talamousse: Give me *all* the firewater, and take my share of the English dog!

Dumais: (*putting away the flask*) No – one more drink, and nothing more!

Talamousse: Give me a drink, then, and take my share. (*He takes the flask with both hands, swallows another good half-pint, and soon falls asleep, drunk. Great Otter* *watches suspiciously, but continues to smoke his pipe in silence.*)

Dumais: Is my brother willing to sell me his share of the prisoner?

Great Otter: What do you wish to do with him?

Dumais: Sell him to Captain d'Haberville, who will have him hanged for betraying the Canadian's cause.

Great Otter: It is much more painful to be burned alive. D'Haberville will enjoy that as much as Talamousse enjoyed your firewater.

Dumais: My brother is mistaken: the prisoner will bear up under all the tortures of the fire like a warrior, but he will cry like a woman if he is threatened with the rope. Captain d'Haberville is well aware of that.

Great Otter: My brother is lying again. All the Englishmen we've burned have cried like cowards, and not one of them sang his death-song like a man. They would have been very happy to be hanged instead! The Indian warrior is the only one who prefers the fire to the shame of being hanged like a dog!

Dumais: Let my brother listen and pay close attention to the words of the paleface: this prisoner is not English, he's a Scot, and the Scots are the Indians of the British. My brother need only look at the prisoner's clothing, and he will see that it's almost like an Indian warrior's.

Great Otter: That is true: he is not constricted by his uniform like the English soldiers, or those of the great Ononthio[28] who lives across the Great Water. But what difference does that make?

Dumais: The difference is that a Scots warrior prefers to be burned rather than hanged. Like the Indians of Canada he believes that only dogs should be hanged, and that if he visited the land of the dead spirits with a rope around his neck, the other warriors would refuse to hunt with him.

Great Otter: (*shaking his head*) My brother is lying again. The Scots-Indians are palefaces just the same, and they cannot have the courage to endure torture like red-skinned Indians. (Dumais, *exasperated, grasps the handle of his axe. Changing his mind, he stirs up the ashes of the fire with his huge, club-like pipe, feigning indifference.*)

Dumais: When Great Otter fell ill with smallpox near the South River, along with his wife, his father, and his two sons, Dumais went to fetch them, running the risk of catching the disease and giving it to his own family. He brought them to his own wigwam, where he cared for them for three moons. It is not Dumais's fault if the old man and the two boys died: Dumais had them buried with candles burning about them like Christians, and the Black Robe prayed to the Great Spirit for them.

Great Otter: If Dumais and his wife and children had fallen ill in the forest, Great Otter would have had them carried to his wigwam, would have brought them fish from the lakes and streams, would have hunted in the woods for game, and brought them firewater, which is the medicine of the Frenchman, and he would have said to them: 'Here – eat and drink, brothers, and recover your strength!' Great Otter and his squaw would have stood guard day and night at the bedside of his French friends, and Great Otter would not have said, 'I've fed you, cared for you, and bought for you with my furs the firewater which is the medicine of the paleface.' (*He stands proudly.*) Let my brother take the prisoner: the Indian now owes the paleface nothing. (*He sits and smokes his pipe in silence.*)

Dumais: Listen to me, brother, and pardon Dumais for the fact that he has hidden the truth from you. He will now speak in the presence of the Great Spirit who is listening, and the paleface never lies to the Great Spirit!

Great Otter: That is true. Let my brother speak, his brother listens.

Dumais: I have lived forty-five winters, and what I will now tell you happened fifteen winters ago. I was returning to my wigwam at the end of the last month of the season of snows, and I ventured onto the ice about half a mile south-west of the settlement of Saint-Thomas.[29] The ice, softened by the sunlight and weakened by the waters of the river, suddenly gave way and your brother disappeared under the water. I managed to jump on to an ice floe, but not without breaking my leg, just above the ankle.

Great Otter: Great Otter has seen his brother's scar, and felt sorry for him.

Dumais: I began to shout for help. Soon the banks were covered with palefaces. Suddenly there was a roar from beneath, followed by an explosion like a thunder-clap. The ice floes, piled on top of each other, had formed a dam which suddenly burst with a terrible sound. And there I was, driven fast as lightning in the direction of the falls. The only obstacle on my way was a giant cedar tree, standing on a tiny island in the middle of the river. I was able to grasp the old tree and to hold on for dear life with both hands. At that point I could see my wife and children in the agony of despair, and could hear the voice of the Black Robe, like an angel of mercy, recommending my soul to the Great Spirit. So I offered to God the sacrifice of my life and waited calmly for the end. Suddenly I felt myself being seized by a strong arm and dragged into the water. My rescuer, with as much strength as he had presence of mind, managed to reach the bank in spite of the ice and the current, and a few minutes later I had escaped from the jaws of death and was embracing my wife and children!

Great Otter: There is nothing my brother should ever refuse for the man who saved him from becoming food for the creatures that dwell in the waters!

Dumais: (*stands, doffing his cap*) Well, your brother declares, in the presence of the Great Spirit, that the prisoner is the very man who saved his life! (*At these words the Indian gives a loud whoop, leaps to his feet with drawn dagger and rushes towards the prisoner. He cuts* Archie *loose, and shakes his hand vigorously, with great demonstrations of joy, then pushes him into the arms of* Dumais.)

Archie: My saviour!

Dumais: (*clasping* Archie *tightly*) My dear friend! Lord, I prayed to You to stretch out Your hand and protect this noble, generous young man. Thank You, Lord! for I was about to commit a murder to save his life!

Archie: Dear, noble Dumais, you've now done a hundred times more for me than ever I did for you! You've rescued me from a cruel and shameful fate; and by saving my life you've given me a chance to justify myself one day to the people who were so kind to me. (*The cries of Indians are heard.*) What are those cries?

Great Otter: Those are our warriors from Marigotte. (*To* Dumais.) Brother, let us go to meet them, so that they do not see your brother the paleface.

Dumais: Yes, let's go, brother. (*To* Archie.) Farewell, noble young man!

Archie: Farewell, my saviour! And don't forget this unfortunate outcast!

Dumais: You and I are bound together, in life and in death. Farewell! (*He leaves.*)

SCENE IV
Archie, *alone, watching* Dumais *leave*

Farewell, kind and faithful friend! (*He moves to stage front.*) Here I am, free and able to hope again. How good it is to be liberated suddenly, after coming so close to death! Lord, I had offered up my life to You; since it's Your wish that I live on, may Your name be praised a thousand times! I pray to You, please watch over noble Dumais; take care also of the house of my second father, Captain d'Haberville. Grant that one day I may be loved and accepted again by that family, which is so dear to my heart! For the moment I feel relieved and more resolute than ever. Something tells me better days are coming for me. – But I hear someone coming! (*Seeing* Montgomery *enter.*) Good heavens! It's Montgomery! I'll pretend to be perfectly calm, so he won't know how troubled I feel ...

SCENE V
Archie, Montgomery

Montgomery: (*harshly*) What are you doing here?

Archie: (*restraining himself*) I've left my troops to rest near a river a few hundred yards from here, where I intend to spend the night. Waiting for dusk, I decided to come and revisit this area, which brings back so many memories for me.

Montgomery: It's not very late in the day. Now that your men are rested, they can still march quite a distance. Take them to the place that's called the Plains of Abraham, and set up camp near there. And on your way, you are to set fire to every dwelling you encounter belonging to the French swine. I shall be following close behind you.

Archie: Is it really necessary to burn down even the houses of those who offer no resistance? They say there are only women, children, and old men left in those houses!

Montgomery: Your orders, it seems to me, are quite precise and clear. Set fire to everything you find. Or perhaps I'm forgetting about your great love for our enemies ...!

Archie: (*biting his tongue and restraining himself with difficulty*) Two of those properties, that group of houses you see yonder, along with the mill on the river where we were going to camp, belong to the Seigneur d'Haberville, the man who took me in during my exile and treated me like his own son. In the name of God, Major, I beg you, give the order for the destruction of that property yourself!

Montgomery: I would never have believed that an officer of His Majesty would ever dare speak such treason towards the Crown!

Archie: (*barely restraining himself*) You forget, sir, that I was a mere child at the time. Again, in the name of all that you hold dear, give the order yourself! Don't force me to offend against my own sense of honour and of gratitude by making me burn the houses of the very people who were so kind to me in my misfortune!

Montgomery: (*sneering*) Oh, I understand! The gentleman would like a door kept open, so he can crawl back into favour with his friends when the occasion arises! (*He leaves.*)

SCENE VI
Archie, *alone*

(*He strides back and forth for a moment, then suddenly explodes.*)

That prophet of doom who made the prediction to me long ago must have been inspired by hell itself! 'Keep your pity for yourself, Archibald Cameron of Locheill,' he said to me,[30] 'for the time when, forced to carry out an inhuman order, you'll tear at that chest of yours which contains such a noble, generous heart!' And you have a long memory yourself, Montgomery: you haven't forgotten the blow my grandfather gave yours with the flat of a sabre in an inn in Edinburgh! But I have a good memory too, and sooner or later I'll double that dose on your back, since you'll be too cowardly to meet me face to face! One day I hope you will wind up more wretched than those you leave homeless here! And on your death day, may you not have a single stone to put under your head! May all the furies of hell – (*He struggles to control himself.*) What a contrast between the cruelty of this bloodthirsty man and the generosity of the races we call barbarians! (*The militiamen are heard, singing as they march, 'Noble, lovely land.'*) But what's this sound? (*He listens.*) I recognize that – it's one of the wonderful songs sung by the Canadians, whom I love as well as I do my Scots countrymen! (*He listens again.*) They're coming this way. Time to leave, Archie – you're unworthy of appearing before their eyes! (*He exits in one direction; the Canadians enter from the other.*)

SCENE VII
Saint-Luc *and the* Canadian Soldiers

Saint-Luc: Halt, here, friends! We'll rest awhile, and wait for Captain Jules.

José: He won't be long comin', 'cause I saw him a little while ago an' he says he intends to stick close to us, from now on!

Fontaine: Whew! What a march! I'm pooped out, from head to toe. Ain't it silly to march with our long muskets like this? We keep trippin' over' em, an' that makes us kiss Mother Earth a lot more than we'd like ...

Dubé: You'll get used to it, buddy, with practice.

Fontaine: With practice? I had enough durn practice, I'd say, since I left Saint-Jean-Port-Joli, my home parish!

José: You're just at the beginnin', friend Fontaine. Up to now you've only been tastin' what they call the joys of military service. Before long I hope you get to know, inside out, what a soldier's life is really like! In the meantime, you can rest a bit now.

Fontaine: Gee – thanks a lot for your permission! A bit of a rest wouldn't do me no harm, though. (*All sit down.*) You know, I just had a durn good idea!

The Others: What's that, then?

Fontaine: Here it is: while Papa José is restin' along with the rest of us, why don't he finish the story he was tellin' us about his dear departed dad?

Dubé: Right! Good idea!

Fontaine: I jus' knew everyone an' his brother would agree! It's such a great story, with all them ghosts an' devils, an' y'know, Papa José tells it so well that if we didn't know him, we'd say he's the one that was there!

José: If you've finished with your compliments, friend Fontaine, I'll begin.

Fontaine: I'm all ears, Papa José!

José: If memory serves me right, I had come to the spot where my dear dead departed father heard all the witches singin'...

Dubé: Exactly so.

José: So there he was, listenin' to them irregenerals, when all of a sudden, when he's least expectin' it, he feels two big bony hands, sort o' like bear's paws, grabbin' him by the shoulders. So he turns around, scared as hell, an' there he is face to face with – La Corriveau!!! There she is, tryin' to grab him an' climb up on him! She had slipped her hand through the bars of her iron cage, an' was tryin' to climb up his back! 'Dear François,' says the Corriveau woman, 'do me a big favour, take me singin' with my friends from the Île d'Orléans!' 'Ha! bloody bitch from hell,' shouts my late father (that was the only cuss-word he ever used, the good man, and then only in moments of great stress) ...

Saint-Luc: By hell, it seems to me it was the right time for it, then! If it were me, I would've sworn like a heathen!

Dubé: 'Bloody bitch from hell,' says my late father, 'is that the thanks I get for my *Diaper Fundy* and my other nice prayers? You want me to go to that witches' sabbath with you? An' here I thought you had at least a good three or four thousand years left in purgatory for your little crimes! You only killed two o' your husbands, after all – hardly worth mentionin'! An' here I felt sorry for you, 'cause I always had a soft spot for the fair sex, so I said to myself, "I should give her a hand." An' now there's my thanks: you wanta climb on my back an' drag me into hell like some hairytick!'

Fontaine: He was quite a guy this François, eh? I woulda like to see him square off with ... (*The others gesture to him to be quiet.*)

José: 'My dear François,' says the witch, 'it's impossible for me to cross the St Lawrence, which has been blessed, without the help of a Christian!' 'Cross it any way you want, you bloody bitch from hell, you Judas Chariot!' says my dear dead departed father, 'everybody's got their own problems! You think I'll take you dancin' with them dear friends o' yours, but it'll be on all fours again like a dog, same way you came draggin' your cage, that musta scraped off all the stones an' gravel on the highway! The roadmaster's gonna come by here one of these days, an' won't he be escandalized to see his road in such a state! An' of course it'll be the poor farmer who'll suffer because o' your mischief: he'll hafta pay a fine for not keepin' up his part o' the road!'

Saint-Luc: By gosh, your late father certainly knew how to talk to spooks!

José: Then the drum major points at my dear dead departed father, an' shouts out with a voice like thunder: 'Are you gonna hurry up an' bring our friend across or not? We only got about 14,400 more rounds to do all 'round the island, afore the cock crows! Are you gonna make her miss most of the fun?'

Fontaine: A lotta fun, for sure! I'm quakin' in my boots, just hearin' you talk about it!

José: 'Crawl back to hell, where you an' all o' your kind come from,' my late father shouts back at him, losin' his patience finally. 'Come now, my dear François,' says La Corriveau. 'Be a bit more helpful. You're actin' like a child, makin' a lot o' fuss about nothin'! You can see time's a-flyin'! Come on, son, just a little effort on your part!' 'No! you daughter of Satan!' says my late father. 'I wish you was still wearin' that nice collar the hangman slipped 'round your neck two years ago – you wouldn't be singin' the tune you're singin' now!' An' while they was talkin' back an' forth like that, the witches an' sorcerers on the island started singin' their chorus again:
   Let's dance all around it,
      Toura loura!
   Let's dance all around it!
'My dear François,' says the witch, 'since you refuse to carry me across while you're alive, I'm gonna strangle you, and mount on your soul to get to my sabbath!' An' with that, she grabbed him right by the throat, an' strangled him!

All: What! She strangled him!

José: When I say strangled, it's not far off. He passed out completely, the poor guy. An' when he came to, he could hear a little bird singin' 'who're *you*? who're *you*?'

Fontaine: What! You mean to tell me it's a little *bird* that keeps sayin' 'who're you'? I always thought it was the kids doin' that, an' I used to get awful mad at 'em!

Dubé: Fontaine, my friend, please shut up, because if you keep at it, I'll sit you down and shut you up once and for all!

José: 'Well, well!' says my late father, 'so I'm not in hell after all, if I can hear God's little birds singin'!' An' he opens one eye, an' then the other, an' sees that it's broad daylight, with the sun streamin' on his face. So he harnessed his mare, who hadn't twigged to what was goin' on at all, by the look of things, the poor beast, an' he headed for home as fast as he could. He only told us about his adventure a coupla weeks later.

Saint-Luc: Here comes Captain Jules. Everyone to his post! (*All scramble to take post.*)

SCENE VIII
Actors, *as before*; Jules

Jules: Friends, the time has come to do battle. In just a little while the English will once more discover, to their own sorrow, the mettle of Canadian soldiers. Let us march to battle with confidence! Don't let the numbers of our adversaries dismay you: our victory will be all the sweeter! When duty calls, a Canadian soldier does not care about numbers – he thinks of one thing only: victory or death!

All: Victory or death!

Jules: We are the sons of heroes, the sons of martyrs. We shall fight and die, if need be, for God and our country!

All: For God! For our country!

Jules: Now, my friends, let us march on to battle!

End of Act two. During the intermission, volleys of shots are heard behind the curtain.

ACT THREE

SCENE I
Great Otter, Talamousse, *a few other* Indians

(*At the beginning of this scene gunfire can still be heard, along with cries and other sounds of battle. The Indians stand motionless for a time, then give three loud whoops.*)

Great Otter: Enough mourning for the deaths of our warriors, brothers! They have been harvested by war, but like the great oaks in the forest, in their fall they have crushed the palefaces and made them flee like frightened women. Even now they are being welcomed as true warriors into the land of the spirits. Even now, brothers, their shades soar over us, and I seem to hear them cry: 'Avenge us! Don't leave our bones to bleach here, trampled by the English! Take up your dreaded tomahawks once more and shout your war-song again, louder than ever!'

Talamousse: Great Otter has spoken like a man! Indian warriors will never be afraid to march into battle as long as they are led by their brother Great Otter because they know that his courage is like the lion's in the forest!

An Indian: Do the cries of our paleface brothers not reach the ears of Great Otter? Why does he not lead us into battle?

Great Otter: (*he controls himself with great difficulty. After a pause*) Listen to me, brothers! Great Otter had only one son left, whom he loved with all his soul, since he felt his own courage live on in the young warrior. Great Otter has just seen this last son of his fall in battle, like a young cedar swept away by the storm. Now Great Otter is left alone in the world! When the Great Spirit calls him into the land of the spirits, he will not have a single relative to weep over his grave, nor will his blood ever flow in the veins of another! Great Otter was thinking about his misfortune and was overcome for a few moments by the weight of his loss. Let some reproach him, if they wish, for weeping like a woman!

The Indian: Forgive your brother, O great chief! He did not know of the death of his son!

Great Otter: Dreadful is the bite of the serpent as he destroys his prey. Dreadful too is the tiger's rage when he rushes on a herd of timid does. Dreadful is the vengeance of the she-lion when an attempt is made to snatch her young away from her.[31] But more dreadful by far shall be the vengeance of Great Otter! Yes, he shall drink his fill of English blood, appeasing the spirits of his warriors and the cries of his own soul! As long as the Great Spirit shall leave a breath of life in Great Otter's body, even so long will his fearful war-axe lay low his enemies; even so long will he slake his thirst in the chalice of revenge!

Talamousse: (*after a pause*) Who was the English warrior who fought so bravely during the battle? Fast as lightning, he was everywhere danger called. More than once he rushed towards our Indian warriors, but each time he turned away as though an invisible spirit had pushed him back!

Great Otter: That warrior was not English, but Scots. It's the prisoner whose life we spared. Great Otter recognized him and admired his courage. (*The sounds of battle draw nearer. Canadian soldiers are heard shouting for help. The Indians all rise, give a great war cry, and rush off. The sounds grow distant and gradually cease.*)

SCENE II
Montgomery, An English Soldier

Montgomery: Well now! Is my vengeance achieved? Has Archibald of Locheill fallen into the trap we set for him?

Soldier: No, sir. I don't know how he escaped, since he was the only one of his group to survive when the explosion went off; all the others were struck down in a flash!

Montgomery: (*aside*) He will die, I swear it! (*To the soldier:*) Has General Murray heard anything about this?

Soldier: He heard the sound of the explosion, sir, but he has no idea where it came from.

Montgomery: (*aside*) My vengeance is assured! (*To the soldier.*) Good! – now leave me. And above all, be discreet!

Soldier: You can count on me, sir! (*He leaves.*)

SCENE III
Montgomery, *alone*

So Murray heard the explosion but doesn't know who caused it! And Archibald was the only one of the group to survive? No matter – let's go find the general. This will be the finest day of my life, since it will see me avenged! (*He exits in one direction;* Jules *and* Saint-Luc *enter from the other. Their uniforms are in disarray, and they have both been wounded in the face.*)

SCENE IV
Saint-Luc, Jules

Jules: (*speaking quickly*) My dear Saint-Luc, there's no sense trying to deceive ourselves: the battle is lost! Montcalm has fallen, along with a large number of our brave comrades, and now our soldiers are exhausted and without ammunition. Any further resistance would amount to useless bloodshed. I see our soldiers coming – have them rest here. I have a few orders to give for the care of the wounded, but I'll be back in a moment.

Saint-Luc: Very good, Captain. (Jules *leaves.*)

SCENE V
Saint-Luc, Canadian Soldiers (*they seem overwhelmed by their defeat*)

Saint-Luc: Friends, let us rest here awhile. (*All sit.*) Further resistance is useless: no use deceiving ourselves, we have lost the battle. But there is no cause for despair. Remember, as long as a soldier can fight on, he can still hope for victory!

José: You're darn right, sir! What use is there cryin' an' lamentin' our lot? The best thing is to console ourselves, an' do it fast, 'cause when your heart is sick you can't do nothin' right!

Dumais: How can we help but be sad, thinking of all the misfortunes we have just endured? After seeing some of our bravest leaders fall on the battlefield? What a terrible loss we've suffered!

Saint-Luc: Brave Montcalm! Yes, he's fallen, along with many of our bravest soldiers, but don't we still have a Lévis and a d'Haberville left? With men like that, we Canadians can still accomplish wonders – and indeed we shall!

Dubé: But who will take care of our wives and children? Who will feed them, when hunger racks their bodies?

José: God will take care of them, my dear Dubé. He knows very well what we need an' He never abandons no one. He watches over all His children, an' especially over the families of soldiers who've sacrificed everythin' to defend their religion an' country. That's what I always heard, an' from my own experience, it's absolutely true.

Fontaine: Anyways, here we are, an' the battle's over. Ain't it funny how you imagine a whole bunch o' things when you never tried them! I always believed you couldn't go to war without comin' back missin' at least one or two legs. But thank God, here we all be with nothin' missin'! 'Minds me of what our *curé* said to us: 'Friends, you're off to war? It's a difficult task! But what do you expect? Every man who comes into this here world has to follow his own dustiny!'

José: Well said, my dear friend Fontaine!

Fontaine: You mean you're surprised by that, Papa José? You know durn well I'm a guy what thinks deep thoughts, I am!

José: (*after a pause*) Listen, if it's all right with you, I'm gonna sing you folks a nice little song, not too happy, but not too sad, neither. It'll relax us a bit, an' drive away our sadness, an' it'll show our English friends how Canadians bear up under the misfortunes that come along, like good Christians should.

All: Motion carried!

Dubé: Go ahead, Papa José – sing us one of them songs you know so well!

José: With pleasure, friends, although my singin' ain't what it used to be. (*José sings, with all joining in the chorus.*)
　　First Verse
　　When Heaven in its grace
　　Showers us with blessings
　　We spend our time happily,
　　Livin' like Canadians!

　　Chorus
　　So let us not lose heart,
　　Good friends, in present sorrow!
　　When the storm is over
　　We'll be out pickin' flowers!

　　Second Verse
　　An' when life's bitter moments
　　Bring hardships to afflict us,
　　While we're alive down under
　　We'll bear 'em all with courage!

Chorus
So let us not lose heart, etc.

Third Verse
We always showed our courage
When battle's trumpet sounded,
So undeserved defeat
Will never make us cower!

Chorus
So let us not lose heart, etc.

Fontaine: How lucky you are, Papa José, to have a nice voice like that. An' ain't it a nice song, with a chorus too! (*He sings the chorus.*) 'So let us not lose heart,' etc.

José: Ah, if only you had heard me when I was younger, I could really carry off a tune like that!

Dumais: Thank you, José, your song has cheered me up.

José: Maybe I'm just a poor ignorant lout, but I think that, just 'cause we got beaten, we ain't got no reason to pound our chests an' cry 'mea cool-paw'!

Saint-Luc: Quite right, José – all of you behaved bravely. I really admire that simple, strong faith I see in you people and which – alas! – is rarely found among those who call themselves learned!

José: Well, you see, sir, faith ain't somethin' you learn in books, it's somethin' that's passed down from father to son.

Fontaine: I see our captain, Monsieur Jules, comin' this way. Now there's a brave one for you: on the battlefield he was like a lion, no other way to put it! You might say, if he's still alive it's 'cause death was afeared of him!

José: Yes sir! What a man our young captain is! With a hundred like Monsieur Jules you could go anywhere, by gum!

Saint-Luc: What's surprising about that? Isn't he a d'Haberville? (*Jules enters.*)

SCENE VI
Actors, *as before*; Jules (*all rise to greet him*)

Jules: Don't put yourself out for me, friends: you must need rest after the bloody battle you've just been through, after the superhuman efforts you've all made to secure a victory which – alas! – did not rally to our colours today. We have been beaten, it is true, but we have no reason to reproach ourselves, for we have done everything that brave men could do!

Dumais: Sir, whatever fate brings us now, our hearts and our arms will always serve our country. Is that not so, friends?

All: Yes! Our country forever!

Jules: Keep that noble spirit alive in you! All is not lost, you can be sure of it! Let's make use of the time at our disposal, and prepare to avenge our defeat with a shining victory! When I think of our misfortunes, of the treachery of the man who claimed to be your friend and mine, that vile outcast whom we treated like a native son, then I feel only one desire – for revenge!

José: That fellow Archie, the scoundrel, has strangled every last shred of gratitude in his heart! An' I must say, what he done is an awful surprise to me, 'cause he always seemed so kind, so nice!

Jules: My dear José, that was the kindness of a hypocrite, flattering his friends as long as he needs them and ready to tear them to bits like a tiger when he can do without them.

Dumais: If you will allow me, sir, I would like to tell you frankly what I think of this person, whom you used to love like a brother and to whom, as far as I'm concerned, I've sworn eternal gratitude for saving my life.

Jules: Go on, Dumais – speak your mind!

Dumais: Well sir, let me tell you I cannot share the hatred and the desire for revenge you feel against Archie. (Jules *appears surprised.*) Instead of cursing him as an enemy, as a traitor, I feel heartfelt sorrow for him, as for an unfortunate friend. I am certain, sir, that Archie is not as guilty as appearances suggest. He must have been forced to act as he did. You are familiar with the laws governing military discipline: a subordinate *must* obey his superior, in each and every circumstance! I have no doubt that was the situation Archie found himself in. He was merely the unwilling instrument of the acts of vengeance carried out in his name by the English troops. I'm firmly convinced of that, and my conviction is based on my own knowledge of Archie's noble character, on his love for this country, his enthusiastic passion for this land. You may be sure, sir, that men of Archie's stripe don't change as quickly and as radically as that!

Jules: (*after a few moments' reflection*) Dumais, you're letting your noble sentiments and your gratitude get the better of you. Archie is nothing less than a traitor! – And now, my friends, in just a few hours we must leave to join up with General de Lévis's army. But first, Monsieur de Saint-Luc, take your men and return to the battlefield, to Dumont's mill, where the fighting was so intense. There you will probably find wounded men in need of help. Have them brought to a safe place.

Saint-Luc: Very good, sir. (*To the soldiers.*) By the left, in single column, forward – march!

SCENE VII
Jules, *alone*

I need to be alone for a while. My heart, after the storms it has suffered, yearns for a moment's calm. Can it really be true that Archie is guilty of the serious sin of ingratitude I impute to him? Oh the traitor! Why didn't I get to meet him face to face! Why didn't I get a chance to drown his vile treachery in his own blood? ... But now we've been defeated. The force of numbers has triumphed over courage. And Montcalm, brave Montcalm, has fallen on the battlefield! I was present for the hero's last moments. And I shall never forget his last words. Seeing that the battle was lost, and once they had told him that his wound was fatal, he exclaimed: 'All the better – I won't see the capture of Quebec!' and he died a few moments later. Oh, why didn't I die in that murderous battle as well! Am I now condemned to see the flag of Albion wave proudly over the fortifications of New France? Ah! better to die a thousand deaths! ... (*He collapses on a bench.*)

SCENE VIII
Jules, Archie

Archie: (*not noticing* Jules) The sounds of battle and the intoxication of victory haven't succeeded in quieting the terrible pangs of remorse eating away at my heart! They remind me of my cruelty towards people who loved me, whom I loved, whom I continue to love, as God is my witness! (*Bitterly.*) Oh, the honour of bearing arms for proud Britain has cost me dearly! Won't I even have a chance to find my brother Jules and tell him of the grief that has torn – that continues to tear at my heart? ... (*Seeing* Jules.) What's this? Who is this soldier? Good Lord! – it's Jules d'Haberville! (*He takes a few steps in* Jules's *direction.*)

Jules: (*without turning around*) It is he! ... (*He stands, stares at* Archie, *makes a gesture of revulsion, and turns away.*) Dare I believe my eyes? Is it really you, Archibald Cameron of Locheill? Was it not enough for you to see the people who loved you as their own so cruelly betrayed? Have you come now to feast your eyes on the spectacle of my own misfortune? Have you come to add insult to injury? Archibald Cameron of Locheill, up to this point I've hated you as an enemy; now I despise you as a coward!

Archie: Jules, my friend, you've judged me without a hearing!

Jules: 'My friend'? Don't dare call me your friend, you vulgar outcast! Get away from here – don't insult my eyes any longer with your presence! What are you doing here, in any case – you've seen the utter downfall of the proud Jules d'Haberville, and your heart should be content with that. Are you looking for more houses to burn, more mothers and young children to slaughter? Alas! our women and children have been driven into the woods by your brave soldiers, our homes have been put to the torch! You must have taken particular pleasure in seeing the great manor of the d'Habervilles collapse in flames. Rejoice, Archie! You've been victorious! Canada will long wear the glorious proofs of your victory: your swords and torches have demonstrated all too well the gratitude of noble, *generous* Cameron of Locheill!

Archie: Enough, Jules, I beg you! Enough of these bitter accusations – they're too much for me! If only you knew how much I've suffered, and continue to suffer! (Jules *turns his back.*) He won't even hear me out! Lord, what shall I do? Jules, don't send me away without allowing me to explain how I was forced to do what I did. It's an explanation I owe to your wonderful family, to you – and to me! It will relieve me of a dreadful, heavy burden. Ever since we parted, Jules, I've led a miserable existence. I had hardly taken up my father's sword when I learned that my regiment was to join the expedition against New France. Oh, how I regretted then the decision I had made to serve in the English army! But my word was given, and I had no way of foreseeing the vandalous acts to which I would later have to consent. So I embarked for Canada. A cruel, infamous monster by the name of Montgomery was commander of the division to which my regiment belonged. He it was who put the torch in my hand and forced me to become the persecutor of the very people I love. How can I describe to you my anguish, my anger, my despair on hearing those inhuman orders? Jules, you're perfectly familiar with the laws of war and military discipline. I *could not* refuse! Fighting against myself, I gave the orders. If I had refused to obey, I would not only have been put to death, I would have been dishonoured, would forever have stained the glorious name of the Camerons of Locheill! As God is my witness, Jules, I was more sorrowful than sinning! Yes, I know that the evidence is against me, that in your eyes everything I've done is condemnable – and that is what most overwhelms me. But in the name of our former friendship, of the wonderful years we spent together, I appeal to you! You loved me then, Jules! You said – I quote your very words – that the nobility of my character had won your heart!

Jules: Cameron of Locheill, don't lift the veil covering the past. I did love you, I confess, but times have changed!

Archie: Yes, times have indeed changed, but *my* heart has not! I'm still the same person, Jules! Still ready to shed my last drop of blood for you and your noble family! If I can't justify myself in your eyes and obtain forgiveness from you, then I'm leaving Canada forever, as soon as possible. But wherever on earth I roam, my greatest joy, my greatest happiness will be to learn that the d'Haberville family has regained its former glory, that better times have returned to the manor of Saint-Jean-Port-Joli, happy, gentle times that the people living there deserve. But surely I won't be reduced to that, Jules? Surely you'll follow the goodness of your own heart, and see in me a friend far more sorrowful than guilty! Thank you, noble friend, for having consented to hear me out. Now what must I do to obtain pardon from you? Beg you? Kiss your knees? Here I am at your feet: I beg of you, tell me you've forgiven me!

Jules: (*struggling with his emotions*) Stand up, Cameron of Locheill!

SCENE IX
Actors, *as before*; Montgomery

Montgomery: What's this I see! Archibald Cameron of Locheill, an officer of the British Crown, at the feet of an enemy, a miserable, *defeated* enemy!

Jules: (*drawing his sword*) Major Montgomery, who gave you the right to come here and insult me? If your insolence it not matched by your cowardice, prepare to defend yourself!

Archie: What are you doing here, you vulgar spy! There's no use trying to create foul suspicions against me any more – your own cowardly conduct during the battle is now known to everyone and you'll soon be rewarded for your actions, you faithless, dishonourable wretch!

Montgomery: Locheill, if I treated your remarks with the scorn they deserve, you would pay dearly for your insolence! You should be aware that I enjoy the highest credit in the eyes of General Murray, despite your accusations, and that I could destroy you with a single word to him!

Archie: Destroy *me*! Ha! I'm not afraid of you, Montgomery. You talk about your credit, but don't you realize that the credit of a coward doesn't last long? Do you even know what credit is? Would you like to find out? (*He hands him a letter.*) Do you recognize that signature? It's General Murray's! Now listen to this, Montgomery. (*He reads.*)

'Archibald Cameron of Locheill, I watched you in action today, and you conducted yourself most nobly. You have certainly refuted the suspicions Montgomery has tried to spread about your courage and your loyalty. It is in fact he who is a coward and a traitor, and he will be punished as he deserves.

Until His Majesty's Government can do much more for you, please accept the rank of major, of which Montgomery has shown himself to be unworthy. I salute you, Major Archibald Cameron of Locheill!'

There now! Did you understand the contents of this letter? If you don't believe me, here – read it for yourself! (*He hands him the letter.* Montgomery *scans it rapidly, then throws it on the ground.*)

Montgomery: I have been betrayed!

Archie: No, you have betrayed yourself, Montgomery: we now know you for what you really are!

Montgomery: I'll have my revenge! ...

Archie: But don't imagine that I'm about to accept a title and rank that you've borne so disgracefully. You won't see Archibald Cameron of Locheill begging for the insignia of a Montgomery. I've already answered General Murray, thanking him for his praise as well as for the promotion he offered me. I told him that since

I had now given ample proof of my courage and my loyalty in this battle, and since I have now served the two years of my commission, I no longer wish to bear arms against those to whom I am so heavily indebted.

Montgomery: Aye, I shall have my revenge! You'll see what a Montgomery's fury can accomplish!

SCENE X
Jules, Archie

Jules: Is that really true, Archibald? Are you refusing the promotion your courage deserves? Why are you doing this?

Archie: *Why?* Can you doubt for a moment why, Jules? You certainly don't know my character very well, if you suppose for a single second that I would lead the English on to pillage Canadian soil! The love and friendship I feel for you and your illustrious family are much more important to me than anything I might gain from any sort of promotion. I would be happy to do the same again and again, if by doing so I could obtain forgiveness from you. (Jules *appears more and more moved.* Archie, *yielding to sudden impulse, rushes to take* Jules's *hand, but his gesture is not reciprocated.* Archie *sighs deeply.*) Alas! Jules, my friend, my brother, can nothing persuade you? Is everything finished between the two of us, forever? Oh, if only you knew how deeply you have wounded me! ... Farewell, Jules, farewell forever to the person I used to call my brother! ... Since all is finished between us, the only thing left for me is to pray on my knees to God that He grant His blessings to a family I love so dearly ... And so, for the last time, farewell Jules! (*He turns and begins to leave.*)

Jules: Halt, Archibald! (*He turns aside, pressing his chest with both hands, as if to drive out the bitterness which remains.*) No – anyone who sacrifices his finest and most legitimate aspirations to his feelings of friendship and gratitude cannot be as guilty as appearances suggest! (*Holding out his arms.*) Archie, my friend, my heart pardons you!

Archie: (*rushing to embrace him*) Your words make life worth living again! Dear Jules, I feel like a different man!

Jules: As for me, my dear friend, don't you think the love and friendship I felt for you caused quite a conflict in *my* heart?

Archie: The very thing that made me despair has now become cause for my greatest joy, since a friendship that has overcome trials as terrible as ours is destined to last eternally! We shall soon see better days, Jules,

Jules: Yes indeed, we *shall* see better days! (*The Indians enter.*)

SCENE XI
Actors, *as before*; Great Otter; Talamousse; Other Indians

Great Otter: (*seeing* Archie, *he shouts for joy and rushes to embrace him. To* Jules) Listen to me, brother! Your Scots friend is a true man; his heart is a generous as a lion's! As long as the waters of the Great River shall flow to join those of the Great Water, so long will Great Otter hold this Scotsman dear to his heart, for if it were not for him this Indian chief would be rotting in a vile dungeon, shackled with shameful chains! Just as I was leaving your wigwam, brother, I was captured by English warriors, and as they were about to put me in irons the Scotsman happened by and made them set me free. May the Great Spirit reward him for what he has done!

Archie: Great chief, I did no more than pay back a debt I owed you. but is there something wrong? You seem so sad!

Great Otter: Brother, I once had ten children. Every evening, as night drew near, I could look proudly upon them. But only one of them was left. I used to take him everywhere hunting with me; I would arouse his noble heart with tales of the exploits of the great warriors of our nation. I loved that son more than a fish loves the clear, sparkling water of the lake it inhabits, for I felt myself live on in him. He was my pride and joy! In the evening, when others would see the two of us sitting on the same mat, peacefully smoking our pipes, they would say, 'Great Otter can certainly be proud of his son!' Alas! my son fell in this battle, and his soul has gone to the land of dead spirits! (*He hangs his head in sorrow.*)

Archie: Great chief, your son is alive!

Great Otter: What did you say, brother? Repeat it, I beg you!

Archie: I swear to you, in the presence of the Great Spirit, that your son was only wounded. He is now recovering in my wigwam, and will be back with you before nightfall. (*The Indians give a loud whoop and surround* Archie.)

Great Otter: Noble warrior, Great Otter will never be able to repay what you have done for him! He can only pray that the Great Spirit will shower upon you the abundance of his blessings!

Jules: Archie, you are indeed still the same person, thinking of everyone but yourself! (*The Canadian militia is heard approaching.*) Good! Here comes Saint-Luc with his soldiers. They will all be happy to hear of the wonderful things that have just happened!

SCENE XII
Actors, *as before*; Saint-Luc; José; Fontaine; Dumais; *and* Canadian Soldiers

Jules: Come quickly, friends, so that I may present to you Archie, my friend and yours. No need to add, he is *not* guilty of all the wrongs we had accused him of!

José: What? Is what you say true, sir? By cracky, I'm sure happy, then! Dear Archie, that I used to like so much, and thought I had lost forever!

Archie: Do you think I would have forgotten all the fine lessons you taught me? (*They embrace.*)

Dumais: (*taking his hand*) How happy I am to have been proven right on your account, my generous friend!

Saint-Luc: Well now, am I the only one to be left out of this general celebration? Archie, please forgive me for the terrible suspicions I entertained concerning you!

Archie: You were perfectly right to entertain them! (*He takes his hand.*)

Jules: Time is precious. While we await our signal to depart, let's celebrate the return of our friend Archie.

All: Yes, yes!

Fontaine: All the happier to do so, since I can rest my weary legs a mite. If this keeps up, I'm gonna forget what it means to take a rest! (*All surround* Archie: Jules *on his right,* José *on his left,* Saint-Luc *on Jules's right, with his soldiers behind him,* Dumais *to Saint-Luc's right,* Great Otter *to José's left, with his Indians behind him and* Talamousse *and* Ouabi *to his left.*)

Archie: Friends, you're too kind to me! This is one of the happiest days of my life, and one I shall treasure forever!

CURTAIN[32]

Notes

Prologue

1 In various issues of *Canadian Drama* (which ceased publication in 1990) and in volume 4 of *Canada's Lost Plays: Colonial Quebec: French-Canadian Drama, 1606 to 1966* (Toronto: Canadian Theatre Review Publications 1982), ed. Anton Wagner, now out of print; nineteenth-century plays included in the latter are Joseph Quesnel's *The French Republicans* (1801), Antoine Gérin-Lajoie's *The Young Latour* (1844), Louis Fréchette's *Papineau* (1880), and Elzéar Paquin's *Riel* (1886).

2 In *The Oxford Companion to Canadian Theatre* (1989), ed. Eugene Benson and L.W. Conolly, and in my book, *Theatre in French Canada: Laying the Foundations, 1606–1867* (Toronto: University of Toronto Press 1984). See also the Suggestions for Further Reading below.

3 First published in Lescarbot's *Histoire de la Nouvelle-France, contenant les navigations, découvertes & habitations faites par les François ès Indes Occidentales & Nouvelle-France souz l'avœu et authorité de noz Rois Très-Chrétiens* (Paris: Millot 1609). The most recent translation is by Eugene and Renate Benson in *Canadian Drama*, 8, no. 1 (1982), 87–95, reprinted in *Canada's Lost Plays*, 4: 35–42.

4 *La Réception de Mgr le vicomte d'Argenson par toutes les nations du païs de Canada à son entrée au gouvernement de la Nouvelle-France*, ed. P.-G. Roy (Québec: Brousseau 1890); re-ed. (with emendations) by Luc Lacourcière in *Anthologie poétique de la Nouvelle-France* (Québec: Les Presses de l'Université Laval 1966), 58–74.

5 Pierre-Joseph de La Chasse, 'Réception pour Mgr de Saint-Vallier,' in *Monseigneur de Saint-Vallier et l'Hôpital Général de Québec* (Québec: Darveau 1882), 263–9. No translation of this text has been published to date.

6 *La Conversion d'un pêcheur* (Montréal: n.p., n.d. [1869?]; republished without music in *Mes rimes* (Québec: Delisle 1876), 117–47; with music, introductory essays, commentary, and notes by L.E. Doucette and Timothy McGee in *Theatre History in Canada/*

Histoire du théâtre au Canada, 5, no. 2 (1984), 132–71. No translation has been prepared to date.

7 *Le Jeune Latour* (Montréal: Cinq-Mars 1844). Translated by Louise Forsyth, in Wagner, ed., *Canada's Lost Plays*, 4: 111–39.

I: Anglomania, or Dinner, English-Style

1 The only surviving manuscript is a copy in the Archives du Séminaire de Québec in the heterogenous collection in forty-three volumes assembled by Jacques Viger over three decades, which he entitled 'Ma Saberdache' and which he subdivided in 1839 into a 'Saberdache bleue' and a 'Saberdache rouge.' The copy of Quesnel's play, in 'Saberdache rouge,' vol. P, 69–113, was completed in September 1847, thirty-eight years after the author's death. It bears the title, 'L'Anglomanie ou le dîner à l'angloise, comédie en un acte et en vers, 1802,' and it is on this basis that the date 1802 has frequently been ascribed to the play. But internal evidence is strong that the work could not have been completed before 1803, since it refers explicitly to Ross Cuthbert's poem *L'Aréopage*, which was not published until March 1803. See David M. Hayne, 'Le Théâtre de Joseph Quesnel,' in *Archives des lettres canadiennes*, vol. 5: *Le Théâtre canadien-français* (Montréal: Fides 1976), 109–17.

2 It was published twice, in separate journals: without an editor's name over three consecutive issues of *Le Canada français*, December 1932–February 1933; and in *La Barre du jour*, 25 (1970), 113–41, the latter edited by Claude Savoie. The first is more faithful to the manuscript, but there is considerable question as to some of the readings of the 1847 copyist. Both published editions contain variants and notes from the manuscript.

3 See J.M.S. Careless, ed., *Colonists and Canadiens, 1760–1867* (Toronto: Macmillan 1971), 64; Mason Wade, *The French Canadians 1760–1967* (Toronto: Macmillan 1968), 1: 99–100.

4 Jean-Pierre Wallot, 'Robert Shore Milnes,' in *Dictionary of Canadian Biography* (hereafter *DCB*), 7: 613–16.

5 As early as 1780 a group calling itself Les Jeunes Messieurs Canadiens had appeared, staging plays from standard French repertoire in various venues in the capital. Historians are still uncertain as to whether the designation (it reappears intermittently until at least 1817) represents merely a generic description (given the loose usage of capital letters in French – as in English – at the time), or an amateur troupe or series of troupes. Since the title is also applied to the Théâtre de Société founded in Montréal in 1789 with Quesnel as its director (the same troupe is referred to as Le Théâtre Canadien in 1792), and since none of the names of the six known members reappear after 1809, it seems unlikely that the term designates a continuing affiliation.

6 After Charles-Simon Favart assumed management of the Opéra-Comique in Paris in 1757, and especially after its fusion with the Comédie Italienne in 1762, there was a

veritable invasion of operettas and light comedies with musical components in France. As a historian of the period observes, 'L'opéra-comique devient véritablement un genre littéraire et la musique, sous forme d'ariettes, prend, dans les pièces nouvelles, une place que certains jugent abusive ... Jusqu'à la fin du siècle, paroles et chant seront souvent intimement liés pour satisfaire un public passionné à la fois de musique et de théâtre.' Pierre Larthomas, *Le Théâtre en France au XVIII*ᵉ *siècle* (Paris: Presses universitaires de France 1980), 53.

Light musical comedy remained in vogue long after Quesnel's last visit to his native land. A contemporary complaint is noted elsewhere: 'le goût du siècle pour l'opéra-comique a détruit celui que la nation avait pour les chefs-d'œuvre de l'esprit humain.' C.D. Brenner and N.A. Goodyear, *Eighteenth-Century French Plays* (New York: Appleton-Century-Crofts 1927), xvii.

7 *Colas et Colinette ou le bailli dupé. Comédie en 3 actes et en prose, mêlée d'ariettes* (Québec: John Neilson 1808). Despite the date of imprint it was not in fact published until 1812, primarily because of problems arising from printing the musical score. See John E. Hare, 'Les difficultés techniques de l'édition québécoise au début du XIXᵉ siècle: Joseph Quesnel et l'impression de la musique de *Colas et Colinette* (1808),' in *Revue de l'Université d'Ottawa*, 49 (1979), 104–7. Quesnel's text was republished in both editions of James Huston's *Répertoire national* (1848; 1893). An English translation of the dialogue by Michel Lecavalier and of the songs by Lecavalier and Godfrey Ridout was published in 1974 (Toronto: Thompson). The Recording is by Select, CC15001.

8 Yves Lefier has identified a Canadian element in *Colas et Colinette* that would have had significant interest for contemporaries: the introduction of new rules for the formation of the French-Canadian militia in the 1780s; see '*Colas et Colinette ou le bailli dupé* et la réalité canadienne,' in *Revue d'histoire littéraire du Québec et du Canada français*, 12 (1986), 211–34.

9 '*Les Républicains français*,' ed. Baudoin Burger, in *La Barre du jour*, 25 (1970), 60–88. An English translation by Louise Forsyth appears in *Canada's Lost Plays*, 4: 94–110.

10 'Joseph Quesnel et l'anglomanie de la classe seigneuriale au tournant du XIXᵉ siècle,' in *Co-Incidences*, 6, no. 1 (1976), 23–31.

11 Roch Legault and Luc Lépine, 'François Vassal de Monviel, *DCB*, 7: 883–5.

12 None of the poems published in Quesnel's lifetime in various newspapers bear his own name. Most of those published in John Neilson's *Gazette de Québec* are identified only by the initial 'F,' and in the long poem 'Le Rimeur dépité' (also known as 'Le Dépit ridicule') which is important for *Anglomania* (see note 6 to the translation below) he appears as 'Monsieur François.' See *Les Textes poétiques du Canada français*, ed. Jeanne d'Arc Lortie with Pierre Savard and Paul Wyczynski, vol. 1 (1606–1806) (Montréal: Fides 1987), esp. pp. 468–9.

13 The French term, 'la Douairière,' is as quaint and archaic as it sounds in English. Robert's *Dictionnaire historique de la langue française* (1992) defines it as 'une veuve

jouissant d'un douaire ... une femme âgée et riche de l'aristocratie ou de la haute bourgeoisie.'

14 Claude Savoie, in his edition of the play in *La Barre du jour*, misreads the word as 'Pennkrène.' The first edition (in *Le Canada français*) has the correct form. In the manuscript a note by Jacques Viger explains that the real-life model is 'docteur Stubinger, ci-devant des troupes hessoises' (formerly with the Hessian troops), who were stationed in Canada, misread by the anonymous editor for *Le Canada français* as 'troupes belgoises' and by Claude Savoie as 'hefsoires,' two adjectives that make no sense in French.

15 François, seeking to 'butter up' a rich, potential patron calls him 'Monsieur *de* Primenbourg,' appending the particle associated with French nobility.

16 Quesnel himself is the author of this French version, which further strengthens the link between himself and his *alter ego*, the poet François. The Lande collection in the National Archives of Canada in Ottawa has a copy in Quesnel's own hand, entitled 'Imitation de la chanson anglaise God Save the King.' The text is reproduced in *Les Textes poétiques du Canada français*, ed. Lortie with Savard and Wyczynski, 1: 381.

17 The seventeenth-century critic Nicolas Boileau-Despréaux, frequently cited as an authority by Quesnel.

18 The 'insolent tale' referred to is a long poem by Quesnel entitled 'Le Rimeur dépité' (one version has the title, 'Le Dépit ridicule ou le sonnet perdu: dialogue entre Mr. François et Made. Françoise') in which 'François', i.e. Quesnel, makes the rounds seeking someone who will listen to his latest poem. Among those he importunes is 'Docteur Bustenger,' whose preposterous German accent and skill at preparing pâtés identify him as our Dr Pennkrève, and 'Monsieur d'Imberville.' Here is the episode:

Je suis allé tout droit chez Monsieur d'Imberville,
Il montoit en voiture, il alloit à la ville;
Je voulus l'arrêter pour lire mon sonnet,
Mais lors, à son cheval donnant un coup de foüet,
Il part comme un éclair et me laisse derrière.

Les Textes poétiques du Canada français, 1: 475.

19 Jacques Viger's note in the manuscript reads, 'Par M. Ross Cuthbert, 1803,' and that is indeed the date of first publication of this curious, satirical poem (Québec: Neilson, 13 pages), comprising 144 lines plus explanatory notes in French and English.

20 Viger's second note on the poem observes, 'C'est vrai: ce sont des alexandrins monstres de 14, 15 et 16 pieds ... au besoin!' Alexandrines, the best-known and most classic of poetic verse forms, are of course restricted to precisely twelve feet (syllables) per line.

21 Vielmont is probably referring to military events which led to the the brief armistice signed between Great Britain and France at Amiens in late March 1802. Between April 1802 and mid-May 1803 there were no armed hostilities between the two nations. See J. Mackay Hitsman, *Safeguarding Canada, 1763–1870* (University of Toronto Press 1968),

65–7. In that case, the date 1802 appearing on the manuscript appears well founded, with reference to Cutherbert's *L'Aréopage* appended as an afterthought.

22 'Dinner' was at this time normally a mid-day meal in refined society (as it remains, in popular usage, in English and French, in most of non-urban Canada).

23 Viger's ms note identifies 'Mont Frédérick' as 'Le Baron F. de Schaffalisky, noble Hongrois.' Historical and biographical sources provide no further clues. Some of Quesnel's satiric poems are signed 'Frétérick,' perhaps in reference to this colourful local character.

24 Viger's note explains that she had a birthmark in the shape of a mouse.

25 The fact that 'François'/Quesnel makes fun of this misshapen poem does him credit, of course; and the Colonel's resolute defence of it has the opposite effect.

26 'It will supply the finishing touch.'

II: The Status Quo Comedies

1 The *Mercury*, the first true party organ in French Canada, had been founded in 1805. *Le Canadien* was established the following year, mainly to counter the *Mercury*'s reactionary and often intemperate stance.

2 For *Le Canadien*'s early dramas and its attacks on de Bonne, see my *Theatre in French Canada*, 89–90.

3 The exception is the French immigrant Firmin Prud'homme's *Napoléon à Sainte-Hélène*, published in 1831, the same year he arrived in Canada, and probably composed before his arrival. See ibid., 103–7.

4 Biographical information on these and other individuals appearing or mentioned in the five plays is provided in the Notes following the translation of each play.

5 Thus Dionne's résumé of the fifth comedy ('cette dernière pièce était plutôt une prétendue représaille des écrits très spirituels publiés dans la *Gazette de Québec*') in *Les Trois Comédies du 'Statu Quo' [1834]* (Québec: Laflamme & Proulx 1939), 40, is repeated verbatim by Thérèse Ouellet in 'Bibliographie du théâtre canadien-français avant 1900' (MA thesis, Université Laval 1949), 11, and E.-G. Rinfret in *Le Théâtre canadien d'expression française: Répertoire analytique des origines à nos jours* (Montréal: Leméac 1975–8), 1: 58.

6 For Faribault, see article by Yvan Lamonde in *DCB*, 9: 249–51.

7 Claude Vachon, for example, writing in *DCB*, 11: 261–2, states: 'On 25 April 1834, following the presentation in the house of the Ninety-Two Resolutions, *La Gazette de Québec* published a short play entitled "La première comédie du Statu Quo," written by Louis-David Roy, a lawyer, and Georges-Barthélémi Faribault, clerk of the House of Assembly.' In fact, the correct date is 26 April, *La Gazette*'s comedy was untitled (it was Dionne who called it 'La Première Comédie du Statu Quo' for identification purposes, seventy-five years later), and Faribault was not yet clerk of the Assembly. Vachon seems here merely to be following Dionne in *Les Trois Comédies du 'Statu Quo' [1834]*, 39–40.

8 For Angers, see the article by Aurélien Boivin in *DCB*, 7: 16–17. As author, he is best

known for his *Les Révélations du crime, ou Cambray et ses complices: chroniques cana-diennes de 1834* (Québec: Fréchette & Cie 1837), a partly fictionalized account of a sensational series of crimes in the Quebec area.

9 See my *Theatre in French Canada*, 84–5.

10 Labelle's text is reproduced, with introductory articles by Doucette and McGee, *Theatre History in Canada/Histoire du théâtre au Canada*, vol. 5, no. 2.

11 Graduate students I have taught at the University of Toronto consistently deduce, upon comparing the text of *La Dégringolade* with Gurik's play, that the latter is derivative of the former, or that at very least Gurik was conversant with the *Statu Quo Comedies, Tuque Bleue*, and *La Dégringolade*.

12 See, for example, Mary Elizabeth Smith, '*Measure by Measure* and Other Political Satires from New Brunswick,' in *Theatre History in Canada/Histoire du théâtre au Canada*, 5, no. 2 (1984), 172–84.

13 'P ... t' is Etienne Parent (1802–74), lawyer, editor, and essayist, of whom Jean-Charles Falardeau has written (*DCB*, 10: 579): '[His] thought dominated the first half of the French Canadian nineteenth century. This man incarnated as did no one else the ambi-tions of a new social type, that of the intellectual and political élite, which at the turn of the nineteenth century was replacing the gentleman class of land-owning seigneurs, and along with the ecclesiastical leaders, resolutely taking hold of the destiny of the French Canadian people.' Parent had become editor of *Le Canadien* at the age of twenty (its publication was suspended the following year). The intellectual leader of the Patriotes throughout this period, he was much more moderate than the party's political leader, Louis-Joseph Papineau, and sought to avoid unnecessary conflict with the opposition in and outside the Legislature. He had been made official librarian of the Assembly in 1833.

   'B ... d' is Elzéar Bédard (1799–1849), lawyer, politician, and later judge. He was one of four men who provided funds to re-launch *Le Canadien* in 1831, and he remained a staunch supporter of the Patriote cause after his election to the House of Assembly in 1832. The Ninety-Two Resolutions were drawn up, it is reported, at his home, and they were introduced in the house by Bédard himself. Generally considered to be the leader of the moderate wing of the party within the House, he was the first per-son to be elected mayor of Quebec City in 1833. Defeated the following year, he retired from municipal politics in 1835, and in 1836 accepted appointment as judge of the Court of King's Bench. See Claude Vachon's article in *DCB*, 7: 61–2.

   'H ... t' is Hector-Simon Huot (1806–46), lawyer and member for Portneuf in the House of Assembly. Married to a cousin of Étienne Parent, Huot was deeply concerned with the state of public education in French Canada and strove to improve it throughout his political career.

   'D ... e' is Charles Deguise (1798–1860), lawyer and municipal politician.

   'F ... t' is Louis Fiset (1797–1867), lawyer, political organizer for various Patriote candidates in the area of Quebec City, and later a judge (1844).

'G ... ' is François-Xavier Garneau (1809–66), the great historian of French Canada. After travelling in Europe, he had become private secretary in 1831 to Denis-Benjamin Viger, official agent of the Assembly in London, returning to Lower Canada in 1833. A great admirer of Papineau, Garneau nevertheless took little active part in politics. At that moment, he was working as a notary in the office of Louis-Théodore Besserer (see note 26 below).

'W ... r' is Pierre Winter (1808–91), lawyer and in 1858 a judge. A colourful but minor character in local politics, he moved to Gaspé the following year and out of the political spotlight.

'M ... l' is Étienne Martel (1805–76), lawyer and minor politician. Like Winter, he moved to the Gaspé Peninsula in 1835 and exercised his profession there until his death.

14 Jacques Viger (1787–1858). A cousin of Denis-Benjamin Viger and Louis-Joseph Papineau, he had been editor of the first *Le Canadien* in 1808–9, and first mayor of Montreal, 1833–6. Viger had frequently been referred to as a 'Témoin banal' ('banal witness') by the 'Friend of the Status Quo' in his letters in *La Gazette*, and the *Mercury*, 27 March 1834, p. 1, col. 3, calls him Papineau's *'fidus Achates*, Jacques of the Red Stockings.'

15 This was the derogatory term applied to the close circle of Papineau supporters (such as Jacques Viger), later to be called Papineau's 'family.'

16 Louis-Hippolyte Lafontaine (1807–64), the great politician and statesman, at this time an ardent admirer of Papineau and an active Patriote. As the prospect of armed rebellion approached, however, he would dissociate himself from Papineau and seek more moderate political goals.

17 Édouard-Étienne Rodier (1804–40), a strong Papineau supporter and radical Patriote, member of the Legislature for L'Assomption, and future militant in the Rebellion of 1837–8. See Richard Chabot's article in *DCB*, 7: 757–9.

18 Founded in 1826 to replace *Le Canadien*, *La Minerve*, owned by Ludger Duvernay, was the voice of the Patriote party in the Montreal area.

19 Bédard, the first mayor of Quebec City, had just been defeated, 31 March 1834, in his attempt to seek re-election to that post.

20 Fiset, apparently through ignorance, deforms the proverbial expression 'ne te laisse pas manger la laine sur *le dos*' by substituting *la tête*. His stumbling syntax is further illustrated in the next sentence when he mentions the electoral district 'dont je ne me rappelle pas le nom dans le moment actuel d'actuellement.'

21 Denis-Benjamin Viger (1774–1861), cousin of Jacques Viger. He had been appointed official agent of the House of Assembly in London in 1831, and retained that post until the fall of 1834.

22 The source of this amusing description is made clear in an item in the *Quebec Mercury*, 22 March 1834, p. 3, col. 2, entitled 'Some Particulars on the Meeting Held at the School House in Glacis Street on Sunday Last,' translated from a report in *La Gazette* of 18 March, p. 2, col. 3: 'This assembly took place on Sunday [16 March] after Vespers on

the invitation of a certain young lawyer distinguished by a tricoloured ribbon, the Gallic Cock, and Napoleon on his breast. (Q[uer]y – would not a *Napoleon* be better placed in his pocket?) A youth who, in his patriotic frenzy, it is said, has sworn on the graves of the victims of the 21st May to revenge the shedding of Canadian blood, though he should in achieving the deed, swallow a Highlander alive, kilt, phillibeg [filibeg], and hose, with cap and feathers to boot. It must be confessed that such an example of patriotism was never before seen!'

The communication is signed, as usual, 'A Friend of the Status Quo.' The reference to the 'victims of the 21st May' is to the violent incident that had taken place in Montreal two years earlier, during a heated by-election. To quell an apparent riot, British troops under the orders of a Colonel MacIntosh had fired on a crowd in the streets, killing three French Canadians.

23 On Winter's warlike speech, see the letter signed 'Friend of the Status Quo' in *La Gazette*, 27 March 1834 p. 2, col 1: 'During the debate on the famous Resolutions one member of the House, Mr G ..., I believe, made the remark, "Well, it's war they want, then!" or words to that effect; whereupon our hero [Winter], who had been perched on a window sill in the chamber, said, loudly enough to be heard by several people present, "Yes! Yes, that's what we want!"'

For the 'Napoleon' on Winter's chest, see preceding note. The word refers also to a gold coin worth 20 francs.

24 'Convention' and words like it are of course meant to suggest the worst terrors of the French Revolution.

25 'M' is the signature used by a regular contributor to *Le Canadien* throughout this period. He frequently takes the 'Friend of the Status Quo' to task for remarks made in *La Gazette* without, generally, the wit and style of the 'Friend.'

26 Louis-Théodore Besserer (1785–1861), notary and member for the County of Quebec. Although a 'Resolutionary,' Besserer would distance himself from Papineau and the Patriotes before the Rebellion and end his days in Ottawa as a confirmed anglophile. (See article by Jean-Yves Gravel in *DCB*, 9:48).

Dr Jean-Baptiste Grenier was born in 1811 but his date of death is unknown and there are few details of his career. He was a cousin of Étienne Parent.

N.-E. Dionne, in his re-edition of the text, lists Elzéar Bédard and F.-X. Garneau as characters in this play as well. Although Bédard is referred to, he does not actually appear, and neither does Garneau.

27 Edward George Geoffrey Smith, Baron Stanley and 14th Earl of Derby, colonial secretary.

28 Grenier's letter, as read here, appeared in *Le Canadien* on 21 April, p. 2, col. 3. In *La Gazette*, 17 April, the 'Friend of the Status Quo' had called upon Grenier 'd'assermenter ce qui suit: "J'étais présent à l'assemblée qui a eu lieu en la paroisse du Château-Richer mardi le 1er avril 1834 ..."'

29 The Château Saint-Louis had been the residence of governors-general since the seventeenth century. Ironically, it had recently been destroyed by fire (23 January 1834).

30 'U.A.F' stands for 'Une Autre Fois' ('Another Time').

31 Joseph-Thomas Amiot (1810– ?), admitted to the bar in 1833. Named clerk of the court the following year, he moved to Montreal in 1847.

32 Amiot had a cast in one eye, and the author is playing on this misfortune.

33 Jean-François-Joseph ('Johnny') Duval (1802–81), lawyer and member for Quebec's Upper Town, a seat he would lose in October 1834. He would later be named chief judge of the Court of Queen's Bench.

34 There were two Mondelet brothers active in politics at this time, Dominique (1799–1863), lawyer and Member for Montreal, and Charles-Elzéar (1801–76), who opposed the Ninety-Two Resolutions but wound up as defence lawyer for the Patriotes after the Rebellion. Dominique had split with the Patriotes in 1832, and was at this time a member of the Executive Council. He appears to be the one alluded to here.

35 P[apineau], [D.-B.] V[iger], [H.-S.] H[uot], [Elzéar] B[édard], [Étienne] P[arent], and [Louis-Théodore] B[esserer].

36 Duval's lameness probably explains the epithet 'Vulcan,' but given the general malice of these texts, there may also be reference to marital problems.

37 André-Rémi Hamel (1788–1840). He had been appointed advocate-general of Lower Canada in 1832, and had stood for election in the Île d'Orléans. Hamel is the central target in the fifth comedy.

38 Hamel had been formally censured by the House of Assembly on 19 February 1834 for interfering in the election process. At the governor's request he had written a legal opinion concerning the Stanstead election declaring its outcome illegal. Hamel's letter to the returning officer appears, in English, in the *Quebec Mercury*, 8 March 1834, p. 3, col. 2.

39 Nicolas Boileau-Despréaux Boileau, (1636–1711). *Le Lutrin*, 1: 32–3:
> Et son corps ramassé dans sa courte grosseur
> Fait gémir les coussins sous sa molle épaisseur.

Our anonymous author writes:
> Tout son corps ramassé dans sa courte grosseur
> Fesait [*sic*] gémir la *barre* sous sa molle épaisseur.

putting thirteen syllables in the second line, in what should be alexandrine, or 12-syllable verse; whence Amiot's comment about 'murdering Boileau.'

40 Louis-Édouard Glackmeyer or Glackemeyer (1793–1881), notary, musician, and member of the Quebec City Council from 1833 to 1845.

41 Frederick John Robinson (1782–1859), created Viscount Goderich in 1827, later Earl of Ripon. He was British colonial secretary at the time.

42 The author plays on the proverbial French expression, 'C'est Gros-Jean qui en remontre à son curé,' substituting 'Thomas' for 'Gros-Jean.'

43 Andrew William Cochran (1792–1849), civil secretary to Governors Sherbrooke and Dalhousie, member of the Executive Council, 1827–41.

44 In French it reads:
>   On le tient, ce nid de fauvette,
>   Ils sont deux, trois, quatre petits,
>   Depuis si longtemps qu'on vous guette,
>   Pauvres oiseaux, vous voilà pris!

I have not been able to identify the source of this quotation.

45 In *La Gazette* for 13 May, p. 1, col. 4, there is a long letter (signed, as the character in *Le Canadien*'s first playlet, 'Thomas A ... t'), in which Amiot decries the practice of eavesdropping and then reveals it was Bédard who had overheard the conversation between himself and Duval: 'Il ne fallait rien moins qu'un célèbre personnage comme M. Elzéar Bédard, membre de la chambre d'assemblée, pour se rendre coupable d'une action qui ferait rougir un homme qui ne serait pas perdu à tout sentiment d'honneur.' Bédard responded on 15 May, p. 2, col. 1, with a letter in the same paper admitting that it was he who, quite inadvertently, had overheard a conversation and the reading from the 'Friend of the Status Quo' letter.

46 Boileau, *Satires*, 1 11: 51–2:
>   Je ne puis rien nommer, si ce n'est par son nom;
>   J'appelle un chat un chat, et Rolet un fripon.

47 Robert Christie, *A History of the Late Province of Lower Canada* (Quebec: Cary 1850), 3: 556–7, states: 'Among the anomalies of the session deserving of notice, is the reprimand by the speaker, of Mr. Hamel, a barrister residing in Quebec, and his Majesty's advocate general, for a *law opinion* in relation to the rights of certain voters at an election for the county of Stanstead, which, by desire of the governor, pursuant to a call from the returning officer he had given. It was resolved by the assembly:
>   That André Rémy Hamel, Esq., in having, as one of the officers of the crown, given an opinion to the governor in chief, on the subject of the proceedings at the said election, to be transmitted to the said returning-officer, has been guilty of a breach of the rights and privileges of this house.
>   And that the said André Rémy Hamel, Esq., be taken into the custody of the serjeant at arms, and be brought to the bar of this house, and admonished by the speaker.'

48 Hamel had been unsuccessful in his attempt at election on the Île d'Orléans, and indeed had lost his deposit.

49 Amiot. Thersites was a Greek soldier (*Iliad*, 2: ll. 211–77) who was described by Homer as lame, misshapen, and low-born, and as much given to reviling the leadership of his army.

50 Jacques Cujas (1520–90), renowned for his fine theological and legal distinctions.

51 Jacques Crémazie (1810–72), lawyer and author of legal texts, brother of the poet,

Octave. He would become the first professor of law at Université Laval after the foundation of that faculty in 1854, and, in 1866, dean of the faculty.

Louis-David Roy (1807–80), lawyer and later (in 1852) judge.

52 A full description of the formal censure imposed upon Hamel, including Speaker
Papineau's speech, appears in the *Quebec Mercury*, 22 February 1834, p. 2, col. 4. The
author is here parodying details and vocabulary of that speech.

53 The letters referred to here appear in *La Gazette* 13 May, p. 1, col. 4, (Amiot's), and in
Le Canadien, 14 May, p. 2, col. 4 and *La Gazette*, 15 May, p. 2, col. 2 (Duval's).

54 Amiot apparently supplemented the meagre income from his practice – in a city filled
with lawyers – by selling used clothing and lending money at high interest. In his letter
in *La Gazette* Amiot protests vigorously against these allegations, maintaining he was
merely seeking an 'honest living.'

55 *La Gazette*, 3 April 1834, p. 2, col. 2, speaks of 'la célèbre poudre politique de Perlimpinpin composée des 92 ingrédients hétérogènes des Messieurs P.B.M. G. & B.'
'Poudre de perlimpinpin' is a comic, derogatory term for a useless medication or solution. The letter signed 'Un Autre' is in the same paper for 25 March, p. 1, col. 4.

56 The reference may be to Napoleon's *Essai sur l'art de rendre les révolutions utiles*, written
in collaboration with J.-E. Bonnet, 2 vols. (Paris: Maradan 1801).

57 *L'Ami du peuple, de l'ordre et des lois*, published twice weekly in Montreal (1832–40), a
highly conservative newspaper antagonistic to the Patriotes.

58 This *Vaudeville*,

Car si vous avez terni le barreau

C'est la faute à Papineau!

in the French sense of a comic or satiric song sung to a well-known tune (in this case the
popular song 'Voilà l'effet de l'argent'), seems to have been widely known at the time
and verses are frequently quoted in *Le Canadien*. Jacques Viger, writing to his wife on 17
February 1834, had included a printed copy of 16 stanzas, 6 lines to a stanza.

III. The Donation

1 Baudoin Burger points out that in the absence of any contemporary reference to the
appearance of the play, one cannot be sure when it was actually published. He reminds
us that Joseph Quesnel's *Colas et Colinette*, although it bears the imprint '1808,' was not
released for publication until 1812. See his 'Théâtre, littérature et politique en 1837–
1838,' in *Aspects du théâtre québécois*, ed. Étienne-F. Duval (Trois-Rivières: Université du
Québec à Trois-Rivières 1978), 3.

2 Initially he worked as a minor copyist in the office of the clerk of the Court of King's
Bench in Quebec. Joseph-François Perrault (1753–1844), who had founded a system of
primary schools, one of which Petitclair himself attended, took a keen personal interest

in the young man, helping him to learn English and encouraging him to continue his education. It was apparently at his urging that Petitclair went to work in the law office of Archibald Campbell, who is the known model for Villomont in this play (2, 20–3). The latter's description of his clerk, more interested in reading Marryat's *Jacob Faithful* or the cookbook *La Cuisinière canadienne* than law books (2, 20), is usually taken as a portrait of Petitclair himself, who seems to have abandoned his legal studies as soon as he entered Campbell's employment.

3 Louis-Michel Darveau, who claims to have known Petitclair personally and who devotes a chapter to him in his *Nos hommes de lettres* (Montréal: Stevenson 1873), 61–74, describes him as follows: 'With genius enough to spare, compared with a lot of people of lesser talent who were given precedence over him, he refused to make any public display of his own worth. He may have been aware of his own strengths and merits, but he lacked self-confidence. Whenever it came down to his own personal interests, even those most dear to him, he would become shy, embarrassed, and fearful. A mere child was enough to distress him and make him take to his heels.' A few lines late Darveau adds, 'he lacked the sort of audacity one needs to fight and to perish or triumph. As the saying goes, he didn't have the nerve, the guts for it. He was totally lacking in what the English call "pluck."' In the same chapter he analyses *The Donation* and reproduces several scenes from it (2, 14–17).

4 For this and other aspects of *Griphon*, see my *Theatre in French Canada*, 116–21, 238–9.

5 Prud'homme, an actor and playwright, arrived in Montreal in 1831 and performed briefly in Quebec in February 1832. Leblanc de Marconnay, editor and author, arrived in 1834 and soon established an amateur dramatic society that was particularly active. Both men composed plays while in Montreal and had them performed and published there, significantly modernizing francophone repertoire in the process. See ibid., 103–14.

6 Aubin is the subject of a useful study by J.-P. Tremblay, *À la recherche de Napoléon Aubin* (Québec: Les Presses de l'Université Laval 1969). For Aubin's imprisonment, see his chapter 3: 'Satire et châtiment,' 27–44; for the Amateurs Typographes, see 131–2.

7 Jean-Claude Noël, 'Pierre Petitclair, premier dramaturge canadien-français' (PhD thesis, Université d'Ottawa, 1973). In a more recent article, Noël reaffirms, 'C'est un fait, le théâtre de Petitclair dénote un souci de neutralité,' in *Bulletin du Centre de recherche en civilisation canadienne-française*, no 19 (December 1979), 27–9.

8 Burger, 'Théâtre, littérature et politique en 1837–1838.'

9 *Le Canadien*, 7 November 1836, p. 2. I have speculated elsewhere (*Theatre in French Canada*, 238, n56) that the play for which support was sought may well have been *Griphon*, under a different title.

10 André Beaulieu et Jean Hamelin, *La Presse québécoise, des origines à nos jours* (Québec: Les Presses de l'Université Laval 1973–), 1: 121–2.

11 *L'Artisan*, 15–29 December 1842; *Le Répertoire national*, ed. James Huston, 4 vols.

(Montreal: Lovell & Gibson 1848–50), 2: 234–70, and (Montreal: Valois 1893), 2: 262–304.

12 Noël, 'Pierre Petitclair,' p. 92.

13 Strong melodramatic elements are visible in the plays by the French expatriates Firmin Prud'homme and Hyacinthe Leblanc de Marconnay, written and performed in the previous decade in Montreal, especially in the latter's *Le Soldat* (1836). See my *Theatre in French Canada*, 103–14.

14 *L'Artisan*, 29 December 1842, p. 2.

15 'Lac Calvaire' is today Lac Saint-Augustin, a few kilometres east of Petitclair's birthplace. The location seems to have had particular appeal for him, since it is the setting for his third and last surviving play, *Une partie de campagne*.

16 Rue Champlain, following the waterfront from the base of Cap Diamant, was famous for its drinking establishments. In 1836 there were fifty on this street alone, as reported by J.P. Tremblay, *À la recherche de Napoléon Aubin* (Québec: Les Presses de l'Université Laval 1969), 20.

17 All three editions of the play (in *L'Artisan* and in both editions of Huston's *Répertoire national*) have 'la promesse que j'ai faite à Auguste,' but this is patently impossible. I have substituted 'Bellire.'

18 In *L'Artisan*'s edition, Susette's name is mistakenly omitted before this reply, which then appears to be Delorval's.

19 Martel pretends to hear the name as 'sucette,' a babies' pacifier, a dummy, or soother (from sucer: 'to suck').

20 *Mérope*, 2: 7. There is no record of this play's performance in Canada to this date, on public, private, or college stage, so the quotation from it suggests a reading knowledge of Voltaire.

21 The poetry of Louis Racine (1692–1763), son of the great playwright, had remained very popular in France, often in anthologized form, throughout the eighteenth century. With its strong emphasis on traditional, particularly religious, values, it is not surprising that it occupied a privileged place in the curriculum of *collèges classiques* in Canada as well to the end of the nineteenth century. This quotation is from his longest (some two hundred pages) and best-known poem, *La Religion* (Paris: Coignard 1742, chant 6), a work that was reprinted several dozen times by the end of the nineteenth century. In this context, it is curious to see the Jansenistic Louis Racine contrasted with the notorious freethinker, Voltaire.

22 According to Noël, 'Pierre Petitclair,' 216, note, the Union Hotel, built in 1805, had changed its name to Payne's Hotel about 1840.

23 *Jacob Faithful*, 3 vols. (London: Saunders & Otley 1834), by Frederick Marryat (1792–1848), is one of many now forgotten novels by this author who was then very popular on both sides of the Atlantic. Incidentally, Captain Marryat, who happened to be on a tour of New York when renewed hostilities broke out in Lower Canada in the autumn of

1838, had hurried north to serve under Sir John Colborne in an expedition against the Patriotes. His *A Diary in America, with Remarks on Its Institutions*, 3 vols. (London: Longmans 1839) recounts his travels, and his *The Settlers in Canada*, 2 vols. (London: Longmans, Green 1844) gives his firm views on the situation in this country. *La Cuisinière canadienne*, reprinted frequently throughout the century, was a cookbook. Since the description of this clerk is generally taken as a portrait of Petitclair himself, the diversity of his reading is of particular interest.

24 This was, in 1842, a very topical reference. Towards the end of 1840 Alexandre Vattemare (1796–1864), a French artist, philanthropist, and popularizer of science, had come to Montreal and then Quebec City, where he announced his intention of establishing a scientific and cultural institute with a library, an art gallery, a museum, a lecture hall, and an ongoing display of the most recent scientific inventions. Aided enthusiastically by Aubin and *Le Fantasque*, Vattemare did his best to arouse local support for the project, but was forced to leave Quebec in March 1841 without success. The defeatist tone one discerns in this reference by Villomont no doubt reflects the disappointment of Petitclair (and of Aubin) at the failure of the venture.

25 These directions appear in the edition of the play published in *L'Artisan*, 29 December 1842, p. 2, but not in either edition of the *Répertoire national*. Their inclusion reminds us that unlike *Griphon*, never performed as far as one knows, *La Donation* had already been staged twice before publication, to enthusiastic response. Its status as theatre, not merely drama, had thus been demonstrated.

IV: A Country Outing

1 There is no doubt that, apart from a playlet or two attributed to the French immigrant Leblanc de Marconnay, the political drama published in French Canada before Confederation was the work of native Québécois. See my *Theatre in French Canada*, 82–125, 152–82. The publication of Petitclair's *Griphon* attracted no attention in 1837, and the play has apparently never been performed.

2 Every critic or historian who has dealt with *A Country Outing* (they are not many!), including myself, has been distracted to varying degrees by the perceived similarity of theme and treatment to Quesnel's play; perhaps the most notable recent example is Elaine F. Nardocchio who, in her *Theatre and Politics in Modern Québec* (University of Alberta Press 1986), accuses Petitclair of plagiarizing Quesnel's text (p. 13). Even the scholar who has worked most intensively on this author, Jean-Claude Noël, has affirmed, in 'Pierre Petitclair,' 132, where he writes: 'Petitclair doit à son prédécesseur l'idée de dénoncer l'anglomanie ...,' that the basic idea for *A Country Outing* came from Quesnel.

3 Some other inaccuracies that should be identified in this context: Léopold Houlé's erroneous attribution to Quesnel, in his *Histoire du théâtre au Canada* (Montréal: Fides

1945), 48, of a play entitled *La Partie de campagne*, an error further disseminated by Claude Savoie in his re-edition of *Anglomania* in *La Barre du jour*, July–December 1965, 113–41; and the surprising affirmation by Jean Du Berger in *Dictionnaire des œuvres littéraires du Québec* (Montréal: Fides 1978), 1: 733, that *A Country Outing* had first been staged in 1842 ('*Une partie de campagne* ... aurait été créée dès le mois de novembre 1842 par les Amateurs typographes, au Théâtre Royal de Québec'), an obvious confusion of this play with Petitclair's *The Donation*.

4 *Le Canadien*, 27 April 1857, p. 2. The brief report is signed 'Un Spectateur.' *Le Journal de Québec* had advised its readers on 21 April that the performance would be held the following evening, but its account of the production is even briefer than *Le Canadien*'s, without any reference to the Canadian author. On page 2, under the heading 'Faits Divers,' it reports: 'Théâtre – Les amateurs canadiens ont joué avec succès, mercredi soir, trois jolies pièces intitulées *La Partie de campagne* [*sic*], *Le Sourd* et *La Sœur de Jocrisse*.'

5 The advertising campaign began on 12 April 1860 in *Le Journal de Québec*. Petitclair's play was to be preceded by a speech from the president of the Société Saint-Jean-Baptiste, there would be comic songs in the intermissions, the society's entire marching band would perform, and 'deux chambres, l'une pour les Dames et l'autre pour les Messieurs, seront à la disposition des personnes qui désireraient ôter leur pardessus.' But even before the advertising campaign a reader of the same newspaper had challenged the Amateurs Typographes on 5 April, asking if that group, 'qui s'est acquis une si brillante réputation sur notre théâtre, voudrait bien nous dire, par la voie des journaux, si, à l'exemple des Amateurs Canadiens, il entend, lui aussi, mettre sa main puissante à l'œuvre si patriotique du monument de Sainte-Foye.' (I have found no evidence that the Amateurs Typographes responded on this occasion.) The same expensive ads began in *Le Courrier du Canada* on 13 April, continuing in both papers until the performance on 28 April. One should point out the relative modernity of this program compared with that of the 1857 première, Monnier and Vaez's play having been first published in 1853 (Paris: Levy), whereas Desforges's had first been performed and published in the 1790s. Like most of the plays by Monnier, *La Grandeur et décadence de M. Joseph Prudhomme* is a 'comédie bourgeoise' satirizing the middle class in contemporary France. There are no Canadian resonances in it, and its theme has only remote parallels with Petitclair's. I mention this because Monnier had also written a comedy entitled *La Partie de campagne (Dans la cuisine)*, published in his collection *Comédies bourgeoises* (Brussels: Gans 1857), but again there is little in common with Petitclair's play, apart from the title; and if *A Country Outing* was indeed composed in 1856, as Joseph Savard affirms, its title predates Monnier's use of it.

6 I exclude texts published in Canada by two recent French immigrants, Hyacinthe Leblanc de Marconnay – *Valentine, ou la Nina canadienne* (Montréal: L'Ami du peuple 1836); *Le Soldat* (Montréal: Bowman 1836) – and Firmin Prud'homme – *Napoléon à*

Sainte-Hélène (Montréal: La Minerve 1831). And, of course, one must exclude the many political playlets published before 1860.

7 See my *Theatre in French Canada*, 116–21.

8 J.-C. Noël has identified a probable real-life model for William: although baptised 'Guillaume,' one of the sons of the Labadie family, for which Petitclair was employed as tutor after 1837, had changed his name to 'William' by 1858. Noël, 'Pierre Petitclair, 170.

9 There are reminiscences of Scribe, especially of his *Malvina, ou un mariage d'inclination* (1828), but they are immaterial to the central plot of *A Country Outing*.

10 'Le Théâtre de Pierre Petitclair,' in *Archives des lettres canadiennes*, 5: 127–36.

11 History has not confirmed Joseph Savard's generous opinion of the French author Louis-Adolphe de Puibusque (1801–63), a decidedly minor journalist, essayist, and poet. De Puibusque visited Canada, and is the author of a brief account, *Notes d'un voyage d'hiver de Montréal à Québec (Canada)*, published in Paris in 1861. The article from which Savard quotes had first appeared in the Parisian newspaper *L'Union*, 30 July 1855.

12 Reference is to the novel *Charles Guérin*, by Pierre-Joseph-Olivier Chauveau (Montréal: Lovell 1953). David M. Hayne has pointed out that the review by L.-A. de Puibusque is probably the first of a French-Canadian novel in a Paris newspaper. *Dictionnaire des œuvres littéraires du Québec*, 1: 104.

13 Savard is no doubt thinking of Philippe Aubert de Gaspé *père* (1786–1871), author of the most important novel of nineteenth-century Quebec, *Les Anciens Canadiens* (1863), but Aubert de Gaspé's son with the same name had published, in 1837, the very first novel by a native French Canadian, *Le Chercheur de trésor, ou l'influence d'un livre*. The other authors alluded to are François-Réal Angers (1812–60), poet, novelist, and journalist, who is often associated with the *Status Quo Comedies*; the novelist Georges Boucher de Boucherville (1814–94), best known for his *Une de perdue, deux de trouvées* (1849–51); Eugène L'Écuyer (1822–98), journalist and novelist, author of *La Fille du brigand* (1844); Joseph Doutre (1825–86), also a journalist and novelist, probably the author of the *Tuque bleue* political playlets of 1848 (see my *Theatre in French Canada*, 157–65); and Patrice Lacombe, author of the novel *La Terre paternelle* (1846).

14 Jean-Claude Noël has pointed out in his thesis, 'Pierre Petitclair, premier dramaturge canadien-français,' 23n2, that there is confusion between the geographical homonyms Pointe-aux-Peaux and Pointe au Pot, both in the same area of Labrador. It seems certain that the former is where Petitclair died.

15 Lac Calvaire is today known as Lac Saint-Augustin, a few kilometres east of Petitclair's birthplace. The location seems to have had particular appeal for him, and is mentioned in his *The Donation* as well.

16 One assumes, at least, that Brown is English Canadian and not British. But in Quebec then as now, an 'Anglais' can be any English-speaking person, of whatever derivation or nationality.

17 Joseph, here and elsewhere, observes the rural custom of identifying locals by appending the father's and grandfather's names to their own.

18 Appropriately, William uses the fashionable English word 'spleen.' This diatribe against country life and manners, at a time when the long-lived messianic agriculturalist tradition was already well founded in Quebec, would be surprising coming from anyone except the anglophile William.

19 The song here deformed remains even today one of the most popular of the traditional Québécois repertoire, 'En roulant ma boule, roulant/En roulant ma boule ...'

20 The apparently illiterate Baptiste says 'Jeanne Sure et Victor Gigot,' meaning the two most popular French writers of the time, Eugène Sue and Victor Hugo (a *gigot* is, of course, a leg of mutton – something the speaker is obviously more familiar with).

21 The dramatic irony of this passage is unique in nineteenth-century French-Canadian theatre. Merely by associating the continental French (and *ipso facto* suspect) authors Sue and Hugo (the latter a major dramatist as well as novelist and poet) with a person who also goes to see plays and even performs in them, Petitclair suggests the type of attitude then prevailing in Quebec society, at least among 'right thinkers,' including most members of the ecclesiastical hierarchy.

22 An obvious slip on the author's part. Surely Flore has not forgotten that Joseph is her father, not her uncle!

23 The apparently ephemeral names of local reels and, probably, accompanying dances. An accomplished musician and composer himself, according to his biographer Louis-Michel Darveau, Petitclair would appear from this passage to have had little respect for popular rural music. Darveau, *Nos hommes de lettres*, 65.

24 'Roule ta bosse' ('roll your hump') is another traditional French and French-Canadian song, here somewhat cruelly sung by the Hunchback ('le Bossu'), with obvious reference to his own condition.

V: Félix Poutré

1 *Échappé de la potence: souvenirs d'un prisonnier d'état canadien en 1838* (Montréal: Imprimé pour l'auteur par DeMontigny et cie. 1862), 130 pages; reprinted in 1862 (Montréal: Senécal), 47 pages; in 1869, in 1884, and in 1885. *Escaped from the Gallows: Souvenirs of a Canadian State Prisoner in 1838* (Montreal: Printed for the Author by DeMontigny & Co. 1862), 48 pages; reprinted 1865 (Beauchemin & Valois), 160 pages.

2 An unusually long critique of the first performance appears in *Le Canadien* for 24 November 1862, p. 2. Another report on the performance of 19 January 1863 appears in *Le Canadien* on 21 January, p. 2, in which the anonymous reviewer goes out of his way to praise the impressive performance of one Paul Dumas, who played the lead role.

3 'Jean Béraud' [pseud. Jacques Laroche], *350 ans de théâtre au Canada français*

([Montréal]: Cercle du Livre de France [1958]), 53–4. The last reference to a stage performance of the play that I have found is in 1929.

4 The 42-page typescript, entitled '*Félix Poutré*, Comédie en 4 actes de Louis Fréchette,' is in the National Archives in Ottawa, Fonds Louis Fréchette, and is available on microfilm (call no. C13990). The adaptation was by Guy Dufresne, a well-known dramatist and script-writer, and it was directed by Guy Beaulne, with Jean Lajeunesse as Félix, Gilles Pelletier as Béchard, and Rolland D'Amour as Camel. The play was broadcast on 2 August 1953 as part of the series 'Le Théâtre Canadien.' Despite necessary compression, the script remains very close to Fréchette's text.

5 Typical is the judgment of George A. Klinck: 'Cette petite comédie bouffe est une dramatisation presque textuelle des *Souvenirs* de Félix Poutré, le patriote prétendu de 37,' in *Louis Fréchette, prosateur* (Lévis: Le Quotidien 1955), 180.

6 This deduction is based on the series of advertisements which began appearing on 8 November 1862 in *Le Journal de Québec*, where the play is described as a 'Grand Drame Historique en trois Actes et un Prologue.' See also the essay by Paul Wyczynski, 'Louis Fréchette et le théâtre,' in *Archives des lettres canadiennes*, 5: 137–65.

7 See Richard Chabot, 'Cyrille-Hector-Octave Côté' (1809–50), a 'teacher, physician, politician, Patriote, journalist, and Baptist minister,' in *DCB*, 7: 208–11. Initially a strong supporter of Papineau and the Patriotes (and a particularly virulent opponent of the Catholic hierarchy in Quebec), he turned against Papineau after the unsuccessful armed rebellion of 1837. Despite his best efforts he was unable to obtain armaments for the uprising of November 1838, and retreated to the United States after the battle at Odelltown. He was granted amnesty in 1843.

8 Dr Robert Nelson (1794–1873), born in Montreal, had studied medicine there under Dr Arnoldi (see note 13 below), who appears in such a bad light in this play. He was the younger brother of Dr Wolfred Nelson, the latter a close ally of Papineau and the hero of the successful defence of Saint-Denis against British troops in November 1837. Robert Nelson and Côté were responsible for organizing the armed insurrection of November 1838, which quickly deteriorated into disaster. He then sought refuge in the United States, refusing to return to Canada even after official pardon in 1843.

9 Saint-Jean-sur-Richelieu, on the Richelieu River some forty kilometres south-east of Montreal. A large number of American loyalists had settled in the area after the Revolution. The historical Poutré had married in, and settled near, this town.

10 *Escaped from the Gallows* (1862), 6.

11 For example, the song sung by 'un Patriote' which opens act 2, scene 1:
    En avant! marchons! (*etc.*)
    O Canadiens, peuple de braves,
    La liberté rouvre ses bras!
    On nous disait: soyez esclaves
    Nous avons dit: soyons soldats!

This is obviously borrowed, with appropriate changes, from a song in Delavigne's *La Parisienne*:

> Peuple français, peuple de braves,
> La liberté rouvre ses bras;
> On nous disait: soyez esclaves!
> Nous avons dit: soyons soldats!
> Marchons!

12 The notary Joseph-Narcisse Cardinal, who was thirty years old at his execution, had been recruited by Robert Nelson and soon became one of his principal deputies. Leader of the Patriote forces at Châteauguay in November 1838, he was captured and sentenced to death. According to Michel de Lorimier, *DCB*, 7: 150, he said nothing before his execution ('he said not a word and died bravely'). Joseph Duquet or Duquette, also a notary and a friend of Cardinal had taken part in Nelson's ill-fated invasion of Lower Canada from the United States. It is again interesting to contrast his portrayal by Fréchette (the scene is not in Poutré's memoirs) with the authoritative *DCB*'s: 'In accordance with the sentence of the court, Cardinal and Duquet had to mount the scaffold on the morning of 21 Dec. 1838. Cardinal was executed first. When it was his turn to climb the steps, Duquet began to shiver and his teeth chattered. He had to be supported. When the trapdoor was sprung, the noose, which had been badly adjusted by the hangman, Humphrey, slipped and caught under the nose of the condemned man, who was thrown violently to one side and hit the ironclad framework of the gallows. His face battered and bleeding profusely, the hapless Duquet had not lost consciousness and was moaning loudly. The onlookers began yelling: "Pardon! pardon!" This agony was prolonged, it was said, for some 20 minutes, the time it took for the hangman to install a new rope and cut down the original one.' Article by Gérard Filteau, *DCB*, 7: 265.

13 Daniel Arnoldi (1774–1849) was not the mere buffoon portrayed here. Born in Montreal, he practised medicine in Rivière-du-Loup and in Upper Canada before returning permanently to Montreal where he enjoyed considerable prestige, being elected chair of the Montreal Board of Medical Examiners in 1834 (the Patriote hero Dr Wolfred Nelson had nominated him for this position). Initially sympathetic to the Patriote cause, he seems to have moved away from it as armed hostilities approached. He was appointed doctor to the Montreal Jail in 1833. According to Gilles Janson, in *DCB*, 7: 26: 'Following the uprising in 1837–38 some Patriotes accused Arnoldi of having failed to look after the prisoners incarcerated in the Montreal jail for participating in the rebellion. Others, however, praised him for displaying humanity in these circumstances.' At the time of his death Arnoldi was president of the College of Physicians and Surgeons of Lower Canada.

14 It is interesting to note that the Radio-Canada version broadcast in 1953 expands upon these physical assaults on representatives of British colonial authority, 'milking' them far more than Fréchette had done.

15 The most revelatory studies are by Paul Wyczynski, 'Dans les coulisses du théâtre de Fréchette,' in *Archives des lettres canadiennes*, 1: 100–28; and 'Louis Fréchette et le théâtre,' in the same series, 5: 137–65. According to Wyczynski only *Papineau*, published and performed in 1880, can lay claim to any originality, a statement that I think requires reconsideration with respect to *Félix Poutré*.

16 Fréchette's name did not in fact appear on any edition of this play in his lifetime. The first edition (59 pages), undated and without printer's name, appeared in Montreal in 1871; the second, by the publisher Beauchemin, appeared the same year (47 pages). A second printing of the second edition by Beauchemin is dated 1878. The first edition appears to have been 'pirated' by an unscrupulous publisher, a not uncommon occurrence before modern copyright laws were enforced.

17 Poutré himself indicates in act 4, scene 12 that he is seventy years old ('there's my reward for seventy years of honesty and hard work'). The ages of the other historical characters given here (Cardinal, Duquette, Arnoldi) are only approximate (Cardinal was in fact thirty years old in 1838, Duquette twenty-three, Arnoldi sixty-four).

18 Toinon is entirely Fréchette's creation, a useful stereotype intended to serve as comic foil for Félix and the other 'serious' characters in the play.

19 The underground organization known as the Frères-Chasseurs, and in English as the Hunters' Lodges. Formed by expatriate rebels and sympathizers in the border states and in both Canadas in the spring of 1838, they remained a threat to the British administration in North America until 1841, when they were ordered disbanded by Washington. Cardinal, Duquette, Côté, de Lorimier, and Robert Nelson were active in recruiting for the Frères, which were intended to serve as a sort of fifth column when invasion was launched from across the United States border. Membership, at its height, was estimated at some 50,000.

20 The fact that Félix does not actually swear the oath detailed here is unlikely to represent a mere oversight on the dramatist's part. The omission probably reflects a concession to the sensitivities of an influential Catholic hierarchy that had from the beginning been firmly opposed to the Patriotes' military ventures and which, in any case, would have taken offence at the portrayal of a solemn oath-taking ceremony on-stage. And since Félix's ultimate betrayal of the pledge for which he is present will diminish further his tenous 'heroism,' perhaps his passive comportment here is intended to mitigate that negative aspect of the protagonist's character.

21 In Poutré's memoirs this entire exchange is between Félix and Robert Nelson and it is Nelson who administers the oath to Félix on his father's farm near Saint-Jean-sur-Richelieu. Poutré, *Escaped from the Gallows* (1862), 7–8.

22 The sansculottes were the working-class militants of the French Revolution, and the song sung here (drawn from the jingoistic *La Parisienne* by French author Casimir Delavigne, with echoes of 'La Marseillaise') has many similar revolutionary resonances in French.

23 The battle at Odelltown, a few miles north of the border with New York State, took

place on 9 November 1838. It proved a disaster for the disorganized and poorly armed
Patriote forces led by Robert Nelson, Cyrille Côté, and Charles Hindenlang (for the latter, see note 28 below).

24 The two passages in italics are borrowed directly by Fréchette from Poutré's *Échappé de
la potence*. The same passages are reproduced here from the English edition of 1862, 9–
10, to show the disruptive effect of these insertions in act 2. (In fact the French is even
more dissonant because of the literary tenses Fréchette retained from the original, which
had disappeared from the spoken language more than 250 years earlier.)

25 This is a mocking line from a traditional folk-song. The full verse is as follows:

> J'ai trouvé le nique [nid] du lièvre
> Mais le lièvr' n'y était pas;
> Le matin, quand il se lève,
> Il emport' le lit, les draps.

Ernest Gagnon, *Chansons populaires du Canada* (Beauchemin 1955), 153–4, reproduces
words and music.

25 Duquette was in fact twenty-three years old at the time of his execution.

27 Charles Richard Ogden, born in Quebec City, had entered politics as a Tory after a
lucrative law career in Trois-Rivières. He had been appointed attorney-general of Lower
Canada in 1833 and was chief prosecutor of the rebels arrested in 1837–8.

28 Charles Hindenlang or Hindelang was born in Paris and had served as an officer in the
French army before emigrating to the United States in the mid-1830s. Recruited to the
Patriotes in 1838, he was one of the leaders of the failed attack upon loyalist forces at
Odelltown. Captured and imprisoned soon afterwards, he was hanged on 15 February
1839. According to Claude Galarneau in *DCB*, 7: 411–12, he made a short speech
before mounting the scaffold, and then shouted 'Vive la liberté.'

29 'Thou shalt sprinkle me, Lord [with hyssop],' first words of the Latin anthem sung while
the priest sprinkled holy water as a purification rite preparatory to saying Mass.

30 Henri IV, one of the most beloved of French kings, assassinated in 1610.

31 Sir John Colborne, 1st Baron Seaton (1778–1863), had been lieutenant-governor of
Upper Canada from 1828 to 1836, and then was appointed commander of the British
forces in both Canadas. His role in suppressing and punishing the Patriotes, especially
during the second rebellion in 1838, has generally been perceived as excessively severe by
French-Canadian historians.

32 François-Marie-Thomas-Chevalier de Lorimier, an early supporter of Papineau and the
Patriotes and one of the leaders of the uprising of 1837, after which he escaped to the
United States. One of the founders of the Frères-Chasseurs, he was an organizer of and
participant in the attempted invasion of Lower Canada in the autumn of 1838. Arrested
on 12 November, he was hanged on 15 February 1839. Fréchette was the editor of de
Lorimier's 'Dernières lettres d'un condamné: M. de Lorimier annonçant sa mort à sa
cousin. Prison de Montréal, 12 février 1839' (Montréal: Demers [1893?]).

VI: Archibald Cameron of Locheill

1 The first edition (Québec: Desbarats et Derbishire 1863) was followed the next year by a second, revised by the author (Québec: G. et G.-E. Desbarats 1864), and thereafter by regular re-editions (1877; 1886; 1899; 1913; 1916; 1925; etc.; plus several undated) in French. The first English translation, by Georgiana M. Pennée, came in 1864, as *The Canadians of Old* (Quebec: G. & G.-E. Desbarats). Charles G.D. Roberts brought out a more literary version that was closer to the style of Aubert de Gaspé, first with the same title *The Canadians of Old* (New York: D. Appleton & Co. 1890; 1897; 1898), then as *Cameron of Lochiel [sic]* (Boston: L.C. Page & Co. 1905; 1910).

2 The first edition is as follows: '*Les Anciens Canadiens. Drame en trois actes tiré du roman populaire de P.A. de Gaspé*. Montréal, C.O. Beauchemin & Fils, Libraires-Imprimeurs, 256 et 258, Rue Saint-Paul. 1894.' This is what appears on the *cover* of the 1894 edition, which is nothing more than a pamphlet. The microform version does not reproduce the cover, and begins instead with the title-page which bears no date and reads: '*Les Anciens Canadiens. Drame en trois actes par* [my emphasis] *P.A. de Gaspé*. Montréal. En vente chez tous les libraires'; this has led to confusion, with some writers interpreting the microform as a separate edition *by* Aubert de Gaspé.

The second edition is as follows: '*Les Anciens Canadiens. Drame en trois actes, tiré du roman populaire de P.A. de Gaspé*. Montréal, Librairie Beauchemin Limitée, 79, Rue Saint-Jacques. 1917.'

3 Both manuscripts are retained at the Collège de L'Assomption in L'Assomption, Quebec. For the copy of the 1868 version, which is the basis of my translation, I am indebted to a graduate student at the University of Toronto, Liane Marie, whose MA thesis, 'Étude préfacielle de la pièce *Archibald Cameron of Locheill ou un épisode de la Guerre de Sept Ans en Canada (1759)*' (1994), offers a critical comparison of the various manuscripts and published versions of the play. I wish to express my thanks as well to the librarian at the Collège de L'Assomption, Réjean Olivier.

4 Reine Bélanger, for example, writing in the authoritative *Dictionnaire des œuvres littéraires du Québec*, 1: 38–9, concludes: 'L'adaptation théâtrale ne méritait pas tant d'éloges. Sa trop grande fidélité au texte original minimise l'action dramatique, sans cesse arrêtée par des dialogues plutôt livresques. Il s'agit avant tout d'un exercice de collège où les "acteurs se forment surtout à l'éloquence."' ·

5 'La Corriveau,' or Marie-Josephte Corriveau (1733–63) is a personage who is both historical and legendary. Convicted of murdering her husband in 1763, she was hanged and her body exposed in an iron cage as exemplary punishment. Many popular legends and superstitions soon arose concerning her, and these were revived after the discovery about 1850 of what was probably her cage. Apart from Aubert de Gaspé's novel and the play, various other literary and popular references exist. See, for example, *The Canadian Encyclopedia*, s.v. 'Corriveau, La.'

6 The Montreal newspaper *La Minerve* ran a series of advertisements on 22, 24, and 31 January 1867 for an 'evening of dramatic and musical entertainment' to be held at the Collège Sainte-Marie on 31 January that would include '"Les Volontaires en Crimée" (comédie)' and '"Les Sorciers de l'Île d'Orléans," drame tiré des *Anciens Canadiens* de M. P.A. de Gaspé.' A brief review in the same paper on 5 February praises the performance, without providing any further information on content. Interestingly, the evening's entertainment was under the auspices of the bishop of Montreal and of a Colonel Dyde, commander of a military or paramilitary company, the Bishop's Guards. As with the performance of January 1868, the evening seems to have had a decidedly military flavour, the reviewer describing in detail the magnificent costumes worn by the Guards and the impressive spectacle of the drills they performed on-stage. The first play referred to is probably *Le Conscrit, ou le retour de Crimée* by Ernest Doin, author and adaptor of many short 'curtain-raisers.'

7 This Montgomery is a fictitious character invented by Aubert de Gaspé, but with some basis in history. In his notes to *Les Anciens Canadiens* the author quotes from the diary of Colonel Malcolm Fraser (who may himself have served as a model for Archibald of Locheill) of the 78th Fraser's Highlanders: 'There were several of the enemy killed and wounded and a few taken prisoners, all of whom the barbarous Captain Montgomery, who commanded us, ordered to be butchered in a most inhuman and cruel manner.' (Note b. to Chapter 14.) See also the translation of Aubert de Gaspé's *Mémoires* by Jane Brierly where this Captain Alexander Montgomery is identified as the elder brother of General Richard Montgomery, who led the unsuccessful American attack on Quebec City in December 1775 in which he was killed. *A Man of Sentiment* (Montreal: Véhicule Press 1988), 409, notes H and I.

8 See my *Theatre in French Canada*, 130–1.

9 *Le Jeune Latour* (Montréal: Cinq-Mars 1844), reprinted in 1969 (Réédition-Québec), with a brief introduction by Baudoin Burger. An excellent translation by Louise Forsyth is found in vol. 4 of Wagner, ed., *Canada's Lost Plays*, 111–39.

10 See my *Theatre in French Canada*, 137–40.

11 *L'Ordre*, 23 janvier 1865, p. 2.

12 Apart from reports in the newspaper *La Minerve*, 14 juillet 1865 and, more extensively, 26 octobre 1865, the most complete description of this occasion is in the curious collection of ephemera entitled *Bibliographie et oraison funèbre du Révd. M.F. Labelle et autres documents relatifs à sa mémoire, ainsi qu'à la visite de Philippe Aubert de Gaspé, Écr., au Collège L'Assomption, suivis d'une lettre de Mgr. de Montréal et d'un bref du Souverain Pontife* (Montréal: Imprimerie de la Minerve 1865), especially pages 2–15: 'Compte rendu des exercices littéraires au Collège l'Assomption les 10, 11 et 12 juillet, 1865'; pages 50–4: 'Prologue du mélodrame intitulé *Archibald Cameron of Locheill, ou un épisode de la Guerre de Sept Ans en Canada*'; pages 55–67: 'Discours à la mémoire du Révd. M.F. Labelle et en l'honneur de Ph. Aubert de Gaspé, Écr., prononcé par le Révd. M.N. Bar-

ret, supérieur du Collège, immédiatement après la distribution des prix, le 12 juillet 1865'; and pages 67–8: 'Réponse de M. de Gaspé à M. le Supérieur.'

13 After the full title on the 1868 manuscript appears the note: 'Arcade Laporte, priest, and Camille Caisse, subdeacon, instructors at the Collège de L'Assomption, sketched out the plan and completed the composition of this drama in 1864.' But on the previous page there is another, later note: 'N.B. Contrary to the note that follows, only the overall plan was sketched by the Reverend Arcade Laporte. Plot development and actual composition are entirely due to Camille Caisse, subdeacon. Both are instructors at the Collège de L'Assomption. 1864. L. Casaubon, priest.' Finally, on the next page, in another hand: 'I, the undersigned, declare that the foregoing observation is absolutely correct. P.A. Laporte, priest.'

Subdeacon is the last, highest stage before ordination in the Catholic Church (Caisse was ordained priest in 1865). After graduating from L'Assomption in 1861, Caisse taught literature there while studying for the priesthood. Father L. Casaubon taught introductory Latin at the college.

14 The Zouaves were volunteer troops (mostly amateurs) recruited between 1868 and 1870 to defend the papal lands in Italy against invasion from republican forces under Garibaldi. Some four hundred Canadians enrolled, most arriving too late to prevent Rome's capture. The bishop of Montréal, Ignace Bourget, was the principal force behind this movement.

15 In the 1864 manuscript 'Fontaine' was 'Tontaine,' which had better comic resonance in French.

16 The role of Ouabi, who has a few lines in the 1864 manuscript, is retained here inadvertently since he has no specific role in the 1868 version of the play. A more significant change between the 1864 and 1868 manuscripts is the elimination from the latter of the role of a stereotypical comic Englishman, Dog Lotchill, whose massacring of the French language is as exuberantly caricatural as was Brown's in *A Country Outing*. His absence has no effect on the action of the play.

17 Since both printed versions refer only to the battle of Sainte-Foy, they are consistent in substituting 'Murray' for Wolfe and 'Lévis' for Montcalm in Jules's response.

18 On the south bank of the St Lawrence, approximately one hundred kilometres east of Quebec City.

19 This stage direction, and others like it, is missing in the published editions. One suspects the military exercices described were performed by the Papal Zouaves themselves, in full uniform.

20 This song is almost identical to the one sung in act 2, scene 1 of *Félix Poutré*. In 1759 its resonances of the French Revolution are obviously anachronistic!

21 Bellona was a Roman goddess of war. Ganymede, a mortal of whom Zeus became enamoured, was carried off by him to Olympus and made cup-bearer to the gods. This exchange is omitted from both published editions of the play.

22 Latin for 'Sweet milk.' José, of course, misunderstands.

23 For La Corriveau see the Introduction to this play.

24 'Diaper Fundy' is José's deformation of the Latin prayer based on Psalm CXXX which begins, 'De profundis clamavi ad te, Domine ...' It forms part of the Catholic service for the dead.

25 Words and form inspired from the traditional French song, 'C'est dans la ville de Rouen,' as recorded by Ernest Gagnon in his *Chansons populaires du Canada* (Montréal: Beauchemin 1955), 119–20.

26 The episode in which Dumais is rescued from certain death by drowning, inspired directly from the novel, is recounted at length in act 2, scene 3.

27 Le Petit-Marigotte was, according to Aubert de Gaspé, a pond much frequented by wild-fowl, located about one and a half kilometres south of Lac des Trois-Saumons, near Saint-Jean-Port-Joli, in L'Islet County, the author's home. I do not know why the reference becomes 'La Marigotte' in all versions of the play. There are at least two sites called 'La Marigotte' in Quebec today, one a hamlet in Lotbinière County, the other a cove in Maskinongé County.

28 An Algonquian word meaning 'Great Mountain' that was applied to the governors-general sent out from France and to the ultimate source of their authority, the King.

29 Saint-Thomas is today the town of Montmagny.

30 An interesting example of the length to which college theatre went in nineteenth-century French Canada to obliterate female reference: in the novel (chapter 9), it is 'she,' referring to a sort of madwoman or witch living on the d'Habervilles' property, 'la sorcière du domaine.'

31 Here, as in Talamousse's preceding speech and elsewhere, the references to lions and tigers seem dissonant in the mouth of a Canadian Indian.

32 The manuscript ends with the Latin abbreviation, 'A.M.D.G.' ('Ad majorem Dei gloriam: To the greater glory of God'), and the note: 'Copied by Odilon Guilbault, priest.' Guilbault, a graduate of the Collège de L'Assomption in 1857, had been ordained in 1864. He taught literature at the college from 1857 to 1891.

Suggestions for Further Reading

I. In English

Ball, John, and Richard Plant, eds. *Bibliography of Theatre History in Canada: The Beginnings through 1984/Bibliographie d'histoire du théâtre au Canada: des débuts – fin 1984.* Toronto: ECW Press 1993. The most reliable and complete source of bibliographic information on drama and theatre currently available. Listings by province, playwrights, and specific themes, with an exceptionally useful index.

Banham, Martin, ed. *The Cambridge Guide to Theatre.* Cambridge University Press 1995. Generic essay on 'Canada: French,' plus individual entries on playwrights. Supersedes previous editions.

Benson, Eugene, and L.W. Conolly, eds. *The Oxford Companion to Canadian Theatre.* Oxford University Press 1989. The most useful and accessible source for information in English on the history of drama and theatre in both languages. Generic essays on 'Drama in French' and 'Quebec, Theatre in (French),' plus individual entries for the plays *Théâtre de Neptune en la Nouvelle-France, Colas et Colinette, La Donation, Le Jeune Latour, Félix Poutré,* and *Archibald Cameron of Locheill,* and the authors Lescarbot, Quesnel, Petitclair, Gérin-Lajoie, Fréchette, and Marchand.

Doucette, Leonard E., *Theatre in French Canada: Laying the Foundations, 1606–1867.* Toronto: University of Toronto Press 1984. All of the authors and plays included in the present volume are discussed in the context of the overall development of dramatic forms and theatrical practices.

Hartnoll, Phyllis, ed. *The Oxford Companion to the Theatre.* Oxford University Press 1983. Generic essay on 'Canada,' plus a few individual entries on playwrights.

Marsh, James H., ed. *The Canadian Encyclopedia.* Edmonton: Hurtig 1988. Generic essays on 'Drama in French,' 'Theatre, French-Language,' and entries on individual authors. Superseded by an expanded and updated CD-ROM version, *The 1996 Canadian Encyclopedia Plus* (McClelland & Stewart 1995); a CD-ROM edition is forthcoming (1997).

Toye, William, ed. *The Oxford Companion to Canadian Literature*. Oxford University Press 1983. Generic essay on 'Drama in French: The Beginnings to 1900,' and a few entries on individual playwrights. A new edition is currently (1996) in preparation.

Wagner, Anton, ed. *Canada's Lost Plays*. Volume 4: *Colonial Quebec: French-Canadian Drama, 1606 to 1966*. Toronto: Canadian Theatre Review Publications 1982. Includes translations of Lescarbot's *Theatre of Neptune in New France*, Quesnel's *Colas and Colinette, or the Bailiff Confounded*, *The French Republicans, or an Evening in the Tavern*, Gérin-Lajoie's *The Young Latour*, Fréchette's *Papineau*, Paquin's *Riel*, plus useful introductory essays and notes.

Journals: *Canadian Drama/L'Art dramatique canadien*; *Theatre History in Canada/Histoire du théâtre au Canada*; *Theatre Research in Canada/Recherches théâtrales au Canada*.

II. In French

Burger, Baudoin. *L'Activité théâtrale au Québec (1765–1825)*. Montréal: Parti pris 1974. The most complete treatment of texts, authors, and general theatrical activity in the period indicated.

Duval, Étienne-F., ed. *Anthologie thématique du théâtre québécois au XIXᵉ siècle*. Montréal: Leméac 1978. Short extracts from fifty plays by thirty-one authors, with general introductory essay and a paragraph on each author.

Laflamme, Jean, et Rémi Tourangeau. *L'Église et le théâtre au Québec*. Montréal: Fides 1979. A study of the uneasy relationship between Catholic authorities and the theatre.

Legris, Renée, Jean-Marc Larrue, André-G. Bourassa, et Gilbert David. *Le Théâtre au Québec 1825–1980*. Montréal: VLB Éditeur 1988. Useful essays on a variety of topics and good photographs, but less comprehensive than title suggests.

Lemire, Maurice, ed. *Dictionnaire des œuvres littéraires du Québec*. Montréal: Fides 1978. Volume 1: *Des Origines à 1900*. Excellent source of information on individual plays. Volume arranged alphabetically, by title of work. Good bibliographic information.

In French only, the most useful journal is *Jeu: Cahiers de théâtre*, although its principal focus is contemporary.

Index

Doutre, Joseph 138, 308
Drapeau de Carillon, Le 134
Du Berger, Jean 307
Ducis, Jean-François (translations of Shakespeare) 40
Dufresne, Guy 310
Dumas, Paul 309
Duquette, Joseph 186–7, 311–13
Durham Report ix
Duval, Étienne-F. 303
Duval, Jean-François-Joseph 36–9, 59–67, 73–82, 301
Duvernay, Ludger 299
Dyde, Colonel 315

Edinburgh 273
Édouard le Confesseur xi
Escaped from the Gallows/Échappé de la potence 183, 188, 309–10, 312–13
Eschambault, Louis-Joseph Fleury d' 7–8
Exil et patrie xi

Falardeau, Jean-Charles 298
Fantasque, Le 87–8, 306
Faribault, Georges-Barthélémi 39, 297
Farrell, Monsignor 246
Faubourg Saint-Jean 62, 77, 80
Faubourg Saint-Louis 86
Favart, Charles-Simon 294
Félix Poutré x, 133–4, 247, 316; Introduction 183–8; text 189–239; notes 309–13
Fille du brigand, La 308
Filteau, Gérard 311
Fiset, Louis 35, 43, 46–8, 298–9
Forsythe, Louise 294–5, 315
France viii, 3–5, 15, 18, 21, 143, 178, 180, 294–5
Fraser, Colonel Malcolm 315

Fréchette, Louis-Honoré x, 133–4, 183–8 passim, 189, 293
French Republicans, The (*Les Républicains français*) 7, 293, 295
Frères Chasseurs. *See* Hunters' Lodges
Fridolinades 41
Frontenac, Louis de Buade de viii, 6, 246

Gagnon, Ernest 313, 317
Galarneau, Claude 313
Garneau, François-Xavier 35, 43, 46–8, 299–300
Garrison theatre viii, 6
Gaspé, de. *See* Aubert de Gaspé, Philippe
Gazette de Québec/Quebec Gazette 33, 35–7, 53, 63, 66, 68, 295, 297, 299–300, 302–3
Gélinas, Gratien 41
Genet, Citizen 5
George III 18
Gérin-Lajoie, Antoine xi, 86, 132, 246, 293
Glackemeyer, Édouard 38, 63, 71–82, 301
Goderich (Frederick John Robinson, Viscount) 64, 301
Goodyear, Nolan A. 295
Grandeur et décadence de M. Joseph Prudhomme 132
Gravel, Jean-Yves 300
Grenier, Jean-Baptiste 35, 51–5, 68, 300
Griphon, ou la vengeance d'un valet 85, 87–8, 131–3, 304, 306
Groulx, Lionel x
Guilbault, Odilon 317
Guilbeau, Major Charles 246
Gurik, Robert 41, 298

Haldimand, Frederick 4
Hamel, André-Rémi 37–9, 62–3, 67–8, 70–83, 301–3